Those Crazy Wonderful Years
WHEN *WE* RAN WARNER BROS.

In August, during an unprecedented heat wave, we were issued new summer uniforms. Note the snazzy WB logo. (Incidentally, in the background is the tennis court, beyond which was the Stars' Dressing Room Building. Our department was at extreme right.) Starting with the back row, from left to right: Stan Frazen, Loux Ferguson, a goofy-looking guy who is guess who, Bryan Hargreaves, Lou Turner and Peter Brooke.

Middle row: Harry Loebl, Bert Dunne, Russ Gustafson, Glen Rosswell, Mel Marks and Dave Beck.

Bottom: Pete Poulton, Morrie Black, Dick Rawlings and Billy Naylor. Inset: Our boss, J. F. Pappmeier.

Those Crazy
Wonderful Years
WHEN *WE* RAN
WARNER BROS.

Stuart Jerome

Lyle Stuart Inc.   Secaucus, New Jersey

For ELAINE and RICK . . . who made me do it
With love.

791.4
J56t
copy 1

First Edition

Copyright ©1983 by Stuart Jerome

Published by Lyle Stuart Inc.
Published simultaneously in Canada by
Musson Book Company,
A division of General Publishing Co. Limited
Don Mills, Ontario

Queries regarding rights and permissions should be
addressed to: Lyle Stuart, 120 Enterprise Avenue,
Secaucus, N.J. 07049.

Manufactured in the United States of America

Library of Congress Cataloging in Publication Data

Jerome, Stuart.
    Those crazy, wonderful years when we ran Warner
Bros.

    Includes index.
    1. Warner Brothers Picture, inc. 2. Moving-pic-
ture actors and actresses—United States—Anecdotes,
facetiae, satire, etc.   I. Title.
PN1999.W3J47 1983   384'.8'0979494   82–19622
ISBN 0-8184-0343-8

Acknowledgments

THIS IS THE PAGE that I usually find to be a bore when reading somebody else's book. So by all means, feel free to skip over it. But now that I have graduated from the ranks of mere "Writer" to that of "Author," I understand the necessity of *noblesse oblige*.

My greatest debt of gratitude is owed to two gentlemen who are now dead: my father, who reluctantly got me the job, and Fred Pappmeier, who—much more reluctantly—kept me on it. I think that Dad might've been amused by most of it, albeit perhaps appalled by my treatment of some of his friends and co-workers. Between stutters and stomach-aches, Fred might've been appreciative of a paragraph or two.

The heroes are my old colleagues in Mailing. Well, if some of them don't exactly emerge as heroes, they are what we used to call "characters." They helped me write this with their experiences, all of which I've tried to re-create with their original zest.

There are some accounts of incidents that we were not privy to. These I have tried to reconstruct from notes made at the time they took place. For them, I was indebted a long time ago to John Huston; makeup artist Perc Westmore; and assistant head of Publicity, Alex Evelove.

There are more: writers Philip Epstein, Ring Lardner, Jr., Richard Macaulay and Robert Rossen; directors William Keighley, John Farrow and Ray Enright; and producers Bryan Foy, Henry Blanke and Robert Lord. They were all very kind to a brash, nosey kid.

I'm sorry that I don't know the full names of others who helped fill in important details of some of our better anecdotes. There was a commissary waitress named Helen; extras Peg and Mary; and an enterprising young grip whom I knew only as "Red."

I also want to thank Bill Schaefer, for over 40 years J. L. Warner's executive secretary, confidant, and probably best friend, for recently taking a long trip with me down memory lane.

Most of the photos are from my family's collection. For the others I am very much obliged to Mrs. Waldon Pappmeier, Fred's sister-in-law; second generation WB executive Terry Dunne, son of my old friend Bert; producer David Lewis; Alan Hale, Jr.; Larry Stromberg; and a scrawny kid messenger named Dickie Selzer, somewhat better known today as *Mr. Blackwell*.

Contents

Foreword

ONCE UPON A TIME . . . Since this is a factual accounting, it seems to be a contradiction in terms to use that old fairy tale phrase, but I really don't know any other way of trying to conjure up the necessary mood of romance and adventure that I want to convey. First of all, this is about the long ago . . . the *very* long ago. Moreover, it deals with the archetypal subject matter of fairy tales: legends. The only difference is that this is true. It all happened exactly as I am about to tell you.

By way of prologue, the very first time I visited the then-Warner Bros.-First National Studios was in 1929 when my father, M. K. Jerome, was signed as one of the first contingent of Broadway songwriters to work on the newfangled talkies. As I roamed the lot that day, a strange thing happened to me. I experienced a feeling of *deja vu*, only in reverse. That is, at the age of nine, I suddenly felt an exultant certainty that I was destined one day to return and that it would become my home.

Nine years later, it came to pass. After graduating from high school and before starting college, I persuaded my parents to let me take six months off to do whatever I wanted. By then I had a long-range goal. I was determined to become a writer, specifically a screenwriter. To achieve that end, I knew that any working experience I could get in a studio would be helpful.

Thanks to Dad's help, I got a job. In the Mailroom. It was supposed to only be temporary, as per my promise, but I soon realized there was nothing in the way of a college education comparable to the practical knowledge of film-making that I was learning daily. Within a few months, I abandoned the idea of college altogether, much to the regret of my folks. Especially my mother, who had long harbored the hope that I would become either a doctor or lawyer. "I'm sorry, Mom," I told her, "but I couldn't even make it as a quack or shyster."

In a lifetime filled with sins of omission and commission, I've had no regrets. And, oddly enough, in all the years since then, working on movies whose locations have taken me to some of the more exotic places in this world, and in writing several hundred TV scripts, memories pale in comparison to those of my halcyon youth. I had no idea then, of course, that those days would turn out to be The Time of My Life, but it was all so fascinating that I started keeping notes, then diaries of our adventures. It became a habit that stayed with me.

9

This is the result. A kind of collective, informal record—or, according to the dictionary, a *gallimaufry*—of some of the people and events that helped shape our lives during the years 1938–42.

One important caveat: This is not to be construed as a *historical* record. We were certainly wrong in our dislike of a number of people; and many of the stories are recounted solely from our immature points of view. But I have not made any attempts at revisionism; to rewrite or change in any way our original thoughts and impressions would totally violate the purpose of these remembrances. Nor have I toned down any of the rough language. I'm as tired of the usual assortment of four-letter words as most readers are (when I was a kid, *the* four-letter word was exciting; years ago it gave way to the word *Residual* on Writers Guild envelopes), but again, since that was the way we talked, they all demanded to be used.

We were a motley crew—sometimes irresponsible, usually irreverent, and *always* prejudiced. All of which can be blamed on our youth. For most of us, all between the ages of 16 and 25, this was our first job, and it is necessary to bear in mind the fact that as $16-a-week "Junior Executives" we were plunged, headlong and unprepared, into a dazzlingly improbable fantasy world.

But then again, maybe we weren't quite as madcap as memory serves. The one indisputable fact that should be noted is that the era during which this all happened coincides with the production of some of our best movies.

Could it have been more than mere coincidence? I mean, in all modesty, could it have been accomplished without our help? Don't laugh. As you'll see, *we* were really running the place.

Once upon a time . . .

"My only advice is, don't let the glamor you'll be surrounded by go to your heads. You boys might think it's all gonna be just a lot of fun, but you'll learn otherwise. Be respectful, work hard and try to conduct yourselves as junior executives. Now, welcome to Warner Bros."

—J. F. Pappmeier
Feb. 14, 1938

Surrounded by towering old fir trees and wide expanses of lawn, from the outside our Main Administration Building projected an ambience of serenity and charm. But inside, it was another matter; many of its inmates commonly referred to the studio as "San Quentin."

1

Cary Grant, Roz Russell & Other Pains

A DESOLATE DECADE was winding down. The Spanish Civil War was raging, and apocalypse lay ahead, but 1938 dawned promisingly. FDR was into his second term, the Great Depression was over and prosperity was actually starting to turn the corner. And taking to heart the slogan "Motion Pictures Are Your Best Entertainment," 85 million American moviegoers turned out weekly to pay tribute to the 356 features that annually came off the major studios' assembly lines.

All things considered, it seemed a very good time to be 17. And when the phone call came for me that morning, I knew the best was yet to be.

Some of the nicest things in my life have happened to me on St. Valentine's Day. I sold my first script, got married, and started at Warners all on that romantic holiday. Though not at the same time. First things first.

My employment began on Monday, February 14th, 1938, as one of four new messengers hired to replace a quartet who had been promoted into other departments. (In my case, it might have been more appropriate if I had been hired on April Fool's Day.)

There were 24 of us, including our department head, John Frederick Pappmeier, and his two office assistants, Bates Bowers and Ed Haldeman. Pappmeier was about 40, of medium height, inclined toward plumpness, wearing wire-framed glasses that magnified his watery blue eyes. He resembled the archetypical Dutch burgher right down to his omnipresent pipe and air of pleasant, calm stability.

By nature he was a pleasant man, but his calm stability turned out to be a thin façade which was constantly shattered, almost always by something we had done but shouldn't have, or vice versa. Suffice it to say that earlier than most of my colleagues, I contributed more than a normal share of his daily woes.

Ours, I quickly learned, was the busiest department on the lot, a beehive of activity from eight a.m. until the seven p.m. closing. I have only montage-like recollections of my first few days, the most outstanding being that by mid-afternoon of the second day, my feet were so painfully swollen that I could barely shuffle along, forcing me to discover various hideouts that even our veterans weren't aware of. Over the next two weeks, the condition of my feet worsened into a continual agony until, at the end of the second week, the pain suddenly disappeared. As had been predicted, my feet were finally broken in. I could now lay claim to officially being a messenger.

If, during those first two weeks the pain could never be ignored, it could be lightened to some extent by the various experiences of each day. It was fun walking down a street and getting a smile or nod from such familiar faces as Fredric March, Joan Blondell and Jimmy Cagney. Or, better yet, delivering mail to the Writers Building and hearing the anguished cries of artists giving birth to new creations.

At left foreground is our Commissary. On the right, the infamous Sydney Greenstreet phone both.

Best of all was having occasion to enter one of the cavernous sound stages. It was there that I was always transported back to 1929. It came about through a combination of odors that existed no place else: a mixture of old dust, fresh lumber and paint, stale makeup, perspiration and coffee. The hot lights, acting as a catalyst, somehow achieved the alchemy of changing them into a mystical fragrance. For me, it was as if all the colors of the rainbow had been distilled into the most exquisite perfume.

There was a thrill in watching such top directors as Raoul Walsh, Lloyd Bacon and Edmund Goulding instruct their casts and crews during the short bursts of shooting that finally followed the long, enervating periods of new camera set-ups, light adjustments and technical problems. Walsh, a burly, handsome man who wore an eyepatch, had started out as an actor before an auto accident deprived him of an eye, and seemed to enjoy acting out each role for the benefit of his cast. Bacon, casually lounging in his canvas chair, was more interested in seeing that his actors hit their chalk marks. And Goulding, a perfectionist, would fuss with vases and furniture, moving them an inch one way or another, for what purpose I never could figure out. All three of them were alike in one respect, possessing infinite patience with the fluffs made by their stars, who often blew the simplest lines.

One fluff, above all, stands out in memory, when, for the first time in my sheltered life, I heard a lady utter The Ultimate Four-Letter Word, not in ecstacy, but exasperation. It was demure little Priscilla Lane. Having a bad time with a line, she finally cried out, "Oh, fuck it!"

I don't know which shocked me more, her utterance of the word in mixed company or the total lack of reaction from the crew. When I recounted the incident to my colleagues, hoping they would find it amusing, I was met with blank stares. Russ Gustafson, one of our veterans, expressed the feelings of the others. "You said she kept blowing up, so what the fuck did you expect her to say?"

That same day Mike Liss, one of the trio who started with me, achieved a degree of status by telling us something that he had

It was the first time I had ever heard it spoken in public exasperation rather than private ecstasy, when demure Priscilla Lane bellowed the Ultimate Four-Letter Word.

witnessed. Delivering mail to costume designer Orry-Kelly's office, he entered to find him in the act of dressing Bette Davis. More accurately, *undressing* her, since at that moment Davis was clad only in a pair of high-heel shoes.

As Mike graphically described it, he was prepared to make a sudden exit upon her first outraged cry, but since neither of them paid him the slightest heed, he managed to steal several long, hard looks while pretending to leaf through his letters.

One heretofore unknown fact emerged from Mike's brief encounter: Davis was not a real blond.

Speaking of Jack Orry-Kelly, an Australian with the battered visage of a one-time prizefighter, as our reigning costume designer he was talented, highly emotional and short-tempered. In all respects, to an extreme. If one was only a witness to and not the recipient of his anger, his tantrums were a wonder to behold. Early on we learned one sure means of provoking him into such a state. All we had to do was innocently mention, in some slight context, the name of Cary Grant.

"Grant!" he would scream. "Don't talk to me about that louse! I knew him when his name was Archie Leach, and that's all he ever was—a goddam *leech*! I befriended him when he didn't have a pot to piss in, let him stay in my apartment, fed him, bought him clothes! Not alone he never repaid a penny of what he owes me, but now the cheap shit pretends he doesn't even know me!"

The diatribe would occasionally vary in details and degree of wrath, but the gist of it remained the same. It was always an awe-inspiring performance.

Only once did I incur his displeasure, luckily not to the extent of an anti-Grant-type outburst. It was on my third day, and I was sent to First Aid on a rush, where the nurse handed me two manila envelopes. One was for Rosalind Russell, the other for Orry-Kelly. My first stop was Stage 22, where I found Russell completing a scene with Walter Connolly. I presented her with the envelope, basked in her gracious smile of thanks and quickly departed for my second stop.

Orry-Kelly was hunched over his drawing board as I deposited the second envelope and headed for the door. I was brought to a sudden halt before I reached it.

"What kind of a goddam joke is this supposed to be?" he demanded. I turned around. He was holding three Kotex pads. It sickeningly dawned on me that somehow I had accidentally switched envelopes.

"I think I might've made a mistake," I mumbled.

"I think maybe you're right," he replied acidly. "The pain's in my ass, not my twat!" He looked at the name scrawled on the envelope. "Roz Russell. Ha! The old broad's showing off again!"

I snatched the pads away, muttering something about coming right back. Russell was awaiting my return, this time without the gracious smile, as I handed her the pads and received in return a tube of rectal ointment. At least she had the good manners not to make any comment.

When I returned to our department, thankful that at least matters had been corrected before Pappmeier was notified, I found out otherwise. Russell had irately called First Aid, who then called us. Since it was my first offense, I was put on probation for a week.

It was obvious that Fred Pappmeier and some of us held a mutual distrust from the beginning of our relationship. In all fairness, it wasn't entirely his fault. Most of us obtained our jobs through nepotism, and since our benefactors were usually of more importance than him in the studio hierarchy, he seldom had any say in hiring. Also, having worked his way up from a day laborer on the back lot, he knew what it was like to put in a full day's work and expected us to do the same. He was suspicious of "lofty" ambitions, believing that those who aspired to artistic jobs, such as acting, writing, or directing, would soon become goof-offs by devoting their time and energy to furthering their own interests.

In turn, we considered him a neurotic, humorless martinet. While it was true that our sins were visited upon his head, we didn't think it was the end of the world if we missed a pickup at certain out-of-the-way departments or failed to expedite a rush with the mindless efficiency that he demanded. I don't think that Fred began to suspect me of lofty ambitions until I started spending too much of my working day visiting the Writers Building, a habit I didn't fully develop until my third week. In the case of my friend, Mel Marks, the second of my Valentine's Day cohorts, he and Fred had a personality clash within the first hour of our first day.

Mel was a brilliant kid of 18, who had graduated from prep school *cum laude,* and who had then decided that instead of going on to college, or entering the family business (his father had founded the chain of National Shirt Stores), his destiny was in the movie business. Like most extra-bright people, he was terribly intolerant of stupidity and inefficiency, causing him to criticize a certain method of mail sorting which Fred was explaining to us. Although justified from an efficiency standpoint, his criticism was certainly ill-timed. Fred's face turned red, and with the slight stammer that we later came to associate with his low boiling point, he curtly advised Mel to just listen and do as he was told.

A few days later, sent to Publicity to pick up copy from one of the female publicists to take to Mimeo, Mel's intelligence again got in his way. Reading her copy, he pointed out a slight grammatical error. With a notable lack of appreciation, she phoned our department. Since the woman was a chronic complainer of whom Fred wasn't overly fond, Mel received only a 15-minute chewing-out, along with the warning that one more infraction would be his last.

With this admonition in mind, he somehow managed to go about his duties in our prescribed robot-like manner. It was only during the bull sessions in the privacy of our back room that he would give vent to his frustrations, pointing out the inane and wasteful practices that he soon noticed existed in so many departments. His captive audience, however, was far less interested in economics than sex and studio gossip, and after a short time he gave up trying to educate us and devoted his free time to studying.

This continued for about a month, during which time Fred was heard to reluctantly admit that "maybe that Marks kid is finally straightening himself out."

Then, one morning, something happened that caused Pappmeier to abruptly change his mind. Taking the front lot route, Mel checked out at 10:45. His normal return was scheduled for not later than 11:15, after which time an explanation for his tardiness would be demanded.

The deadline came and went with no sign of him, a fact which our front office duly noted. The hands of the clock crept on to 11:30 and beyond. He still hadn't returned. Trying to act casual—a performance he was never equal to under stress—Fred started to inquire if any of us had seen Mel. Nobody had.

Normally, Fred went home for lunch every day at noon, a habit which we characteristically insisted was also for the purpose of having a "matinee" with his wife. On this occasion he sent out for a sandwich and forwent the matinee.

By this time, some of us were concerned. Mel was too smart to think he could goof off for over an hour. No matter the excuse, Pappmeier would have the pleasure of firing him on the spot.

Tension was growing. Seated at his desk, Fred was unusually quiet as he kept an eye on the clock. At 1:03, Mel suddenly appeared in the doorway. Nonchalant, smiling broadly. Fred stared at him, the veins in his thick neck starting to bulge. He opened his mouth but no words came forth. Bates Bowers, usually lenient with us, glared at Mel.

"Where in hell have you been?" he demanded.

Mel's smile never left his face. "Well, here's what happened," he said. "When I dropped off my mail at H. M. Warner's bungalow, the old man himself came out. He had a couple with him—a judge and his wife—and he asked me to show them around the lot and then bring them over to the executive dining room at one. I just delivered them and you know what the Judge gave me?" He pulled a ten-dollar bill out of his pocket. "Whattaya think of that?"

Those of us who heard his explanation decided it was the best lie we had ever heard. Still, in this case it wouldn't do. It was only too obvious that, despite his invoking the name of our president, Fred wouldn't take his word for it. There was dead silence for about 15 seconds as Pappmeier sat there, looking as if he were on the verge of a stroke.

"W-w-w-hy d-d-didn't y-y-you p-p-phone?" His voice sounded strangulated.

Mel shrugged. "I didn't have the chance. Oh, by the way, is it OK if I go to lunch now?"

He interpreted Fred's shaking head as assent and walked out. Instantly, Fred dialed H. M.'s extension and spoke with secretary Marie Orth. No, she hadn't seen any messenger come by, nor did she know of any visitors H. M. had.

A cold calmness descended over Fred as he hung up. "OK," he told Bates. "We know he's lying. Make out the termination notice and I'll sign it."

One of us caught up with Mel in the commissary and told him what had happened. "It was a damn good story," he said sympathetically, "but Pappmeier checked on it. Don't bother rushing back, you're through as of now."

Mel nodded and kept eating.

A few minutes later, Fred got a phone call from Marie Orth. "I have a message from Mr. Warner," she said. "He understands that one of your messengers got in trouble by taking friends of his around the studio without first asking your permission. He doesn't want you to blame the boy. I guess it's also my fault for not telling you that I was out of the office for a few minutes when this must have happened."

To give credit where it's due, Mel didn't crow when he returned from lunch. Fred endured this crowning humiliation stoically, but the termination notice was not destroyed, merely filed away for future use.

Unfortunately for him, his sweet dreams of revenge were not to be. Mel, who had been studying shorthand at night school while some of us were wasting our time carousing, applied for secretarial work at an employment agency. He was hired by Irving Briskin, a top executive at Columbia, and one morning he phoned in to say he was quitting and would Pappmeier please mail him his last check.

2

Love, Hate & the End of Jackie Gleason

H<small>OW DO YOU EXPRESS YOUR LOVE</small> if your're a lowly messenger and the object of your affection is a beautiful movie star? It's not a rhetorical question, it actually happened to one of us.

Herman, as I'll call him, was madly enamored of Olivia de Havilland. It was, of course, unrequited and undoubtedly would have forever remained unknown to her had it not been for a rather bizarre incident.

It started with Herman taking a bundle of fan mail to her dressing room. When the three obligatory knocks on her door failed to elicit a response (it was 10:30 a.m. and at that hour all working actors were on their respective sets), he let himself in with a pass key.

We can only surmise the rapture he felt as he placed the mail on top of her bureau, inhaled her perfume, gazed around the room and prepared to depart. But love is, as a popular song once stated, a funny thing. The rapture that filled Herman's heart became so overwhelming that it grabbed at his very entrails.

Heartache can be endured, but a bowel cramp is an altogether different matter. Now, not too far from the dressing room building was a men's room, which certainly should have been his destination at this point. But in all fairness, can any lover blame Herman for the one unbidden thought that suddenly thrust itself into his mind?

Entering her bathroom, he squatted, his cheeks nuzzling the seat normally occupied by his beloved's.

Alas, why is it that when the moment of serendipity is about to happen, the Fates decree otherwise? It was just then that Herman's love made an ill-timed entrance. Discovering a strange man seated on her john, de Havilland fled. Screaming.

Such aberrant behavior—Pappmeier puritanically called it a "disgusting act of perversion"—normally would have resulted in instant dismissal. In this case, after Herman was interrogated by Security, and the facts forwarded to de Havilland, she interceded in his behalf and he was only given two days' lay-off.

Eventually the contretemps faded from our bull sessions. Not, however, until Herman had been forced to endure six months of our normally addressing him as "Pervert."

Not all of us were sex offenders or even goof-offs. On occasion we could even be unsung heroes. As one case in point, Arnold Laven saved the studio thousands of dollars one day.

Sent on a rush to Stage 4 to pick up a production report on a musical called *Garden of the Moon*, Arno was told by the harried first assistant that the report wasn't ready yet and that he was to wait a few minutes while they got an important scene out of the way. The set was a replica of the Cocoanut Grove, in which two hundred extras in evening clothes were paired off as ballroom dancers. Director Busby Berkeley had painstakingly rehearsed the action several times and was now ready for the take. It was an expensive scene because of the dress extras, and since it was then 4:30, he had to get his master shot and various angles in the can by six, or else go into overtime, a situation that usually resulted in Front Office palpitations.

The extras were instructed to take their starting positions, the overhead arcs were lit, the clapboy slated the scene number, "Take one," and the mixer, seated at the sound console, buzzed twice for speed.

"Action!" Berkeley called.

Mounted on a crane, the camera started on a tight two shot of the stars, Margaret Lindsay and John Payne, in a close embrace, then slowly pulled back, gradually craning upwards as the other dancing couples, smiling and mouthing silent conversations, milled around the floor. The scene climaxed in a long shot of the release of thousands of balloons from the ceiling.

All went well until, halfway through the action, as the balloons were released, a dozen or so started popping. Berkeley called, "Cut."

On the second take, the same thing happened, at exactly the same point as before. Except that this time double the number of balloons exploded.

A hurried conference was held among the director, his assistants and the prop men responsible for releasing the balloons from the overhead nets. After which, Berkeley addressed the extras.

"OK," he said, "I know what's going on. Some of you are deliberately busting those balloons so you can either get overtime or a callback. Well, let me tell you something. We'll be watching all of you, and if it happens once more, you can be goddam sure that whoever's responsible will never work at this studio again!"

It was a frightening accusation. Casting suspicious glances at their fellow players, the extras returned to their starting positions for the third take. By now, what with the retrieval of the unexpected balloons and replacing them all in the net, time was swiftly passing. It was now after five.

The unexpected delays had given the assistant the opportunity to complete his report. Handing it to Arno, he curtly told him to hustle it over to Production.

The climax of this scene from *Garden of the Moon* might never have been shot the way it was intended had it not been for the intercession of a lowly member of our department.

Arno started to leave, but just then Berkeley called for another take. Suddenly believing that he knew what the trouble was and how to solve it, he decided to remain. But how could he, a kid messenger, express an opinion to experienced film makers, all of whom considered themselves resident genuises?

He watched breathlessly as the scene progressed, climaxing with its moment of truth. "Bang!" went a score of balloons in unison. " BANG! BANG! BANG!"" The continuing explosions sounded like a Fourth of July celebration.

Berkeley, whom we always believed to become psychotic under stress, started to froth at the mouth, screaming that this was a personal plot against him! As he started to single out various extras, claiming he saw them breaking the balloons, Arno suddenly knew that, if only out of an act of necessary justice, he must make known his theory.

He sidled up to the assistant. "Excuse me," he whispered, "but I think I know what the trouble is." He pointed overhead to the battery of lights. "It's the arcs. I think the heat they generate is too much for the thin rubber of the balloons. If you keep them a little bit underinflated, I think it'll be OK."

The assistant looked at him thoughtfully, but his only comment was, "Didn't I tell you to get that report over to Production?"

It wasn't until the following day that Arno learned that take four was a print. Not alone the master shot, but two protection angles were in the can before six.

It would be nice to report that his resourcefulness was rewarded in some small measure. Ironically, quite the opposite. Because the Production Department was in a stew waiting for the report, Arno was bawled out for goofing off.

In our lexicon, there were two kinds of directors, the "good guys" and those on our "shit list." In neither case did these terms refer to their directorial ability, it being immaterial to us whether they were creative artists or merely adequate hacks. If a director was friendly and ran an open set he was one of the good guys, such as Raoul Walsh, Ray Enright, Bill Keighley and most of the B directors. Conversely, if he was unpleasant and caused us any trouble, he was relegated to the dungheap, a distinction shared at one time or another by all of our foreign directors, Mike Curtiz, William Dieterle, Anatole Litvak and Robert Florey. (By way of being English, Edmund Goulding was not considered a foreigner, though at times he, too, could be a prima donna.)

We lumped the foreigners together under the generic term "fucking Hungarians," although factually only Curtiz bore that ancestry. If we seemed racially prejudiced, we did have good cause. Early on, we were made aware of their dictatorial harshness. Perhaps it stemmed from their European beginnings, where in the early days Herr Director was all-important. Despite the fact that in our factory they had only a limited amount of leeway as far as script changes, casting and cutting were concerned, they did exert a total authority over everybody on their sets, much in the manner of feudal lords despotically ruling over their little fiefdoms.

They could—and did—insult us in front of our visitors, even eject us from their sets, despite the fact that we had been granted permission to enter by their assistants. But that was where their power ended. So far as we were concerned, away from the sound stages they were only employees, no better than us.

Which was the way our Bud Garson felt when he was sent to William Dieterle's office one night shortly before seven. A tall, glowering Prussian right down to his heel-clicking shoes, Dieterle had a quirk of wearing white cotton gloves on the set, which were freshly supplied by the prop man every morning. Once, one poor satrap accidentally gave him a previously worn pair, for which he received a terrible tongue lashing. Dieterle was also known to be superstitious, starting production only a date deemed to be propitious by his astrologer. (Considering some of the movies he made, that adviser should have been drummed out of the astrological society.)

Still smarting over the humiliation of a few days previously, when without any reason Dieterle had flown into a rage and or-

Director William Dieterle's fetish for white gloves—a new pair every morning—was only one of his idiosyncracies. Another was humiliating us when we brought visitors on his sets, a practice that one of us finally had the courage to do something about.

dered him to get his visitors "de hell ov my set," Bud entered his office to find him deep in concentration at his desk, making notes in his shooting script. Without looking up, he muttered, "Go to de druk store und pick up en order vor me."

He pushed forward a dollar bill. It took Bud only a second to realize that here was a God-given opportunity to get even. Taking a deep breath, he quietly said, "Drop dead, Dieterle."

Startled, Dieterle jerked his head up and stared uncomprehendingly.

"Vat? Vat did you zay?"

I said," Bud repeated slowly, savoring each euphonious word, "drop . . . dead . . . Dieterle."

We were closing for the night when Bud returned to our back room. Changing from his uniform with the rest of us, he seemed to be in an ebullient mood, but made no mention of what had transpired.

The first we knew that something was wrong was the following morning, when those of us on the late shift clocked in shortly before ten and saw Pappmeier standing in the doorway. His stammer was a dead giveaway that something catastrophic had happened.

"G-G-G-Garson, I-I-I w-w-wanna s-s-see y-y-you!"

Later, we learned the whole story. By nine that morning, Tenny Wright, our Production Department manager, was on the phone to our department personally, a chore usually handled by one of his staff. "How dare one of your goddam messengers insult a director," Wright demanded.

Fred worriedly asked for specifics.

"Bill Dieterle!" Wright shouted. "He had some script changes to send to Mimeo last night, and the bastard, snotty kid not alone told him it was too late, but added he should go fuck himself. I don't know what the hell kind of department you're running, but I want that kid fired right now!"

Dazed and shaken, Fred hung up. He had long known there weren't too many evil things we weren't capable of: lying, cheating, stealing, these were all common and endemic. But the kind of insult that Wright had described was unheard of, almost a premeditated death wish.

The previous night's rush sheet contained the necessary information. "6:49: Bud Garson to Dieterle."

Wanting to be fair, Fred granted 30 seconds for an explanation. He listened, wincing in dismay. It was an unbelievably stupid act on Bud's part, but his version differed enough from Wright's to warrant further investigation.

Fred contacted Mimeo. No, they had not been advised last night of any script changes. At the drug store, the cashier recalled that Dieterle had phoned in an order, but it hadn't been picked up when they closed at eight.

Armed with this information, Fred asked for five minutes of Wright's valuable time. He repeated Bud's substantiated version of the incident, subtly concluding with, "Wasn't it your directive last year, Tenny, that the messengers were not to perform any personal service for any employee that would take them off the lot? The boy was only following orders."

Wright thought it over. "Tell you what," he decided. "Get the goddam kid to go over and apologize to Dieterle, and we'll forget it."

Pappmeier breathed a sigh of relief. What a wonderfully easy way out! Except for one thing: he failed to reckon with Garson. With the courage of his convictions, Bud maintained he had nothing to apologize for, not even if it meant losing his job.

Unhappily, Fred sat down at his desk, wrote out a termination notice and left to take it over to Accounting.

For some reason, he never got there. Instead, he ended up on Stage 14, where he introduced himself to the director.

"That messenger who gave you so much trouble last night," he said, "I just want to apologize for his actions, and let you know that I fired him."

Dieterle's ego was soothed, Bud remained his own man . . . and as for our boss, well, he proved that on the very, very few occasions when we were more or less unjustly accused, he was willing to put his head on the block for us. I don't think we were ever more proud of him than on that day.

It's too bad that not all of us possessed Bud's moral standards. I, for example, sometimes found it in my heart to be compassionate enough to bend our inflexible rules. It depended on what was in it for me.

This happened on a Saturday afternoon. Although the pictures in production were required to put in a full shooting day, the executives always left by noon, followed by the writers and then, soon afterwards the frenetic activity of the week gave way to a more leisurely pace. There were few rush calls, and with Fred's early departure, in the privacy of our back room we were soon able to indulge in our strictly forbidden pursuit of gambling.

I was next man up when the buzzer sounded, taking me away from a blackjack game in which I was a three-dollar loser. Nor was I made any happier by Bates' telling me to go to the Lagoon and see the assistant director. The Lagoon, which also served as a lake, riverfront and ocean, was located at the farthest reaches of the back lot, a good five-minute bike ride. To make matters worse, it was a very hot, humid day.

"Have mercy on me, Master Bates," I begged. "That's practically an overnight trek."

Unlike our other desk assistant, Ed Haldeman, who could be sarcastic and inflexible, Bowers was reasonable and good-natured, not even ever objecting to our timeworn joke of addressing him as "Master Bates."

"OK," he said, checking his rush list. "Cutting room nine has 20 reels for the Lab. Take your choice."

Choice? My God! The Lab was even farther and 20 cans of film would mean four round trips!

Ordinarily, I enjoyed the surreal freedom of pedaling across the back lot. There was a time warp as one passed through a New York tenement street of the twenties, to a clearing of African huts, rounding a corner to a street cafe on the Rue de la Paix, beyond which was the moated entrance to Nottingham Castle.

This time there was a notable lack of enjoyment. With more important things on my mind than taking in glimpses of three continents, I cursed my luck as I pedalled at full speed, wiping the sweat off my face. The game would probably be over by the time I returned, and I was in dire need of those three bucks for a date that night with a secretary whom rumor had it became nymphomaniacal only after being taken to a movie and stuffed with popcorn.

The Lagoon had been turned into a tropical beach for a musical called *Navy Blues*.

"The guy you wanna see," said the assistant, "is Jackie Gleason."

Other than knowing he was a newly signed comic, I had no idea what he looked like. He pointed to a chubby fellow in a sailor suit, seated on the sidelines with Ann Sheridan and Jack Oakie.

"Oh, yeah," Gleason said in that expansive manner that was to become so familiar to TV viewers many years later. "Here's the deal, pal. I think I'm coming down with a bad case of laryngitis. Now, according to my eminent friend, Dr. Toots Shorr, the only known cure is to gargle every fifteen minutes with a certain medication called brandy." He took out a five-dollar bill. "How's about being an angel of mercy, pal?"

I was in a foul mood to begin with and his patronizing manner didn't help. "Sorry, pal," I snapped, "but number one, it's against company rules to leave the lot on personal errands. Number two, if I were caught bringing in booze, I'd get my ass in a sling!"

He grunted. "Look at it this way, pal. Unless I get medication, I'm bound to hold up production. . ." His voice trailed off and he eyed me shrewdly. "Tell you what. How's about getting me a pint and whatever's left over from the fin is yours."

It was then I noticed that perhaps his voice *was* a bit hoarse. And wouldn't J. L. be proud to know that he had one messenger with enough initiative to bend a rule in order to avoid an emergency shutdown?

The logical place to go was the drug store, which had a complete liquor department. I was offered my choice of Martell, Hennessy, Courvoisier, All the best unfortunately. At $3.50 for their least expensive brand, I decided that my margin of profit would not be commensurate with the amount of labor involved.

During the filming of *Navy Blues*, a newly-signed young comedian named Jackie C. Gleason prevailed on a member of our department to break a strict rule by leaving the lot to buy some much-needed "cough medicine." The result stands as a lasting testimonial to "The Great One's" constitution.

Across from our Auto Gate were three or four sleazy beer parlors frequented by the back lot workers. Some of them, I had heard, although lacking liquor licenses, sold cheap booze under the table. The first two proprietors, noting I was obviously under the 21-year-old age restriction, invited me to get the hell out forthwith. It was at "Mother's," the sleaziest of them all, that I finally met with success. "Mother," an unshaven, pot-bellied old goat, produced a pint of "Genuine French-type Brandy," made in Azusa, at the right price. Ninety-eight cents.

I might have established a new speed record in pedaling back to the Lagoon, the "medication" safely concealed in a brown paper bag. Gleason was appreciative, hoping that there had been a little of the five left for me. I shrugged, as if to say that it really didn't matter, that I was a man of means in my own right. Which I was . . . now.

Gleason, Sheridan and Oakie retired to the privacy of her portable dressing room, and I was about to depart when the assistant whistled for quiet. They were about to shoot a scene between Jack Haley and Martha Raye. It was a funny bit and would have been a perfect take except, just before the finish, it was ruined by a series of anguished cries coming from Sheridan's dressing room. The trio emerged, staggering, their eyes tearing, incoherently croaking something to the effect they had been poisoned. According to Gleason, it was "bull's piss" and they would all be stricken blind. At which point, realizing I was wasting departmental time, I quickly made my exit.

As for my date that night: well, I was forced to sadly admit the truth of the old saying that ill-gotten gains only benefit the devil. I blew better than half my bankroll on a lousy movie and six boxes of popcorn, all of which the girl devoured without offering me a single kernel, though I must admit my desires lay elsewhere.

As we were leaving the theater, just for protection, I bought her one more box, not realizing until we were in my car that her complexion was turning green. At which point, she proceeded to throw up all over the front seat.

Sunday was not a happier day. I kept worrying about Gleason and hoping that he hadn't died—or that if he had, he'd at least had the decency of taking the secret of how he obtained the "medication" to the grave with him.

On Monday, thankfully, he reported back to work and we learned that director Lloyd Bacon had been forced to close down two hours earlier than planned on Saturday when some of his cast came down with food poisoning. Fearing that for some reason Gleason might have blamed me, I made it a point to stay far away from his set. Then, one day shortly after the picture was completed, I got good news. The Front Office, in its ultimate wisdom, decided that Gleason lacked the qualities of a first-rate comic. His option was dropped and he left the lot.

3

Smoking Can Be
Hazardous to Your Career

In the early 1930's, having finally achieved the status of a major studio, Warner Bros. went on a star-stealing spree, raiding Paramount for three of its top names, Ruth Chatterton, William Powell and Kay Francis.

By 1938, Francis was the only one of the trio still under contract. Although her box office value had long since declined, she was still a star by reason of her $5,250 weekly check, the second-highest salary received by anyone on the lot. (At $6,000 per week, Cagney was number one.)

Therein lay the crux of a situation that developed into one of the more sordid chapters in our history. With 18 months remaining on her contract, vis-à-vis the Sales Department's pronouncements that her pictures ended up in their ledgers in a sea of red ink, the Front Office attempted to effect a settlement with her. Their offers were rejected out of hand. If other fading actors sometimes knew when it was time to depart one studio and start over at another in hopes of rebuilding their careers, Francis apparently realized that her heyday was over, and that there would be little interest, let alone demand, for her services elsewhere. And certainly not at anything like her established salary.

Since there was too much money at stake for us to allow her to graciously decline our final offer of a 50 percent settlement, the only other means at our disposal was to force her to quit. So began a campaign of harrassment and humiliation that eventually would even embroil an innocent member of our department.

First, on the pretext that it was to be redecorated, her belongings were moved from her plush dressing room suite to one room in the Featured Players Dressing Room Building. It *was* redecorated, but for a different tenant, a fast-rising newcomer named John Garfield.

Francis knew better than to complain about this trivial inconvenience. As an old pro who had probably memorized every clause in her contract, she was well aware that there was no written stipulation regarding the size of her dressing room quarters. But that was merely the beginning.

Her next assignment, she was notified, would be to assist a number of young hopefuls who were to be screen-tested for stock contracts. It was unthinkable to use high-salaried actors, let alone stars, for the embarrassing task of playing second fiddle to raw newcomers, but again, contractually, her refusal would have resulted in an immediate suspension. Swallowing her pride and pocketing her pay check, for the next six days she reported to the test stage. Although her call was for nine a.m., she was seldom used before mid-afternoon, at which point she would be called upon to mainly feed lines to the youngsters while the camera focused on them, shooting over her shoulder. Uncomplainingly, she spent her days sitting on the sidelines, knitting and drinking gin from a silver flask, and we wondered if, like Dickens' Madam Defarge, she was inscribing into her afghan the names on her hate list.

How much humiliation would you be willing to put up with in return for money? In the case of Kay Francis vs. WB, for $5,250 a week, a lot. But according to those who knew her, she ended up with a broken heart.

An old-timer, Hobart Bosworth, once a star in the silents, now an atmosphere player in our stock company, commiserating about the way she was being treated, concluded that she was still better off than the stars of his day.

"Back then," he recalled, "if you offended any of the moguls, they could order you to clean out toilets if they wanted to. Our contracts only stipulated that we were hired 'for services rendered.' Kay's lucky that the Screen Actors Guild made them change that clause to 'for *acting* services,' otherwise they could force a showdown by ordering her to report to, say, the commissary as a waitress."

To which another old-timer who had worked with her commented, "Knowing Francis, she would not only report, but she would also keep the tips, right down to the last goddam dime!"

It was about this time that the Front Office began to realize that it had perhaps been over-zealous. Exaggerated rumors began circulating in the trade press and movie columns, picturing poor Kay Francis as the innocent victim of a corporate plot to ruin her career. Moreover, since we had recently adopted the slogan, "Combining Good Citizenship With Good Movie Making," it was evident we were laying ourselves wide open to criticism and ridicule.

Within the studio, sympathy was mostly for Francis. Not that she was especially well liked, but in any feud with the Front Office, the consensus favored the other side. It was necessarily a muted sympathy except for two vocal champions. Openly and vociferously, Bette Davis and Jimmy Cagney let it be known that they considered the studio's vendetta despicable. Deliberately going over J. L.'s head, they sought an audience with Harry, who as our president had the power to override any decisions he disapproved of.

H. M. was supposedly sympathetic, but said that since all production matters were under J. L.'s jurisdiction, he was unable to interfere. (The fact is, it was *Harry* who instigated the campaign. Much as J. L. might have approved, he was carrying out his brother's orders. But this was something we didn't learn until much later.)

In order to counteract the bad publicity the studio was receiving, we put Francis back to work. This time in B's. Designed for the lower half of a double bill, they were uniformly mediocre.

It was towards the end of her contract that one final petty, and certainly unnecessary humiliation, was visited upon her.

It happened one noon-time, while our Bob Gara was relieving in Main Reception. Francis phoned from her set, asking for a commissary pass for two friends. Such requests, even from the humblest stock players, were always routinely granted, the procedure being for the receptionist to phone Production and get the OK from one of the staff.

In this case, the request was denied.

There was no explanation. One was hardly necessary.

Bob had the unpleasant task of relaying this to Francis. He said her only comment was, "I understand. Thank you anyway."

She joined her friends for lunch off the lot, reporting back within the alloted hour.

We were not much given to feeling sorry for actors, especially one who in a week's time made the equivalent of what it took us nearly five years to earn, and we used to make fun of the way she pronounced her R's as W's. Also, there were those who, having known her longer and better, claimed that at her height she had been a bad-tempered, money-mad bitch, who was now reaping her just desserts. Still, solely on the strength of the commissary pass incident, we felt she had gotten a raw deal. We were glad that at least one other minor employee felt the same way.

On her last day, as she was driving off the lot, the cop at the Auto Gate performed an unheard-of gesture to an actor: He saluted Kay Francis.

Although *l'affaire Francis* was an extreme case that was not repeated during our time, there was never a lack of internecine warfare between the Front Office and practically all of the stars. It was a case of cold economics; *everybody* had to earn their keep. One good example concerned Bette Davis and Dick

Powell. With both of them between assignments, and their lay-off time used up, the studio found itself in the unhappy position of having two of its highest-priced actors enjoying paid vacations. A solution had to be found soonest! Producer Lou Edelman became a hero-for-a-day by coming up with the script of *Garden of the Moon* by our ace writing team of Jerry Wald and Richard Macaulay. It was a hastily written first draft, and in common with most of its genre, far from being a finished prod-uct. But it was deemed close enough so that a starting date, two weeks hence, could be chalked in on our master production board. Meanwhile, the writers would continue writing and pol-ishing, sets would be constructed, songs written and recorded and the rest of the casting set. All of which was to be accom-plished during the next fortnight.

J. L. was pleased with the concept. According to our Sales Department, Powell's crooning career was going downhill and would benefit by co-starring with Davis. The only thing they failed to reckon with were the stars themselves. Advised by Le-gal to report for the customary wardrobe tests, they were sent copies of the first draft script. Whereupon they exploded in righteous indignation. It was nothing more, they screamed, than a rehash of every cliche-ridden backstage musical that we had ever done and that the writers' switcheroo of changing the locale from a theater to a Cocoanut Grove-like ballroom could in no way conceal the fact that it was a piece of junk.

Producer Edelman, the recipient of their anger, brought the news to J. L.

"They refuse to do it?" Warner said. "OK, we'll put the sonsofbitches on suspension."

Thus saving some $7,000 a week in salaries. But by now too much had been invested in the property to abandon it. New-comer John Payne and veteran Margaret Lindsay were cast in the leading roles, along with Pat O'Brien playing his umpteenth press agent. It was a typical case of our cliche casting. Lindsay, a far better actress than her second-rate parts ever enabled her to be, accepted stoically, aware that if it wasn't this, it would only be another thankless role. Payne, for whom we had high hopes, was talked into it by Edelman, who predicted it would make him a star.

In retrospect, perhaps it would have been better if our Arnold Laven had minded his own business. Then, instead of ending with a thud, the movie could've gone out with a big bang.

With all the ongoing feuds, Bogart and Peter Lorre were the only ones who actually enjoyed—almost sadistically so— aggravating J. L. which, all things considered, seemed only fair turn-about on their part.

Their best collaborative effort came about as the result of an oft-repeated theory of Warner's. He hated scenes wherein actors smoked, claiming it always caused smokers in the audience to become restive and retire to the lobby to satisfy their cravings. Though there was never an edict banning smoking scenes per se, our directors and writers, aware of The Boss's idiosyncracy, tried to keep them to an absolute minimum. Only Bette Davis, with her small stock of mannerisms, of which smoking was the least objectionable, was exempted from this.

It was during the making of *The Maltese Falcon* that Bogart and Lorre discovered the opportunity they had long been awaiting. In a memo to director John Huston, J. L. noted that he had just seen the first week's rushes and that they looked good. He had only one criticism: why did Bogart and Lorre have to smoke so much? He knew from long experience this could only hurt the mood of the story insofar as audience reaction was concerned. His suggestion was to limit smoking to only when necessary to establish a plot or characterization point. This was all the actors had to hear.

"The creep doesn't like us smoking?" Lorre innocently asked, his sad, doe-like eyes boring into Bogie's.

"Except like he says," Bogart pointed out. "Only for plot or characterization." He lifted his upper lip in that sardonic grin and turned to Huston. "In that case, Johnny, I think I ought to smoke a helluva lot more."

Huston failed to follow his logic. Bogart tried to explain.

"Look, this guy Spade's in a tight spot, right? His partner's just got himself bumped off, Spade's involved with a bunch of cut-throats, and to make matters worse, the cops're starting to roust him around. Now if all that wouldn't make a guy twitchy, I don't know what in hell would. And when you get to feeling twitchy, you just naturally start smoking a lot more, right?" So saying, he lit up.

"Ha, you think Spade's got reason to be nervous?" Lorre complained, lighting a fresh cigarette from the stub he was holding.

"What about Cairo? First, everybody hates the poor creep just because he's a fairy. Then, he knows even if he gets lucky and finds the Falcon, he's still got Guttman and Wilmer to worry about. You ask me, Johnny, Cairo's got a right to smoke not just one but two cigarettes at once in every scene."

Bogart nodded in agreement. "Absolutely. The fact is, Johnny, the mood of your story can only be hurt by these people *not* smoking."

Huston, who had also written the script, pondered these points for a moment. He was well aware of the fact that, since this was his directorial debut, his fledgling career would be off to a dismal start if he set out to deliberately antagonize The Boss. If sufficiently aroused, J. L. might even resort to the ultimate punishment for disobedience by replacing him with another director, a situation that had often occurred in the past with other rebels. Still, Huston was a firm believer in giving his actors the necessary leeway to make their characterizations playable, and this situation certainly belonged in that category, Moreover, in an industry of sycophants, he knew there was no way of fulfilling his dream of putting his own personal stamp on his movies if he was forced to kowtow to the Front Office.

Igniting a match with his thumbnail, he lit one of his favorite Mexican cigarettes and inhaled deeply.

"You're right," he said. "These people *are* nervous. Sure, they'd be smoking up a storm. Fuck J. L."

A sentiment devoutly wished by many, albeit more usually unspoken, it was easier said than done. If not exactly sacrosanct, a Front Office directive could seldom be completely disregarded without very good reason, a fact borne out over the years by a multitude of has-beens whose "fuck J. L." attitudes had only resulted in the sudden demise of promising and/or flourishing careers.

The following morning, producer Henry Blanke came on the set. A German who had arrived on our shores with Lubitsch back in the twenties, Blanke was our oldest supervisor in point of service. An intense but pleasant man, he had a well-deserved reputation for good taste and integrity. Ordinarily affable, on this occasion he was a bit troubled. Having received a copy of J. L.'s memo, he felt that Huston was taking an unnecessary risk by seeming to deliberately cross him.

"I agree with you about the dramatic necessity of *some* smoking," he said, "and I think I can even talk Jack into understanding that. But yesterday, in a scene with all four of your principals, you had every one of them lighting up. I'm afraid he's going to think you're ganging up on him."

Huston had a lot of respect for Blanke; he weighed his words before answering.

"Lord knows I don't want any trouble," he said. "But this is the only honest way to do this story. You understand that, Henry."

Blanke sighed. "Let me see what I can do with Jack."

The Boss was busy on other matters, and it wasn't until two days later that he, executive producer Hal Wallis and Blanke ran the new *Falcon* rushes. J. L. was not pleased with what he saw. Not only had his good advice gone unheeded, but now, he bitterly noted, *all* the goddam actors were smoking in *every* goddam scene.

Blanke's attempt to bridge the gap between Huston's integrity and J. L.'s intransigence was not successful. That afternoon, production on Stage 12 was abruptly halted when the director was ordered to report to the executive suite.

According to authorities who over the years worked at the various majors, J. L.'s sanctum sanctorum was not as elegantly furnished as Louis B. Mayer's; it was not the polo-field size of

Darryl F. Zanuck's; nor did it contain the dais from which exalted height Harry Cohn customarily gazed down upon his minions. Still, with the focal point of a massive desk, above which a strategically placed spotlight could be made to glare into a visitor's eyes with the intensity of a third-degree grilling, it was awesome enough to inspire dread apprehension, especially if the summoned employee had reason to believe that in The Boss's mind he had committed a transgression.

Whatever happened in their 30-minute meeting remained a secret between them. It's doubtful that Huston scored any points, though we were certain he would walk off the picture rather than capitulate to any drastic changes. But the outcome of the discussion—more likely, harangue—became academic when he returned to the stage. The cast principals for waiting for him.

"We've got a confession to make," Bogart said. It was one of the few times he ever showed remorse. "About this smoking, well, we really did it to get the old man pissed off. It was fun needling him, but hell, now we think it's time to put an end to it."

"Bogie's right," Lorre added. "We aggravated the shit outta the creep, so now we're happy."

Mary Astor and Sydney Greenstreet, both of whom had been initiated into the conspiracy, nodded agreement. Unanimously, they agreed that it was hard enough to come up with a good picture under the most optimum conditions without adding the unnecessary burden of Front Office ill will.

For the remainder of that day, plus the following two days, all of the scenes were played without one single cigarette being lit.

If J. L. was satisfied that he had won his point, it turned out to be a short-lived victory. The rushes from those two-and-a-fraction days disclosed that something had gone awry. It wasn't anything drastic, nothing that could even be pin-pointed. The closest anyone could define it was Wallis's "There's a nuance missing." It was so slight a change, argued one executive, that the audience would never notice it. Blanke disagreed. "If we noticed it, they will, too," he said.

Hal Wallis and Blanke spent hours in Projection Room 5 running and re-running the new rushes, then doing the same with the earlier footage and comparing them. Somehow, the mood *had* subtly changed. Cutter Tommy Richards thought that maybe there was something wrong with the rhythm of the new scenes, as if the actors were off a beat in their timing. Wallis had a different theory: could it be a technical problem? Was there, somehow, the minutest change in the lighting or camera work? Veteran cameraman Arthur Edeson assured him there had been no changes.

It was a vexing problem and apparently one without a simple solution. All they knew was that a tiny spark had gone out of the movie, that the promise of something unusual was being lost.

That evening, Huston joined Blanke in the projection room and they ran the scenes again. Depressed, they sat in silence afterwards for a long moment. When Huston finally spoke, it was in a slower drawl than his usual speech.

"You know something, Henry?" he said. "I could be wrong, but maybe the trouble is due to the cast *not* smoking in those new scenes. . ."

Blanke rubbed his bleary eyes. "Oh, God, let's not go into *that* again."

"OK," Huston agreed. "But remember, these people are accustomed to smoking all the time, not just when the camera rolls. It's become an emotional crutch. I think they will just naturally play certain scenes a little bit better if they're holding cigarettes."

Blanke looked at him thoughtfully. "As you say, you could be wrong."

"Sure," Huston admitted. "It's only a gut feeling. There's only one way to prove it—re-shoot and see what those scenes look like when they're smoking."

"Or *disprove* it," Blanke muttered darkly. "How do we tell Jack?"

Huston grinned. "Whatta you mean 'we?' *You're* the fucking producer."

It started out as an ordinary prop, but it has since come to occupy a special niche in *film noir* history. Our Art Dept. came up with the sketch. We delivered it to our Plaster Shop. A mold was cast and six hollow reproductions were turned out. They were turned over to our Paint Shop, where they were sprayed with black enamel. Finally, they were sent to Prop. Total overhead cost of the Maltese Falcon to the final budget: $683.60.

Unfortunately, there is no record of J. L.'s initial response to Huston's theory. But if it was true, as someone once quipped, that he had a whim of iron, it was also true that he was shrewd enough to know when to change his mind. With Huston's promise that the re-takes could be done without adding to the original budget, an OK was given to re-shoot the scenes in question.

A few days later, they saw Huston's hunch pay off, the evidence flashing before them on the screen. The missing nuance was found in a cloud of smoke.

Interestingly enough, has any film historian noted that *The Maltese Falcon* came close to not being released? It's true—that is, not being released under that title. S. Charles Einfeld, our publicity and exploitation V.P., argued that the public would call it *The Malted Falcon* and that in any case it was too esoteric. His suggestion was typical of WB thinking of the period: *The Gent From Frisco*. Thankfully, wiser heads prevailed. Even though it would have been the same movie, under that B title, would it have been the *same* movie?

One final footnote: When our top brass attended its first preview, the verdict was that ". . . it's a pretty good little movie." Nothing special. As a remake of a remake there were no plans to release it as anything more than a quick-A for the top spot on the usual double-feature bill.

Huston believed it deserved a better fate, voicing his opinion to Grad Sears, our V.P. in charge of sales.

"Tell you what," Sears predicted, "I'll bet you five bucks that a year from now nobody'll even remember it."

4

Lifelong Friends
of Henry Fonda

OUR MAILROOM DUTIES were, for the most part, physically wearying and mentally stultifying. The lot was divided into six mail routes, which we covered at scheduled intervals. We were also called upon to deliver rush interoffice memos, bicycle film between the cutting and projection rooms, and relieve the receptionists and a few of the executive secretaries during their lunch hours. Mostly, we trudged our 15 miles a day.

There was one assignment that kept the job from being total drudgery. Rotated among us was the pleasurable task of escorting visitors around the lot. Not alone did it mean exchanging the dullness of routine for 90 minutes of set watching, but far more important, it meant the possibility of added income, something that was all too often a dire necessity between paydays.

Officially, the studio frowned on its "Junior Executives" accepting gratuities, claiming it should be beneath our dignity. Since this was a ukase formulated by one of the $1000 a week executives, we ignored it. Certainly we never felt that accepting cash was in any way demeaning. Loose change, perhaps; crisp greenbacks, no!

To that end, over a period of time, we each perfected our own *modus operandi* of appealing to the fiscal emotions of our visitors. It started when we picked them up at Main Reception. With a great display of ersatz charm, we would welcome them with the hope that this would turn out to be a never-to-be-forgotten occasion. Then, consulting our Call Sheets, we would recite the titles and casts of the pictures shooting on the lot. Mention of such names as Errol Flynn, Rosalind Russell and Patric Knowles in *Four's a Crowd*; George Brent and Humphrey Bogart in *Racket Busters*; and Jimmy Cagney and Pat O'Brien in *Angels With Dirty Faces* were all that was needed to cause instant salivation.

It was always at this point, after a moment's dramatic hesitation, that we would deliver the *coup de grace*, by sorrowfully adding that all sets were *usually* barred to visitors. It was a technique that seldom failed. Inevitably, there would be shocked silence, then consternation.

"You mean we can't get to see Errol Flynn? My brother-in-law manages the Strand back in Far Rockaway and he promised we'd get to meet some stars! . . . I'm president of the George Brent fan club in Keokuk, and I've got to deliver this scroll to him personally—it's signed by all eight members!"

We would stare at them in troubled contemplation, an emotion we learned to accomplish by frowning and biting down on the upper lip in fair imitation of some of our better actors. Then, with a "to-hell-with-the-rules" gesture, we'd declare that we were not going to deprive them of the chance of seeing their idols. Not even—spoken with a slight quiver—if it meant endangering our jobs. Their expressions of gratitude were marvelous to behold, thus establishing, at least tacitly, the understanding of a *quid pro quo*.

Actually, visitors were at least tolerated, if not openly welcomed, on most sets. There were two permanent exceptions: Stage 5, where the process, trick and miniature scenes were filmed; and *every* Paul Muni picture. Fortunately, Muni's refusal to emote in front of strangers seldom hurt us financially. Despite his prestige as an Oscar winner, few visitors ever envinced a strong desire to see him. Still, as our answer to MGM's reclusive Garbo, his cold aloofness didn't exactly endear him to us. Someone once asked his brother-in-law, writer Abem Finkel, if Muni actually took himself that seriously in real life.

"Well," he reflected, "all I know is that in all the years I've been in the family, I've never known him to go to the bathroom."

It was during the filming of *Juarez*, in which he played the Mexican patriot, that I had my one and only personal encounter with Muni. It gave me bad dreams for weeks afterwards.

It happened early one drizzly, fog-shrouded morning as I was making my first mail delivery. Not quite fully awake, I turned the corner of Stage 19, almost colliding head-on with an apparition in a black cloak, stovepipe hat and a greenish face. It was, of course, Muni in costume and makeup. In the split second before I recognized him, I involuntarily yelped, "Oh, Jesus Christ!"

"Wrong!" he muttered, striding on, "Benito Juarez!"

I often wondered afterwards, was there the barest hint of a smile on his face as he said that?

Most of our stars were cooperative about meeting fans. Cagney, Flynn and Dick Powell, the top male favorites in 1938, would give autographs and chat between takes. In Flynn's case, if the fan was young, attractive and female, she stood a good chance of being invited into his dressing room.

On the distaff side, Ann Sheridan's genuine warmth and earthy good humor endeared her to scores of visitors. On one occasion, welcoming a group of vacationing schoolteachers, she served her favorite libation, a glass of milk liberally spiked with scotch. It was a warm day and the refreshing drinks were

"Oh, Jesus Christ!" I cried.

"Wrong," Mr. Muni muttered. "Benito Juarez."

It was Bette Davis's fault that co-star Miriam Hopkins suddenly developed a migraine headache, closing down production for the day during the shooting of *The Old Maid*.

quickly downed. The messenger who took them around said the teachers did a lot of giggling and staggering as they left the lot.

Bette Davis, variously known as Our Queen and/or The Fourth Warner Brother, sometimes tolerated visitors, other times not. It seemed to depend on her mood, or as we less delicately put it, "Whether or not she's got the rag on."

Presumably, she was between menstrual cycles one day during the filming of *The Old Maid,* permitting our Len Mark to bring a young honeymooning Spanish couple on the stage. Moreover, Davis asked the still photographer to take their pictures with her, a courtesy usually extended only to VIPs.

Dourly observing all this from her side of the set was her co-star, Miriam Hopkins. It was common knowledge that a bitter rivalry existed between them, at least on Hopkins' part. Davis was certainly secure enough to be above playing such childish games, but they did keep their distance between takes, with Davis and her entourage on one side of the stage and Hopkins and her people on the other.

Finally, no longer able to sit by ignored while Davis chatted with the obviously entranced couple, Hopkins dispatched an emissary to tell Len that she would be willing to meet them. They understood very little English and her invitation had to be translated. Perhaps it was the fault of the translater—certainly Hopkins was then as well known as Davis—but the invitation was politely declined and they left the set shortly afterwards.

Len's visitors innocently cost the studio some money that day. Right after they left, Hopkins suddenly developed a migraine headache and had to go home early.

Incidentally, her invitation was translated by her co-star.

Mid-afternoon was not usually the best time to take visitors on The Tour. All too often, directors would be fighting losing battles with their shooting schedules, and tempers of cast and crew—the rosy glow of their two-or-three-martini lunch dissipated—were apt to become a bit frayed.

Which was the bleak situation I faced one 3:30, while escorting a pair of matronly ladies. Within our first 15 minutes I had been peremptorily turned away from two stages. Since it was standard operating procedure to first obtain permission from the assistant director before bringing visitors inside, if we were told "No," there seldom was any recourse of appeal. In this case it was especially heartbreaking because the ladies had promised, "A nice couple dollars you'll get if ve can just see a real live star making a movie."

There was one other picture shooting, *The Male Animal*, but I didn't hold out much hope that my third try would be the charm. Under Elliott Nugent's direction, it was both behind schedule and over budget, a combination that always caused a certain amount of tension among the director's staff. Still, with no alternative, I girded my loins, and leaving my visitors outside, dolefully approached the first assistant.

"Excuse me, sir—" It was as far as I got. The assistants knew that whenever we wore our hangdog expressions and called them "sir" that we were about to ask a favor.

"If it's about visitors, kid," he snapped, "the answer is no!"

Dejectedly, I turned away, passing Henry Fonda, seated on the sidelines waiting for the camera crew to finish lighting the set. Suddenly an idea exploded in my mind. It was crazy, even potentially dangerous, but desperate as I was, I couldn't be bothered worrying about the possible consequences.

"ExcusemeMr.Fonda," I said, jumbling the words together in my nervousness.

"Huh?"

"I have two ladies outside," I continued, forcing myself to slow down a little. "They're friends of your family's and I wonder if you would allow me to bring them in?"

He looked at me with sudden interest. "Friends? From Omaha?"

"Yessir," I plunged on. "*Lifelong* friends, I understand."

"Why, sure," he said without hesitation. "By all means, bring 'em right in."

Armed with permission from the star himself, I rushed back to my visitors with the good news, cautioning them, however, that we could only stay for a very short time, and that it was only because of my close friendship with Hank that we were allowed in at all. Appreciatively, they followed me into the dark stage on tiptoes. Far in the distance, lights were focused on the living room set. I slowly continued forward until, still some distance from the perimeter of the crew, they could see what was going on.

A voice called "Quiet for rehearsal," and the ladies strained forward as the lanky figure of Fonda hit his mark. Wide-eyed, open-mouthed, they watched as he went through a long, intricate scene with Eugene Pallette, Hattie McDaniel and Jack Carson. As it ended, and the makeup people started checking them for the take, I realized I had been holding my breath. I expelled a long sigh of relief. What a great idea it had been!

"We'll have to leave now," I whispered and they nodded. They had seen their real live star making a movie and the memory would live on.

We headed back to the door; then hurried footsteps sounded behind us and a familiar voice called, "Hey, wait a minute, I want to say hello."

I felt a terrible compulsion to start running, but it was too late for anything save facing the dread consequences. The ladies turned and stared in awe.

"Hi," he said, unnecessarily adding, "I'm Hank Fonda. I understand you're friends of my folks."

I tried to say something—anything—but discovered I had no voice.

"Your folks?" they responded. "Nu, they live in Brooklyn?"

Fonda stared from one to the other. By some miracle, before he could reply, there was a distant summons, "Ready for a take, Mr. Fonda."

He shook hands with them, saying it was a pleasure to have met them. I started to slink away, but his hand fastened around my arm and he led me out of their earshot. Then he stopped and glared.

"From Omaha, huh? Lifelong friends!" He seemed angry, but then his expression softened into that wonderful slow smile and he released his grip. "Oh, boy!" He shook his head in reluctant admiration. "I guess you had some good reason for all this hog-wash. I just hope I didn't blow it for you."

Somehow, I managed a croaking, "Oh, no, sir."

All the way back to Main Reception, the ladies excitedly re-hashed their meeting not alone a famous star, but one who also hailed from their home town.

If I was slightly embarrassed, the feeling was instantly dispelled with their presentation of two $5 bills as they left the lot.

Of course, things didn't always work out that well. There were many times when, entirely due to circumstances beyond our control, an anticipated tip never materialized, as our Neill Lehr once discovered to his sorrow.

Escorting the mayor of a town in Mississippi, and his wife, Neill knew at once that he had struck pay dirt. They were the unbeatable combination that we always hoped for: prosperous, avid movie fans. By happenstance, their first stop was Stage 2, where a comedy-mystery *The Body Disappears* was shooting, and Mrs. Mayor "oohed" and "aahed" when told that one of her favorite actors, Edward Everett Horton, was in the cast.

They entered just in time to watch a take between Jane Wyman, Horton and Willie Best, in which Best played his usual stereotyped Negro comedy relief. With the announcement that it was a "print," the assistant told Best that his scenes had been completed. Saying goodbye to his fellow actors, he turned to Wyman and kissed her, and she responded with a little hug. In actuality, his was a simple little peck on the cheek, hers a friendly embrace, merely the sort of affectionate gestures most actors normally indulged in. But the horrified look that came over the faces of Neill's visitors said otherwise. Here was a "nigra" brazenly inflicting himself sexually upon a white woman while, even worse, *she* embraced him! In the name of common decency, what kind of people were these movie stars?

If it was a question they didn't actually voice, it was only because they already knew the answer. Suddenly becoming cold and distant, they asked Neill to kindly show them the way out.

Less than 15 minutes after their arrival, they swept out the door without so much as a "thank you." Much less a tip.

Then there was Morrie Black, who took a man I'll call Mr. Smith on The Tour and ended up being the cause of some high-level fiscal intrigue.

Unlike most visitors, Smith, middle-aged and well dressed, was not particularly interested in actors, his only request being that he'd like to see the workings of the studio. Morrie started out by walking him around the back lot sets, a ploy we often used to whet our visitors' appetites by the anticipation of what was yet to come. Nothing was shooting on the exterior sets that day, but Morrie noticed that Smith made constant notations in a little notebook.

They visited two sets. On the first, *No Time for Comedy*, the visitor watched impassively as cameraman Ernie Haller tried to find the source of a hot spot that was casting a slight shadow on Jimmy Stewart's chin, as he rehearsed a scene with Rosalind Russell and Charlie Ruggles. It was the kind of typical delay that most visitors found tedious and boring. Not so with Smith. Interested in the most mundane production problems, he kept asking all sorts of questions, and Morrie, flattered that he was considered an expert, expounded at length on the seeming inefficiency that was part and parcel of moviemaking.

After about ten minutes of repositioning the key light, they were ready for a take. Nay, said the sound mixer, "I'm picking up the drone of an overhead plane."

Smith wanted to know why the sound stage, one of six that had been constructed in the past few years, hadn't been sound-proofed? Morrie explained they had been, at the time. Now, however, with over 20 flights a day departing from and landing at Lockheed Air Terminal, only two miles away, the new generation of tri-motor commercial airlines presented problems that had been unforseen.

Another five minutes elapsed while a second plane was picked up by the mike. Finally, they were ready for a take. It consisted of six lines of brisk dialogue among the three princi-

A certain studio visitor was most interested in, but not entertained by the inordinate number of takes required for one 15-second scene between Jimmy Stewart, Rosalind Russell and Charlie Ruggles in *No Time For Comedy*.

pals, a total contribution of about 15 seconds to the whole movie.

Ruggles fluffed the first and second takes, Stewart the third, Russell the fourth, then Ruggles again. Before the sixth try, the makeup man and hairdresser decided that touch-ups were required. Smith, who had been writing in his notebook during all this, agreed to leave.

On their second stop, *A Dispatch From Reuter's,* another kind of problem was temporarily holding up production. In a scene with Otto Kruger, Eddie Robinson had the line, "It is the consensus of opinion that war is inevitable." Only he refused to say it, pointing out that "consensus" meant the majority of opinion and that therefore the line as written was redundant.

Director William Dieterle was equally insistent that the line be read exactly as it appeared in the script, claiming it was much more dramatic.

"Up yours," Robinson said, disappearing into his portable dressing room.

"Und shit on you!" the director retorted.

Morrie knew the danger signals. Any moment now Dieterle would explode and he wanted his visitor and himself far away when the inevitable happened. Smith agreed to leave.

Ninety dull minutes had gone by when Morrie showed him out the door, not even begrudging the measly buck thrust into his hand. After all, the guy had seen absolutely nothing of interest. Or had he?

Some months later, during the course of our corporation's annual stockholder's meeting in Delaware, Mr. Smith showed up as a minority stockholder of the worst possible kind: a dissident who, in light of our depressed earnings, had some heavy questions to ask of The Brothers.

Consulting a notebook, he began by wanting to know why the expensive standing sets on the back lot weren't utilized more often?

J. L., who was chairing the meeting, was puzzled for a moment, then came up with the ambiguous reply, "Well, they're used according to script requirements, weather conditions and, you know, that sort of thing."

Well, why is it, Smith went on, that the new sound stages, listed on the books as costing $100,000 each, hadn't been sound-proofed against the inevitability of increasing air traffic?

Here J. L. stumbled a bit. "Well, they were soundproofed— except maybe for the roofs." (Laughter.)

Smith continued. Why, he demanded, naming the actors and the circumstances of the scene he had witnessed on the set of *No Time for Comedy*, couldn't high-salaried stars remember of a few simple lines, so that an easy little scene didn't have to be done over and over?

Warner's response was that that was a problem that had always existed and always would. Personally, the only star he had ever completely liked was Rin-Tin-Tin. (More laughter.)

His interrogator was not yet finished. Again naming names and the picture, he brought up the incident between Robinson and Dieterle, adding with some degree of hyperbole that they almost got into a fist fight over a word that audiences wouldn't give a damn about, one way or the other.

Here J. L. was stuck. Lamely replying that he had no knowledge of the incident, he promised that upon his return to the coast, he would investigate the matter. And yes, he would certainly notify the gentleman of the results of his investigation.

Smith's questions, complaints and conclusions were not new; ever since the industry became important enough to attract the attention of Wall Street and the bankers, their efficiency experts had recited the same litany, only to learn, sooner or later, that movie-making was unlike any other business they knew.

The meeting finally adjourned with the incumbent officers re-elected, but not, however, with the harmonious unanimity of prior years.

Upon his return to the studio, The Boss irately demanded to know how that sonofabitch stockholder had learned so much about our inner workings? Luckily, he had more pressing problems and the brouhaha was gradually forgotten. But not by Morrie. Conscientious as he was, for a long time afterwards he worried that he might somehow be pinpointed as the dirty rat-fink who had revealed company secrets.

But Smith never mentioned the curly-haired messenger when he finally wrote to J. L., reminding him of his promise. The letter was turned over to S. Charles Einfeld, our Vice President in charge of Publicity and Exploitation, who replied:

"Mr. Warner has asked me to respond to your important inquiry. The facts are as follows: Mr. Edward G. Robinson and Mr. William Dieterle did indeed have some discussion over the line in question. However, at no time was there any question of fisticuffs. The problem was most amicably solved when it was referred to executive producer Hal Wallis, who suggested that Mr. Dieterle shoot it both ways."

True . . . more or less. There was a 40-minute impasse, after which time someone had the good sense to phone Wallis for his opinion. Interrupted during a story conference, his impatient reply was, "Oh, for crissake, shoot the goddam thing *both* ways!"

Afterwards, the "amicable" settlement between star and director went like this:

Robinson: "Okay, I did it your way. Now up yours!"

Dieterle: "Your vay stinks. Und shit on you!"

Which of the two versions was used? (Oh, please, Mr. Smith, don't despair.) Neither. The scene was deemed redundant and cut out after the first preview.

If we could come to a financial understanding with one or two visitors, it would seem to logically follow that the larger the group, the more our potential loot. In fact, this did not hold true. Quite the reverse. With more than a group of six, it was almost impossible to obtain permission to enter a stage, the end result being that we were forced to walk them around the back lot. If it was a warm day, our visitors ended up dusty, bored and more than a little disappointed. Far worse, we ended up empty handed.

Which is why our Darwin Krystall's heart sank as he opened the door to Main Reception and saw a milling crowd awaiting him. Counting, he came up with an even dozen. With him, it added up to an unlucky 13. It was futile to consider anything more than the walking tour. But after viewing the facades of a dozen deserted streets, with the temperature soaring into the 90's, his people started grumbling.

"Enough of this. . . . No more walking. . . . Where in hell are the stars?"

Apologetically, Darwin had no alternative but to tell them that the pictures shooting were all closed to visitors. In that case, the angered group announced, get us out of this damn oven!

He started leading them back to Main Reception. Just then, a familiar face—the first they had seen—darted out of a stage and hurried down the street. It was Jeffrey Lynn and a collective murmur of interest was heard. Darwin and his people were heading the other way when he happened to turn and saw that one of them, more aggressive than the others, had followed the actor in hot pursuit. Right into the men's room. Which is where he found them, Lynn standing at a urinal, modestly trying to cover himself with one hand, while with the other he signed an autograph book . . . for a middle-aged *female*!

If not the best actor on the lot, Lynn might have possessed the greatest *savoir faire*. While the woman gushingly told him he was her favorite actor, he went on gushing in his own way. It was the kind of nightmare encounter that we had always jokingly said would someday happen. Darwin, red-faced and stammering an apology, had to almost physically eject her.

As the group left, Lynn's voyeur fan pressed something into his palm. A nice shiny quarter.

When we sympathized about what a lousy deal he got, one of us observed that it really was Jeffrey Lynn's fault. How so, Darwin despondently asked? "Well," he was told, "maybe if Lynn had been hung better, you'd have done better."

Then there's the tragic story of Bob Hebert and the Oklahoma oil millionaires, versus a dirty, stinking actor, whose disgusting behavior cost Hebert a veritable fortune.

Is it possible that Jeffrey Lynn was complaining to the cops about his voyeur fan?

The Oklahomans, two stout, middle-aged gentlemen similarly attired in white suits, Stetsons and cowboy boots, let it be known from the outset that they wanted to meet as many stars as possible.

"Tell you what, boy," one of them confided, "as a little inducement, let's say it's worth ten bucks for every head you come up with. OK?"

Luckily, Bob's breath was momentarily taken away, because it gave the other man a chance to speak. "Come on, Jake," he chided, "let's make it worth the boy's while—$25 a head."

Speaking of heads, Bob's started spinning. With four pictures shooting, and at least a dozen stars working on the lot, the possibilities were beyond his mathematical ability to comprehend. All he could think of was that, according to legend, one of our predecessors had once received a $100 tip, a fortune that had never even been approached since then. But now it would be an amount that would pale into insignificant chicken feed if he played his cards right! With visions of undreamed-of wealth flashing before his eyes, and his hands trembling, he consulted the Call Sheets.

Stage 12-A: *The Sea Wolf.* Edward G. Robinson, Ida Lupino, Alexander Knox.

Stage 15: *Knockout.* Arthur Kennedy, Virginia Field, Anthony Quinn.

Stage 22: *Footsteps in the Dark.* Errol Flynn, Brenda Marshall, Ralph Bellamy, Walter Connolly.

Stage 6: *The Wagons Roll at Night.* Humphrey Bogart, Sylvia Sidney.

They came to Stage 12-A. With the huge sliding door open, indicating that they were between set-ups, it was a perfect time to chance a chat with the actors. Dear blessed Lord, thank you, Bob whispered! Seated in a semi-circle were the three principals, Robinson, Lupino and Knox, idly chatting. Seventy-five bucks on the hoof!

Hebert had never before spoken to any of them, but that was of no consequence, not even though it meant interrupting their conversation. Despite being somewhat bemused by his sudden introduction of two strangers, they were at least courteous enough to acknowledge them to sign their autograph books and accept the gentlemen's cards, along with the directive, "Now be sure an' call us, y'hear, next time y'all come to Tulsa."

If his guests seemed happy, Bob was in a state approaching orgasm.

He led them into Stage 15. A scene was being shot, and they had to wait an interminable two or three minutes before a take was okayed and the actors released. The instant that "Cut and print," was called, and before Arthur Kennedy, Virginia Field and Anthony Quinn could move away, Bob had them cornered with the oil men.

As before, the short meeting ended with the tendering of autograph books, business cards and an invitation to visit next time they were in Tulsa, "Ya'll hear?"

Leaving the stage, Jake poked his friend in the ribs. "Boy, are we havin' fun or are we havin' fun?"

He was poked back with the definitive answer. "We is havin' *fun!*"

It was nothing compared with what Hebert was experiencing. Doing some quick mental arithmatic, he calculated that so far he had earned $150. *One hundred and fifty dollars!* And this was only the start! He was well on his way to financial independence!

A quick glance again at the Call Sheets indicated that Stage 22, with its four stars, offered the better return, but Stage 6, despite its meager promise of only another $50, was closer.

Outside Stage 6, the flashing red light gave mute notice that a scene was being filmed. They waited a minute or so, then the light went off and Bob led them inside. From a distance, they heard the echoing command, "OK, once more. Quiet!"

Putting his fingers to his lips, Hebert indicated they were to follow him. Some 50 feet ahead, a blaze of lights illuminated an arena where the circus-background scene was being shot. As they drew closer, in the immediate darkened foreground they made out a number of cages containing a menagerie of lions, tigers and leopards, all peacefully snoring away.

Perhaps it was the Oklahomans' white suits that stood out in the semi-darkness, or perhaps as an actor he was merely giving vent to his temperament. Whatever, one mangy, toothless old lion awakened, and lifting a leg, proceeded at point-blank range to relieve himself with a veritable torrent, all but drowning his victims.

Screaming in outraged shock—never mind that their cries ruined the distant take—they ran for the exit. Outside, drenched from Stetsons to boots, and starting to stink with an unholy fragrance, they suddenly decided they were no longer having fun. Worse, in new-found fury, they blamed Bob. Threatening legal action against the studio, they stormed off the lot, somehow forgetting to pay for services already rendered.

Nor was that the end of it. When Hebert, bedraggled and despondent, returned to our department, he learned that the assistant on *The Wagons Roll at Night* had phoned to complain that a messenger and his drunken visitors had not alone come on the stage without permission, but had ruined an important scene.

He was given the following two days off. Without pay.

Finally, there was the incident that went down in our annals as The Schoolhouse Story.

As a self-contained little city, with our own power station, fire and police departments, we even had our own schoolhouse. Surrounded by a white picket fence, it was The Little Red Schoolhouse of a bygone era, where over the years such moppets as Jackie Cooper, Dickie Moore, Bonita Granville, Sybil Jason and Billy and Bobby Mauch occupied desks for four hours a day, studying text books instead of scripts.

So it was perfectly natural for our Jim Levien to decide to climax a happy tour with a vacationing school principal and his prim wife by taking them inside.

"I think you'll get a kick out of this," Jim said, opening the door.

They followed him into the deserted room and their eyes went to the blackboard. They stared, then gasped. Somebody—we always suspected it was the work of the newly arrived Dead End Kids—had chalked:

SMOKING IS GOOD FOR KID ACTORS. IT STUNTS OUR GROWTH.
JACK & JILL WENT UP THE HILL TO HAVE A LITTLE NOOKY.
I WILL NOT FUCK AGAIN DURING CLASS.

This last was repeated five times.

Jim's attempt at re-creating nostalgia cost him a tip. The couple was not amused.

5

Tony Cohen, Alias Anthony Quinn

KATHERINE HIGGINS ran our commissary. A thin, severe-looking woman who still retained the brogue of her native Ireland, one of her specialties was noted on the menu as "Katherine's Leek & Potato Soup." In making up new menus, someone carelessly misspelled a word, causing it to appear as "Katherine's *Leak* & Potato Soup," thereby considerably altering its ingredients. (There were, of course, those chronic complainers who maintained that it should *always* have been spelled that way.) Another set of menus were hurriedly substituted, but by then the harm had been done, causing us to suspect that its yellowish hue derived from more than vegetables, and the once-popular item was finally dropped from the daily bill of fare.

As with all company restaurants, our commissary was deliberately a losing proposition. In an effort to keep employees from leaving the lot, substantial lunches were offered at bargain prices, ranging from 35¢ at the counter to 90¢ at a table, and upwards for those who desired the a la carte dishes served in the more exclusive Green Room. Although well intentioned, the reason it was unsuccessful was due to a Front Office edict prohibiting the sale of beer and wine. Those who spent tension-filled mornings on the sets wanted the opportunity to unwind a little during their lunch breaks and the only way they could do so was to go off the lot to more liberal establishments. This merely proved how short-sighted our edict was, because the off-lot lunch hour, more often than not, stretched out to 90 minutes and longer, invariably causing afternoon production to resume later than scheduled.

For a time, one of the worst offenders of the late returnees was character actor Barton MacLane, whose typical lunch consisted of four or five martinis and a toothpick. The possessor of an enormous, perpetual thirst, MacLane wasted no time in downing his liquid refreshment. It was the *shmoozing* and contemplative tooth-picking which followed that often caused him to return to his set an hour late. Co-starring at the time with Glenda Farrell in the *Torchy Blaine* B series, with the usual tight budget and short shooting schedule of its genre, MacLane's continual tardiness starting causing problems.

Finally, Executive Producer Brynie Foy issued an ultimatum: during shooting, MacLane was forbidden to leave the lot on his lunch hour. To enforce this, the Auto Gate and both reception rooms were alerted to notify Production if he tried to sneak out.

He never did. Nor did he retire to the privacy of his dressing room, where he could have imbibed in peace and quiet. A gregarious man who enjoyed loud arguments, MacLane surprised us by showing up in the commissary. How, we wondered, would he be able to drink his lunch in that confining atmosphere, with dozens of spies waiting breathlessly to report his first infraction?

The answer was . . . easily.

In a display of sympathy, his cronies elected to remain on the lot with him, all assembling at their own reserved table in the rear. While the others ate, MacLane held forth with the omni-

In this scene from one of the *Torchy Blaine* series, detective Barton MacLane is grilling a suspect. If MacLane looks a little gruff, it's possibly because he was anticipating the lunch whistle, so he could stop grilling and get grilled.

present toothpick stuck in his mouth, withdrawing it only when sipping from a glass of "water," which he constantly replenished from a thermos. Anybody who questioned the aromatic odor emanating from the glass was given short shrift, as was the case of Manager Higgins, whose eyes widened suspiciously the first time she caught sight of the thermos.

"Whattaya mean, it smells like gin?" MacLane demanded. "It's just plain water, with a little perfume to kill the taste of the water. You've heard of non-alcoholic near-beer, haven't you? Well, goddam it, this is non-alcoholic near-gin!"

After that, no one disputed his word. The Front Office knew better, but just so long as he reported back to work on time they were temporarily willing to go along with the gag.

We ate at the counter, of course—an economic necessity on our budgets—our 35¢ lunches consisting of soup or salad, a hot entree with two vegetables, bread and butter, and choice of milk, coffee or a soft drink. If it was payday, or if we were temporarily flush with gambling winnings or a tip, we might splurge on the 50¢ lunch, which included *both* soup and salad, an entree of roast beef or club steak, plus dessert. It might not have been gourmet fare, but since we always worked up ravenous appetites by noon, we were among the minority who considered the commissary lunches satisfactory, if a little skimpy.

The fact that we didn't eat there every day was the fault of Connie Martin, our stalwart cashier, who was adamant about our paying cash on the barrelhead. No credit. No chits accepted. We once complained that since the contract people were allowed to sign their checks, with Accounting billing them semi-monthly, why couldn't we have the same privilege?

"I'll tell you why," Connie patiently replied. "First of all, you're not under contract. Second, if you ran up two weeks' tabs, you couldn't afford to pay them. Third, even if you could, knowing you deadbeats, you wouldn't."

She might have had a point or two or three there.

Which is why, if we didn't have the wherewithal, we were forced to go across the street to the drug store counter. Their lunches were a little more expensive, but at least we were treated as the important people we were by being accorded the courtesy of charging our meals until payday. (After which time, if we didn't promptly settle up, they came looking for us.)

A few of us were eating at the drug store one day when we were joined by a friendly little guy, who mentioned that he was playing a role in the new Jimmy Cagney picture, *City for Conquest*. Short, with wild hair and a big nose, he didn't look like much of an actor, nor did his odd name sound like one. Fresh from New York, he surprised us by his fervant declaration that he loved working in movies. Although most stage actors displayed an open condescension toward Hollywood, he hoped there would be bigger and better parts in the offing and that he would never have to return to the legitimate theater.

Like so many others, his hopes were dashed on the shoals of redundancy. We had more than our quota of diminutive, funny-looking gangster types, and the last time we saw him he said that things hadn't worked out and that he was returning east.

Sometimes, blessings in disguise take a long time to reveal themselves. As an actor, he never could have played more than character parts. It was as a director that he made movie history with, among others, *On the Waterfront* and *East of Eden*.

The funny-looking little guy with the odd name: Elia (Gadge) Kazan.

One day, at a time when production was unusually heavy, Connie decided she could no longer maintain her work load without assistance. Not alone did she have to ring up the checks and make change, but she also had the more time-consuming chore of answering the ever-ringing phones and paging the required people. What with constant emergencies involving casts and crews, there were times when the continuous calls became her number-one priority, causing long, irate lines in front of her counter.

In the interest of improved efficiency, our business manager agreed that her request had merit, and a memo was dispatched to our department, ordering that one of us be made available.

When we knew him as a lowly member of our stock company, his ambition was to become a movie star. With *that* face? we wondered. Luckily, Elia Kazan had another, better talent. As a director, he made film history with *On the Waterfront* and *East of Eden*, among others. Here he appears between Jack Carson and Priscilla Lane in *Blues in the Night.*

Fred generously offered it to anyone who was interested, and it was much sought-after since all we had to do was answer the phones from 11:30 until the 2:30 closing. Moreover, we were provided with a free 50¢ lunch, not to mention the added inducement that no walking was involved.

After a series of try-outs, Connie selected Lou Turner as her permanent assistant. Lou was an excellent choice, unflappable in the face of non-stop life-and-death calls, and possessing good clear diction, an essential requirement considering the din raised by hundreds of voices competing with each other.

If he had one slight fault, it was a common one, endemic to our department. With our accustomed irreverence, he had succumbed to the habit of mispronouncing certain names.

It happened shortly after he started, with a phone call from executive producer Hal Wallis's office. There was a problem with the script of *They Died With Their Boots On*, and they had to reach one of the writers, a dour little Scotsman named Aeneas MacKenzie. Long before, finding his first name a bothersome tongue-twister, we had privately dubbed him "Penis."

Lou switched on the public address and the inevitable happened. "Mr. Penis MacKenzie, telephone," he paged, his dulcet tones penetrating every nook and cranny. "Mr. Penis MacKenzie, telephone please."

Connie was too busy to know what the sudden roars of laughter were all about, and though Lou immediately realized his gaffe, the harm had been done. MacKenzie was not amused, especially when it soon became his common nickname among his fellow writers. It was producer Robert Lord who urged him to accept it philosophically, explaining, "Since the only other mispronunciation is 'Anus,' wouldn't you rather be known as a prick than an asshole?"

One Tuesday in the Spring of 1940—it was the desolate day before payday and only a few of us were lucky enough to have the required 35¢—we entered the commisary at 11:30 and encountered a small miracle.

On the side of Connie's counter was a freshly-painted placard reading: *As our way of saying goodbye to all our friends, please have lunch on us today. Joan Blondell and Dick Powell.*

We knew the Powells had asked out of the remaining months of their contracts, and had in fact already moved off the lot, so this gesture came as a totally unexpected but delightful surprise. Still, before putting ourselves in jeopardy, we had to make certain there were no restrictions. We asked Connie if it was on the level?

"You can read, can't you?" she snapped. "It says *friends!*"

"Oh, great!" Bernie Kotzin cried. "We were practically the most intimate friends they ever had!"

Undaunted by her expression of disbelief, we sat down and grabbed menus. Then, remembering that three of our colleagues, temporarily impoverished, had gone to the drug store, one of us was immediately dispatched to phone them with the cryptic message that if they hadn't ordered yet, they were to get their asses over to the commissary, that it was *Christmas!*

Christmas indeed! Also, Thanksgiving, Rosh Hashanah and All-Saints feast day rolled into one. How beautiful, those unaccustomed words that fell trippingly from our tongues that magical noontime:

Shrimp cocktails all around please. Salad with Roquefort dressing. What, Roquefort is ten cents extra? That's all right, dear, today money is no object. Then we'll all have the New York steaks, medium-rare, with bearnaise sauce, baked potatoes with sour cream and chives, large Cokes and blueberry pie. Oh, make that pie a la mode with ice cream please.

We toasted "Big Tits" and "Dopey"—our departmental nicknames for our hosts—with our Cokes, savored every last crumb, then, though for once satiated, debated whether to order seconds. Jimmy Miller, with an innate sense of fair play, was strongly opposed to the idea, claiming it would look as though we were taking advantage of their generosity. The rest of us took the *pro* position that since this was undoubtedly a once-in-a-lifetime windfall, we should take *full* advantage of it. We were

When Dick Powell and Joan Blondell left the studio, their unexpected farewell gift was one of the most wonderful surprises that ever happened to us.

going to put it to a vote, but by then it had become academic. We had spent our entire hour eating.

When we presented our checks to Connie, she glanced at the totals and muttered one word: "Freeloaders!"

We had each spent an incredible $1.75!

As was usual whenever an actor did anything of a benevolent nature, there were those who looked for an ulterior motive. Some said it would give the Powells a nice tax write-off; others argued that it was a lot cheaper than following the usual custom of buying individual gifts for all their co-workers. Still another group claimed, possibly with some logic, that Powell had specifically chosen that particular day by learning in advance that there would only be one picture shooting on the lot.

Whatever, we never questioned the motive behind anything that was free. For us, it was a day to remember . . . truly Christmas in May.

Although the commissary closed at 2:30, we were not entirely deprived of the mid-afternoon snacks that our voracious appetites demanded. By three, a Mexican bus boy we called Jose started wheeling a cart around the lot, offering candy, fruit and soft drinks. As some of us were availing ourselves of refreshment one afternoon, we were joined by Anthony Quinn, who started speaking to Jose in Spanish. That is, we assumed it was Spanish, but the bus boy only responded with a blank stare. Quinn tried again, with the same result, then was summoned to the sound stage where he was working.

Knowing that Quinn's publicity biography listed his ancestry as Mexican-American, we asked Jose how come he hadn't understood his compatriot? In the few English words that comprised his vocabulary, he replied that it was because the Senor had "No spoke Spanish." Harry Loebl, considered our resident sage by reason of being several years our senior, said, "You mean this Quinn guy doesn't talk like the rest of you Mexicans do?"

Jose shook his head. "Thees kin' talk I no hear never."

During one of our bull sessions in the back room the next day, as we were idly discussing the incident, and wondering why Quinn would pretend to be part Mexican, Harry suddenly snapped his fingers and excitedly interrupted.

"Wait a second!" he cried. "I got it! I got it! All along—ever since this Quinn guy came on the lot—I've had the feeling I knew him from someplace. It just came to me! Five years ago, back in the Bronx, he lived across the street from us! You know what his real name is?" He paused dramatically. "*Tony Cohen*! Get it? Cohen—Quinn!"

We seldom doubted Harry's word on any of the more esoteric subjects and in this case it seemed logical to believe that an actor with romantic-type aspirations might prefer a Latin background to that of the Jewish Bronx. It was interesting enough to warrant our broadcasting it throughout the studio, surprising and delighting a number of Jewish secretaries who had already been attracted to him.

Quinn was then playing the second lead in *Knockout* and one of us persuaded Harry to accompany him to the set in hopes of a confrontation that would force the actor to admit his deception. The closest they came was when Harry approached him between set-ups and meekly asked, "Didn't you used to live near the Concourse in the Bronx?"

"No," said Quinn, thereby ending the conversation.

We accused Harry of being gutless. He should have said, "Hey, Tony Cohen, what gives with all this crap about being a hotsy-totsy Latin? I know better, *lundsman*!"

Harry saw it a bit differently, claiming he had already proved it to his own satisfaction and that there was nothing to be gained by antagonizing a guy who was playing a heavyweight prize fighter.

The subject of Anthony Cohen-Quinn had waned when, a few weeks later, two of us encountered Jose on the lot. No longer pushing the cart or wearing his bus boy's uniform, he was now nattily attired in a suit. He told us that he had just picked up his final check and that his agent had got him a part over at RKO. There was nothing surprising in what he said, since half the people in Hollywood were would-be actors; it was the *way* he said it. In perfect, unaccented English!

Noting our startled reactions, he laughed. "That was a pretty good 'Mex' act I put on, huh? Had to do it to get the job. The only time I was afraid it wouldn't work was when Quinn started talking to me in Spanish. Lucky for me he didn't give me away—all the Spanish I know you could stick in your ear."

After that, Harry wasn't quite so sure that Quinn was the Tony Cohen he had once known.

We never got around to making a general retraction. We were right so much of the time that we felt it would be a disservice to those in the studio who depended on us for the inside scoop to find out that we were not infallible.

6

Will the Real Errol Flynn Please Join In

SHORTLY AFTER our eight a.m. opening, the Burbank Post Office would deliver the usual five or six 50-pound sacks of mail, a procedure that was repeated at 1:30 every afternoon. For the six of us on the sunrise shift, the routine was to break open one sack at a time, spill the contents on the counter, then distribute it in the bins corresponding to the various routes, after which each bin would be broken down to departments and individuals.

With an average of 75 percent of the mail being addressed to actors, the largest bin was, of course, reserved for the Fan Mail Department. After the afternoon mail, it would be overflowing with 1500-2000 letters and postal cards.

Incidentally, the great American public of those days couldn't spell any better than today's college freshmen, forcing us to become adept at deciphering some very weird reworkings of names. There were always those letters addressed to variations of such as Oil Fin . . . Olive D. Have A Land . . . Paul Money . . . Ed Robin & Son . . . Dick Foul . . . Ronald Re Gun . . . Clawz Raynz . . . Piss Ella Lane . . . Ann Shitagain . . . etc. Nothing derogatory intended; these were from fans, albeit typically illiterate ones.

One pencilled name, presumably intended for Bogart, remained our favorite for a long time: *Hump Free Bigot.* It had a nice ring to it.

We always felt it would be appropriate to let our "household names" see how famous they really were. It might have taken some of them down a peg or two. But those never got beyond the guardians of Fan Mail.

Early in 1938 we started receiving mail from New York City addressed to "Julius Garfinkle, Personal." Since we had no record of anyone with that name, the letters ended up in the "Not At" box and were eventually returned to the senders. It caused a bit of a flap when it turned out they were from his family, intended for a newly arrived and newly renamed John Garfield.

Although we never opened the fan letters, there were always enough penny postal cards to provide interesting reading. One, anonymously addressed to Guy Kibbee, declared, "Your face reminds me of my mother-in-law's ass."

Another, to George Raft, complained, "As a gangster, you stink. You don't even know how to hold a gat." Presumably, the writer knew whereof he spoke. It was postmarked Joliet Prison.

Possibly one of the weirdest postal cards we ever received was sent to Errol Flynn from a lady in New Jersey. It was a plea to phone her collect any Tuesday or Thursday at 8 P.M. California time. It was signed only with her first name, Agnes, and a phone number.

Intrigued by the request, and the fact that she was willing to pay for the long distance call, one of our group—I'll call him Sam—adept at doing a passable vocal imitation of Flynn, borrowed the card long enough to oblige the lady. Agnes, he told us, sounded middle-aged, tipsy and spinsterish. At first, that is. After a few moments of small talk, she got to the point. Having

An anonymous fan compared Guy Kibbee's face with a certain part of his mother-in-law's anatomy.

seen all of Flynn's movies, she had noticed that in his costume films his tights had presented a magnificent bulge between his legs. The most beautiful bulge she had ever seen. Was it truly all his?

Of course, Sam stammered, all t-t-ten inches. With that, she commenced moaning, begging him to call her every filthy name he could think of.

Unfortunately for poor Agnes, our imitator lacked the real Flynn's sophistication. Unnerved by the obvious fact that she was masturbating, he suddenly terminated the conversation by hanging up. We were very disappointed in Sam, pointing out that under the circumstances he certainly should have protected our star's reputation by at least joining in with her.

While sorting the mail one morning, an enterprising new-comer, whom I'll call Earl, made the interesting discovery that most of the fan mail letters contained quarters or half-dollars, as payment for autographed pictures. The rest of us had long been aware of this fact, since the weight and shape of the coins were easily detected through the envelopes. But we certainly didn't have to be warned that filching money from the U.S. mails was a federal offense and that it wasn't worth the attendant risk for pocket money.

Earl saw it differently, envisioning larceny on a much grander scale. If there were, say, an average of 500 letters each day containing change, and if he stole only one-fifth of them, his per-diem income could be increased by $25 or more. Of course, there were obstacles to overcome, and some slight danger involved, but nothing that he considered insurmountable. Mainly, he knew he couldn't make the fan mail delivery every day without the risk of arousing suspicion. The Fan Mail Department was located in the Music Building and deliveries were made every afternoon as part of a regularly scheduled route by whichever of us was up next. But often, if he knew it was around the time for fan mail delivery, Earl would volunteer to take the next call, and slothful as many of us were, we were agreeable,

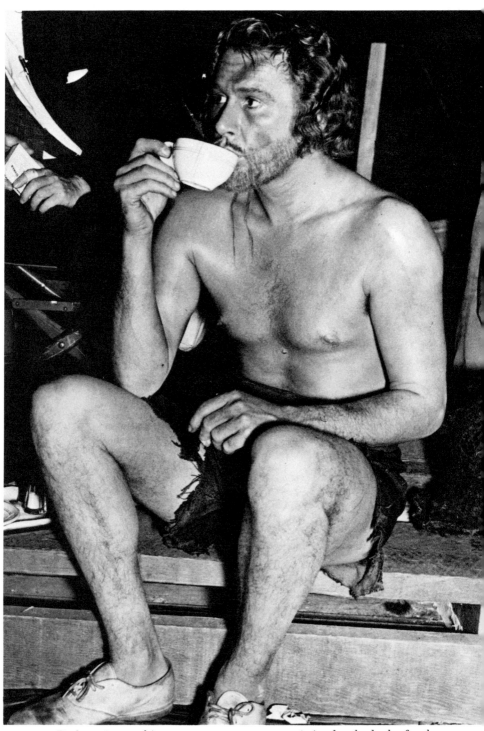

Perhaps it was this costume—or more appropriately, the lack of—that prompted the weird request from a Flynn fan. (Whatever the contents of his cup, it's a sure bet it wasn't coffee.)

attributing his industry to the fact that as a newcomer he was trying to apple polish Pappmeier.

With the accuracy of our records, it was later learned that in one month's time Earl had delivered the fan mail some 18 times. But that was much later. There were no suspicions that the volume of mail had decreased, or that there were fewer letters containing coins. In retrospect, we might have wondered why he was constantly exchanging handfuls of coins for paper money, but with his self-established reputation of being a lucky gambler, it seemed reasonable when he claimed it had been his previous night's winnings at poker or blackjack.

Unlike most criminals, who are supposed to throw away their ill-gotten gains, Earl shrewdly put his loot to work. One day he let it be known that his favorite aunt had died, leaving him a small bequest. Having no special plans for this windfall at the moment, he was willing to lend it to his friends at a slight rate of interest. Since by Monday most of us were dead broke, with Wednesday's payday light years in the future, his generous offer was like manna from heaven.

At first.

In the initial rush of borrowing, we were both unmindful and uncaring of the fact that his interest rates were somewhat more than "slight." Usurious was the word. A $5 loan for one week cost $6; $10 cost $12; or, if the principal was not repaid, the loan could be renewed indefinitely as long as the weekly interest was paid.

This went on for about three or four months, during which time his debtors grew to include the staff in Mimeo and some of the girls in the steno pool. It finally reached the point where Earl arranged to have Wednesday as his permanent day off, whereupon he would spend ten hours in our back room, collecting his debts, issuing new loans, and entering cryptic notations in his thickening ledger, looking more and more, as one of us deep in his web ruefully remarked, "Like a bloated, bastard banker."

By then the old adage about lending money and losing a friend had come to pass. We were beginning to despise our one-time benefactor. Strangely, we never collectively discussed plans to do away with him. It certainly wasn't due to our scruples; where money was concerned, some of us didn't have any.

At that point, enjoying a prosperity that seemed boundless, Earl logically should have put an end to his thievery. Certainly, by then he didn't need the extra money with its attendant risk, however slight, of eventual apprehension. On the other hand, has there ever been an entrepreneur who accumulated enough, even ill-gotten, riches to then call it quits? Take J. Paul Getty, Howard Hughes, Aristotle Onassis, to name a few—apparently their first $100 million only served to whet their appetites for more. Always more! So it was with Earl. With a growing ego, and a greed to match, he brought about his own downfall.

When it happened, it was almost comedic. At the very least, it lacked the dramatic twist we would have given it in a movie. Late one afternoon, the Plumbing Department was called to fix an overflowing toilet in the men's room in the Music Building. The plumber discovered the trouble was caused by dozens of crumpled, waterlogged envelopes and letters clogging the pipes. All fan mail.

Security quietly instituted an investigation. A few days later, Earl was apprehended in the same booth in the act of attempting to flush away more evidence. It was an ignominious ending to a budding financial career. He wasn't arrested, since such action could have resulted in unwanted publicity, but merely fired and warned not to come near the studio again. That was the last we ever saw of him. On the day of his sudden departure, we figured he was owed over $700. But since by then most of it represented interest compounded on top of interest, the fact that he never attempted to collect it bothered our consciences very little. If at all.

Our daily mail always included several dozen letters addressed merely, "Warner Bros. Studios, Burbank, Cal.," and these we were instructed to read, then forward to the proper department or person. Since they usually fell into certain catego-

ries, it rarely required glancing at more than the first few lines
to know the writers' gripe or proposition.

If a letter started out, as so many of them did, "I go to movies
all the time and I ain't never seen a single one as good as what
happened to me in my own life which I will sell you and you can
get Joan Crawford to play me. . ." the envelope would be
marked "Att: Story Dept.," from whence it would eventually be
mailed back to the sender with a form rejection advising that we
did not buy unsolicited material.

Then there were those that threatened lawsuits. "You used
my name in a movie and unless you wanna be sued you better
pay. . ." These went to Legal, with their form response being
that a disclaimer at the beginning of our movies announced that
all names and events were fictitious.

The Music Department came in for more than its share of
junk mail. "Altho not a professional songwriter," the opening
invariably read, "I have just written a great song for one of your
musicals . . . " What *song*, we wondered? Outside of a hack-
neyed title and a dozen cliche lines, there was no indication that
the writers possessed the slightest musical ability. Of course,
that never fazed them; there was usually the P.S. that "your staff
songwriters can fix whatever's necessary."

Leo Forbstein's secretary used to grit her teeth whenever we
brought in a batch of these in our deliveries.

"Damn it," she would complain, "don't I have enough to do
without having to answer these nuts? Why don't you just throw
all that crap away?"

Good question. We would have, except that the Front Office
believed it was good public relations to respond to all inquiries.
Since everybody had something to sell, or complain about, we
couldn't figure out how any rejection, no matter how diplomatically worded, could make friends for us.

If all the correspondents had their hands outstretched with
one gimmick or another, by far the majority offered themselves.
How many thousands of times we must have read, "Dear Sirs:
My family and friends have always told me I look exactly like

(Davis, Gable, Flynn, Garbo, etc., etc.) and I know that I can act much better. I am sending you my picture. If you'll send me expense money to come to Hollywood . . . " The only photo I can remember that bore the slightest resemblance to an established star was that of a balding, middle-aged man with a big nose, who looked a bit like Jimmy Durante. According to him, however, he was Fred Astaire's double.

Laughable and ridiculous as these letters and accompanying photos were, there was also something undeniably poignant about many of them. With most people leading, as Thoreau wrote, "lives of quiet desperation," who could blame them in their pitiful quest of The American Dream?

One such letter stands out in memory, different from the others only because it triggered a chain of circumstances that almost ended in tragedy. Postmarked Hollywood, written in a childish hand, with some of the words misspelled, it was from a girl named Dorothy who had just arrived from Minnesota and wanted to know how she could become an actress? Her qualifications included two years of high school drama, the lead in a church Biblical pageant, and two performances as Meg in a local group's presentation of *Little Women*. There was an enclosed snapshot of a pretty girl of about 17. Blond, bosomy, with a beguiling smile, she was no different from a thousand others we had seen in similar poses.

Normally, we would have scrawled "Casting" on the envelope and that would have been the end of the matter. They received hundreds of identical inquiries each week, all of which, the Front Office notwithstanding, were relegated to the waste basket.

In this case, it was the Hollywood postmark that initiated the incident. A messenger named (as I'll call him) Herkimer happened to open her letter. Instead of forwarding it, he put it in his pocket. That evening after work he phoned her at the boarding house where she was staying. Introducing himself as one of our casting directors, he said he was impressed with her picture and would like to meet her.

Imagine Dorothy's innocent delight. Barely a few days in Hollywood and already a studio casting director wanted to meet her!

Herkimer took her out that night for a hamburger and a drive to the beach, during which he learned she had just turned 18, had no friends or family here and was a virgin. It was this latter fact that decided him against going too far on their first meeting, noting that she froze as he started to reach under her dress. As delightful a morsel as she was—much prettier than her snapshot indicated—he saw no reason to rush things. Rather, he casually mentioned that an actress had to experience *every* kind of emotion before she could truly call herself a professional. She agreed, and he let it go at that. For the moment.

All this we learned in the back room the following day. Herkimer concluded his narrative by saying that he had another date with her tonight. And then, oh boy! He licked his blubbery lips, one of his many repulsive habits.

At first we weren't interested. Herkimer was not one of the more popular of our group. Short, with thinning, dank hair and bad skin, he was boastful and cheap, and we disbelieved his constant bragging about easy conquests, pointing out his ever-present crop of pimples as evidence that he was a compulsive masturbator.

The next morning he seemed a bit preoccupied, and when idly asked how he had made out, he surprised us by shaking his head.

"She got scared," he said. "I bought her another hamburger, then drove up in the hills and parked. When I started pulling down her panties, she got the shakes. Like a goddam spastic! Then she started crying that she'd never done this before and all that kind of crap. I took the cunt home. Screw her!"

We thought that would be the last we would hear about Dorothy. But Herkimer's lust outweighed his anger. He was off the following day. When he returned, he was obviously pleased about something. For the whole morning he remained secretive, smiling and occasionally chuckling to himself. Finally, just before lunchtime, Bryan Hargreaves could no longer stand the suspense.

"Come on, you jerk," he said. "Spill it!"

Herkimer's pretended surprise didn't ring true. "Huh? Spill what?"

"You know goddam well what," Bryan said ominously. "What're you so fucking happy about?"

There were five of us present. The others feigned complete indifference, but in fact none of us moved when the summoning buzzer sounded. If Herkimer wanted undivided attention, he had us in the palm of his hand. First, he licked his lips.

"Well, this Dorothy I was telling you about—" The door was thrown open and Ed Haldeman stood in the threshold.

"Excuse me, gentlemen," he said in his usual, deceptively quiet, sarcastic manner. "I know you all have better things to do, but I've buzzed three times now without getting one teensy-weensy little response. I wonder if I could intrude long enough to borrow three of you for a little work?"

I was one of the three next up, causing me to miss Herkimer's personal recitation. I got it second-hand during lunch.

Following the night when Dorothy panicked, he dwelt on the idea of letting her cool her heels for a few days, certain that the fear of having offended her one studio contact would sooner or later overcome her moral trepidations. But he finally decided against playing the waiting game for two reasons: what if, in her remorse, she tried phoning him at the studio to apologize for her actions? He had taken the precaution, of course, of using a phoney name, but then she would learn that there was no such person in Casting. More important, his lust was still unfulfilled and growing. With the space of a whole day off ahead of him, he made a sudden decision.

Phoning Dorothy, his voice cold and impersonal, he said that he had ordered a screen test set up for her on the following day. Of course, she would first have to study for it, but if she was interested he would pick her up in half an hour.

She was probably standing outside, impatiently waiting moments after he hung up.

If a bit puzzled why Herkimer drove her to a motel rather than the studio, she readily accepted his explanation that the set they were going to use was not ready and that this would be a close approximation.

In the privacy of the sordid little room, he proceeded to set the scene. She would be playing a girl whose husband is about to leave for the army. They meet here, talk a bit and have a farewell drink before parting. Dorothy understood. But what about the dialogue? He said she needn't worry about that just yet; the main thing was for her to get into the mood of the role, and in order to help her, he would play the husband. The only necessary prop was a half-pint of bourbon, which Herkimer had thoughtfully picked up in advance. Pouring two straight drinks, he told Dorothy to drink it in the farewell toast.

They rehearsed it several times. Never having tasted alcohol before, she found the first sips difficult to swallow, but after each she was praised by her mentor, who said she was now starting to loosen up and really act.

There was, at this point, no need to hear the rest. The outcome was only too obvious. She would finally collapse on the bed in a drunken stupor and good old Herkimer would then pounce. No, first he would lick his blubbery lips. The images it conjured up were not conducive to a pleasant lunch.

Our narrator agreed that that was indeed the outcome. Except that Herkimer had, naturally, described the de-floweration in graphic detail.

"Oh, one funny thing," he added. "You know what a cheap prick he is? Well, to save a few bucks, he only rented the room for half a day. So before he can get it up the second time, the manager's pounding at the door to tell him his time's up."

At which point, apparently, he dressed Dorothy, awakened her and drove her home. Time to write her off as another easy conquest.

Unlike most sexual recountings, which could be interesting, even erotic, this one left us with an uncomfortable feeling of disgust. There was nothing exciting about it, and whatever we were, we weren't rapists, a fact we made clear to Herkimer. What conquest? All he had done was commit rape. His jeering response was that we were all jealous.

There was some mild discussion about intending to do something for the girl. Exactly what, we didn't know. Chances are, nothing would have come of it, but in any event we were too late.

The following day, a short paragraph on an inside page of the *Hollywood Citizen-News* told the end of the story. An unidentified starlet had attempted suicide by turning on the gas in her rented room. She had been rescued just in time and her mother was on her way from Minnesota to take her home.

Upon inquiry, we learned from a secretary in Casting that Dorothy had phoned around noon the day of her promised screen test. When told that the casting director she asked for didn't exist, she seemed shocked, then hung up.

"Happens all the time," the secretary said. "Some louse passes himself off as a big shot and takes advantage of these poor kids. But wouldn't you think they'd be smarter than to fall for such an old gag?"

No, maybe not . . . not if you've just turned 18 . . . fresh from Minnesota . . . with stars in your eyes. . . .

We had little to do with Herkimer afterwards. When conscription started, he was one of the first to be drafted and we were glad to see him go.

By some tacit understanding, Dorothy's was the one sex story that we never recounted in our bull sessions.

7

Claude Rains, Herbert Marshall & Other Weirdos

THERE WERE FEW SECRETS our actors were able to conceal from us. We knew who suffered from headaches, heartburn and hemorrhoids; who wore dentures and hairpieces; we knew who were the boozers, drug addicts and degenerates; we knew of one star who wore a prosthesis and carried around a spare; another whose hobby was bathing obese young ladies and then requesting permission to take a little souvenir.

The fact that we were knowledgeable of their physical defects and character foibles came about as part of our normal interests. Well, perhaps "normal" isn't quite the right word. *Abnormal* might be closer.

At least three times a week we picked up stacks of manila envelopes from Fan Mail for delivery to the various dressing rooms. The envelopes contained personal mail, and the more-literate and laudatory fan letters, the latter being as necessary for some of our actors' egos as mothers' milk for newborn babes.

There were very important rules that we had to observe: namely, if there was no response to our three knocks, we were to unlock the door with our passkey, leave it ajar, place the envelopes on the nearest table or desk and then depart. Under no circumstances were we to ever open drawers, look into closets or touch *anything.* Failure to observe any of these rules, we were sternly warned, would result in instant dismissal. Understood?

Right! You bet! Yessir!

The fact is, NOTHING was sacred or safe from our prying eyes. Just as Herman at least once started to enjoy the use of de Havilland's personal commode, so another colleague got his kicks out of the dressing room deliveries by sampling booze, often returning to our department a bit glassy-eyed and unusually happy, a condition that, somehow, Pappmeier never caught on to. Many of us snacked on whatever edibles might be found in the refrigerators and those who smoked made it a practice to filch a pack or two from the ever-present cartons. Above all else, we never minded our own business when it came to learning something about theirs.

The Stars Dressing Room Building was a secluded two-story structure, surrounded by huge old shade trees and fronting on a tennis court. The term "dressing room," at least as far as the stars were concerned, was a misnomer, being in fact commodious apartments, consisting of a living room, bedroom, kitchen and bath. For obvious reasons, all were exactly the same size, the only difference being in the furnishings. Outside of their own personal effects, they were furnished by set decorators from Property according to the tastes of each occupant.

Errol Flynn occupied the downstairs, right-hand corner apartment. The doorway was hidden from view of those trodding the nearby walk to the Writers Building by a high hedge, a small detail Flynn must have appreciated whenever he had feminine companionship.

Quietly sedate and masculine, there was only one bit of evidence in Flynn's dressing room suite that made us aware of his satyriasis.

The oak-paneled living room was decorated with his own art, mostly strikingly handsome nautical prints. Occupying a special place of honor on one wall was a large autographed photo of FDR. As would be expected, there was a well-stocked wet bar. There were also bookshelves, crammed with hundreds of volumes of history, poetry and the classics. One of us, certain that Flynn, above all, would have the definitive collection of pornography, once combed through his entire library and was both amazed and disappointed to find absolutely nothing of a prurient nature. We found it hard to believe, but as one of our more sophisticated colleagues pointed out, Flynn didn't need that sort of thing.

"After all," he said, "when you're Big Prick (our respectful nickname for Flynn) you don't have to build a dame up with sexual fantasies. *You* are the fantasy."

He was right, of course.

It was a masculine apartment, done in quiet, good taste, with only two clues that its occupant might be somewhat less than the sedate, cultured gentleman it suggested: There were always open liquor bottles and half-consumed drinks sitting on the tables. The bedroom—naturally—provided the other clue. Specifically, the double bed. The left side of the mattress sagged precipitously, as if it had been broken down under the long-term stress of too much extra weight. What kind of marvelous positions, we enviously wondered, did he and his bed partners engage in, and why didn't he give equal time to the other side?

In one respect, though, we didn't envy him at all. Judging from the medications he kept on hand, he suffered from hemorrhoids.

Bette Davis occupied the suite above Flynn's. Furnished in spindly, uncomfortable Early American, with antimaccassars covering the sofa, it was cold and austere, her only personal touches being half a dozen family photos and a tea set with a cracked pot. She didn't drink, nor did she eat much; the only edibles we ever came across were hard-boiled eggs and sometimes a little cheese. Her one vice, apparently, was smoking.

Bette Davis thought it was her first husband, bandleader Harmon "Ham" Nelson, when she heard the water running in her dressing room shower.

There were always cartons of Luckies stacked in a corner, this being about the only thing of interest to us. Although some stars ended their working days in their dressing rooms, relaxing and bending elbows with their cronies, Davis seldom spent much time there. Once when she did was a story given us second-hand.

Bandleader Harmon Nelson, then married to Davis, visited the studio one day with a musician friend. The latter had a nephew in our department and we learned this from him. (Normally, unless we could swear to its authenticity, we seldom added incidents to our annals, but in this case, we thought it was amusing enough to pass on to our future departmental generations.)

It seems that while his wife was emoting in front of the camera, Nelson and his friend, being tennis buffs, decided to make use of the nearby court. After a few sets, hot and perspiring, they decided they had had enough and retired to her suite. Finding nothing cold to drink, Nelson decided to go across to the drug store for some beer, leaving his friend to relax. A few minutes later, having wrapped up earlier than expected, Davis entered, and hearing the shower running, opened the bathroom door. Reaching inside the curtain, she fitted action to her words. "Ding-dong, Daddy. Wait a sec and I'll join you."

She was stepping out of her panties when the front door opened and her husband entered.

Claude Rains started out with a room in the Featured Players Dressing Room Building, then was promoted to a star's suite. In both cases, he stank up the joint.

A pompous, posturing, strutting little popinjay, his reputation as a great actor was most assuredly not shared by any of us. As far as we were concerned, the only good performance he ever gave was as *The Invisible Man*.

I had been in the department about a month when Ed Haldeman told me to go over to "Shithead's" dressing room and pick up something for Wardrobe.

I looked at him uncomprehendingly. "Who?"

From his expression, it's possible that Claude Rains was finally becoming aware of something that we had long known—that the aura surrounding him was not the sweet smell of success.

"Claude Rains," he answered impatiently.

I was still new enough to be respectful of, if not my betters, certainly my elders. I knew, of course, that privately we used various nicknames for most of the stars, but this was a new one as far as I was concerned. I wondered why Rains had been awarded that particular appellation. The answer swiftly became apparent when I entered his room.

Talking on the phone, he took a brief second to tell me— *order* me: "Those shoes over there, boy. Take them to wardrobe."

I was by then accustomed to being called son, kid, pal, by those who didn't know my name; "boy" was not to my liking. Nor did I appreciate his lack of common courtesy by omitting "please" and "thank you." But my rising anger became secondary to the more rudimentary sense of smell. I became aware of—no, almost *overcome* by—a horrible, sewer-like odor. It permeated the room, a fetid, rank stink, and I swallowed hard to fight back a sudden nausea.

I soon learned it was a common complaint among my colleagues. Some of them swore that he had some kind of phobia about using the toilet, and that he probably defecated in his living room. I'm sure none of us ever had the stomach to try and prove the theory, but there were times we would talk about leaving an anonymous note for him. It would contain only one word: *Phew!* Of course, we never did. Which was too bad; maybe he'd have taken the hint.

I delivered the shoes to Wardrobe, learning afterwards that Rains, who was very short, was never satisfied that the high heels he insisted on wearing were as high as they could go without his tottering and facing the danger of falling flat on his face.

"These're from 'Shithead,'" I told the wardrobe man. He nodded. No other identification was needed. Obviously, he, too, had been in Rains' dressing room.

Edward G. Robinson's middle initial should have been "C" for Culture. Far from being the crude gangster whose portrayals first brought him to fame, he was, in real life, a mild-mannered

Eddie Robinson didn't have that tender look on his face the day he accused one of us of committing a heinous offense in his dressing room.

little guy. His suite was always crammed with art books, cata-
logues from art dealers all over the world and paintings from his
personal collection adorned almost every square inch of wall
space. Extremely possessive of these, he had typewritten cards
on the walls, warning the night janitors never to dust any of his
art works; this was something entrusted only to himself.

There was a bad moment about that once, when he came in
and found three or four of his paintings slightly askew. As far as
he was concerned, it could only mean that some intruder had
brazenly touched them! To seemingly make matters worse, a
newly arrived manila envelope from Fan Mail seemed to pin-
point the culprit. With a phone call to our department, he demanded to know the identity of the messenger who had delivered his mail and why in hell did he dare touich any of his
priceless collection?

Questioned by Fred, the kid staunchly maintained his innocence, swearing that he had never gone near "the goddam pitch-
ers." Knowing that his artistic interests were limited to poring
over "Tillie & Mac," and "Toots & Casper" porno cartoon book-
lets, we were inclined to believe him.

By an unusual stroke of good fortune, our colleague was
found not guilty by a radio announcement. There had been a
slight earthquake that morning, just enough of a tremor to have
caused the frames to tilt. Did Robinson apologize afterwards? Of
course not. We didn't especially hold it against him; most actors
were, at one time or another, a pain in the ass.

We never thought of Robinson, fat and ugly as he was, as any
kind of a romantic figure, so we were surprised to learn that he
and sex symbol Marlene Dietrich had had an affair. Co-starring
in *Manpower*, it was her last day on the picture. When the company broke at seven p.m., Dietrich brought two picnic hampers
to Robinson's suite. They were not seen again until 11:30 that
night, when they separately drove off the lot. What, we wondered, had gone on? As usual, it was not an idle question.

At least part of it was answered later that day, when one of us
had occasion to drop something off at Robinson's suite. They
had *eaten*. There was ample evidence that Dietrich had pre-

We were certain the occasion was a lot more romantic than this, the night that Marlene Dietrich and Eddie Robinson had an "affair" during the filming of *Manpower*.

pared a complete dinner: hors d'oeuvres, salad, beef Stroganoff, climaxed with a magnificent chocolate torte. The leftovers—at least enough for another full meal—had been neatly stored away in the refrigerator.

What happened after dinner? We never did find out. But it didn't really matter. As one of us succinctly put it, while helping himself to a slice of the torte, "Listen, if I had a dame who could cook like this, the hell with the screwing."

As befitting husband and wife, Dick Powell and Joan Blondell shared the upstairs center suite. If, as was later proven to be the case, their marriage was developing some snags, we suspected one good reason for it: Everything of Powell's, from his correspondence, to the clothes in his closet, to his shaving kit and medications in the bathroom, were neatly, carefully kept in their alloted places. Almost compulsively so. Conversely, Blondell was a slob. The array of stockings, panties and bras drooping from chairs, or dropped on the floor, seemed to be typical female carelessness. But that was far from the extent of it. What with lipstick-smudged bits of toilet paper underfoot, cigarette butts snuffed out in whatever receptacles were handy, and little rat-like bites indented on pieces of candy which were then replaced in their boxes, we were convinced that "Big Tits" must have driven "Dopey" up the walls.

More than most, their dressing room did have a lived-in look. There were always bowls of potato chips, peanuts and pretzels, and in the kitchen soda pop, and often a roast chicken or ham, enabling us to have a nibbling good time. The liquor cabinet was sparse, usually containing one bottle each of gin, scotch and bourbon, replaced only when fully consumed. Not by any of us, however; our resident boozer let it be known that in his expert opinion their brands were strictly second-rate.

The double bed in their bedroom looked as though it had never been used. As a matter of historical fact, during the Powells' last few months with us, we *knew* it wasn't used. Not even once. For some devilish research reason of his own, a colleague inserted a toothpick in the middle of their bed, standing it up between the bedspread and blanket in such a way that if either side was uncovered, the toothpick would become dislodged. Up until the day they left, it remained intact. As tantalizingly sexy a broad as Blondell was, we wondered how come the grinning crooner didn't avail himself at least a few times daily of what was rightfully his?

Then again, thanks to our intrepid investigations, we decided that perhaps he had other things on his mind. There was certain evidence, by way of the contents of his bathroom cabinet, that seemed to lend credence to this theory. It was jammed with a strange assortment of medications: a dozen different laxatives and an equal number of constipation-inducing drugs. Some of them, under prescription, were periodically renewed, leading us believe that whatever he suffered from was chronic.

Powell's alimentary problems were of less than passing interest and undoubtedly would have been forgotten had not one of us become friendly with their secretary. Allegedly, Powell suffered from a rare physical disability, having been born without a sphinctor, the muscle that controls the bowels. Lacking normal control, he was forced to go through life alternately medicating himself to induce constipation, then when his system required it, purging himself with his assortment of laxatives.

Though many of us were at an age when we thought anything scatological was the height of humor, somehow we didn't find this to be funny. Except once, when one of us commented, "Well, now I know why he sounds so strangulated when he sings."

In the privacy of his dressing room, Jimmy Cagney led a secret life. Unfortunately, there was nothing scandalous about it. Having started out as a chorus boy on Broadway, now middle-aged and having trouble keeping his weight down, Cagney was a solitary tap dancer. With the carpeting removed from his suite, he customarily spent his lunch hours tapping his way from room to room. Again, after a day's shooting, while others unwound by drinking, socializing and fornicating, Cagney would switch on his phonograph and unwind to the tune of "Tea for Two." If his efforts wouldn't give Fred Astaire much competition, the constant practice did help to keep him in shape. (It also stood him in good stead a few years later when, as George M. Cohan, he had some strenuous dance numbers in *Yankee Doodle Dandy*.)

Despite the fact that Cagney never gave us any trouble, with our juvenile prejudices we often complained that he was a miserable cheapskate. This solely because, like Davis's, his dressing room was Spartan to an extreme. She, at least, smoked. He didn't smoke, drink, eat, or do anything that we considered normal and/or interesting. One thing he did do was read a lot, mostly law books which, considering his many legal battles with the studio, did seem appropriate.

One of our more important character actors—a gentleman whom we all liked—had a strange, off-beat hobby, as I discovered one day. Noticing the new addition of a cigar humidor in his dressing room, I opened it in hopes of filching a fine Havana or two. There were no cigars, nothing but snippets and clusters of hair, mostly curly, sealed inside small cellophane envelopes. Black, brown, yellow and red hair, each bearing labels of female names. Ah, I thought, souvenirs, probably from his daughters' and grand-daughters' first haircuts. How wonderfully sentimental!

No doubt it was sentimental on his part, but as we later learned, he had no daughters or grand-daughters. Nor did the hair in those little packets come from ordinary haircuts. It was a long time later that the puzzle was solved. He was enamored of fat young women who, for a certain consideration, would allow him to bathe them and then snip off a locket of their pubic hair. That was all he asked. Those that we found out about were waitresses and extras, all of whom had only the most complimentary things to say about him.

One young extra, who must have weighed over 200 pounds, confided, "He's a real gent. He gave me twenty bucks in an envelope. Then I got in the tub and he scrubbed me all over like I was a baby. All he asked was if he could take a little snip of my pussy hair as a remembrance. Little snip? Say, listen, the way that doll treated me, I wouldn't have minded if I'd ended up with a bald-headed snatch."

There were perversions and there were hobbies. In this gentleman's case, we agreed it was the latter. A hobby, simple and innocent.

There was always at least one dressing room suite kept available for the use of any incoming stars, as in the case of Herbert Marshall, who joined us in 1939 to co-star in *The Letter*.

Like his fellow Limeys, the suave, handsome Englishman seemed rather remote and cold, certainly much too dignified to indulge in macabre humor. But there was one incident that made us wonder.

It happened one afternoon when a pair of us encountred our Bert Dunne on the walk near the Stars Dressing Room Building. Normally a happy-go-lucky guy, he was pale and shaken.

"You guys got a minute?" Bert asked. "I just saw something that you won't believe! You gotta take a look, but I'm telling you, you won't believe it.!

No matter how rushed we were, it was a poor imitation of a messenger who couldn't spare the time to investigate something that sounded interesting. Hurrying back with him along the walk, Bert explained that he had been on the fan mail route and Marshall's was his last stop. He came to a halt in front of the door.

"I tell you, you're not gonna believe this," he repeated, turning the key in the lock. He swung the door open.

The drapes were drawn and it took a moment for our eyes to make out the object he was pointing at. Then it took another moment for us to actually believe what we saw. Bert had not exaggerated.

Standing in the rear of the living room, next to an antique desk, shod in a black shoe, and a black sock held up by a garter, was . . . one artificial leg!.

It was true in this case that seeing was not believing. Only upon slowly approaching and then tentatively touching the prosthesis did we finally believe that it actually existed. Grotesque

It might not have been done deliberately, but who would have thought that suave, cultured Herbert Marshall would indulge in macabre humor?

as it was, there was also something sad and forlorn about that poor, disembodied member standing there so quiet and patient. One almost felt the need to solace it.

"There, there, good old leg," one would say comfortingly, "you've stood at attention long enough. Now it's time to get some rest."

So saying, pick it up and gently lay it on the couch. Of course, we did nothing of the kind. As shaken as Bert, we didn't linger.

It was known that Marshall had lost a leg during the First World War and that he wore an artificial one. But since he had been seen on the set that afternoon, *walking*, we had to conclude that this was a spare. Or, perhaps more accurately, his *third* leg. But why had he left it out like that? Was this his *evening* leg, used only for socializing after work? Did he change legs the way we changed socks and underwear? Too bad we never got to know him well enough to ask. Those tantalizing questions forever remained unanswered.

When our favorite bogeyman Boris Karloff checked in to do *Devil's Island*, we naively expected him to live up to his reputation. Surely, we thought, we would contribute something at least as spooky as Marshall's third leg.

Karloff turned out to be a terrible disappointment. A shy, colorless man, who might have been a minor clerk rather than a famous actor, every day he brought fresh flowers from his garden, English water biscuits (which we found to be tasteless) and a thermos of tea. His only other personal possession was a shopping bag, which he toted to and from the studio daily.

It was a week after his arrival before one of us entered his dressing room and checked out the bag. It contained needles, skeins of yarn and a patch of material. He was *knitting* something!

Actors were known to while away the interminable set delays in a variety of ways. Some conducted personal business, others napped or read, a few customarily sought out suitable companionship for a "matinee," but none of the male actors we knew

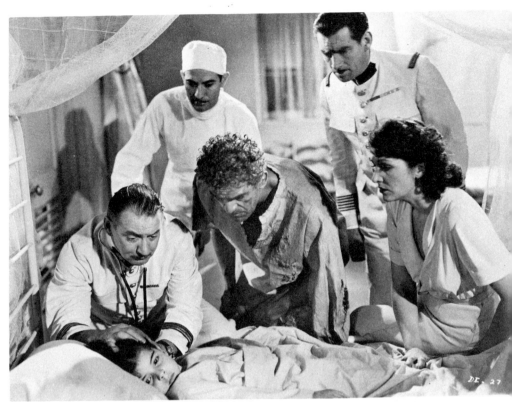

Bogeyman Boris Karloff scared moviegoers in *Devil's Island*, but none of his fans would have believed what he did in the privacy of his dressing room.

indulged in knitting. At least, not publicly. Nor did Karloff; it was an activity limited solely to his dressing room.

We tried to imagine what it might have done to his image if the fan magazines headlined it on their covers:

THE FRANKENSTEIN MONSTER'S SECRET VICE!
EXCLUSIVE PICTURE OF KARLOFF DISPLAYING HIS NEEDLES

At the end of five weeks, when filming was completed, the yarn was taking shape. As a typically British cardigan sweater.

Marion Davies was the greatest star of them all!

Well, if not exactly with the paying public, at least so in the opinion of her good and great friend, William Randolph Hearst. To prove her importance, when she started back in the twenties, Hearst constructed for her a very special dressing room bungalow on the MGM lot. When she moved over to our studio, her status symbol naturally accompanied her. Officially known as her dressing room, it was, in all actuality, a palatial mansion. Of Spanish architecture, it consisted of ten rooms and four baths. The master bathroom, with its gold-plated fixtures and five-foot square Grecian tub, contained a curiosity: twin toilets side by side. In today's spirit of togetherness such a pairing might not be considered unusual, but to us it presented a somewhat bizarre sight. Was it, we wondered, for the simultaneous convenience of Davies and Hearst? Did one of them, perhaps, have a fear of going to the bathroom alone? Or was it planned thus so that if, say, Marion was tinkling, and the Chief suddenly found his bladder about to burst, he could relieve himself without resorting to the gross imposition of knocking on the door and yelling, "For crissakes, Marion, hurry it up or I'll piss in my pants?"

Ah, we thought, what a perfect world He could have created if only God had had Hearst's money.

Off the main entry hall, on the right, was a baronial-sized dining room, beyond that a serving pantry and then a kitchen which would have done justice to a fine restaurant. In the left wing was the sitting room, two more bedroom suites and baths and a wood-paneled study with a walk-in fireplace.

The building had been transported in sections from MGM in 1936, a major feat of engineering considering the fact that it involved a journey of over 20 miles. By the time of my arrival, after four lackluster pictures for us, Davies had decided it was time to retire and the building was now empty and again destined to be moved.

The first time I explored it was at the insistence of my colleague Fred Schmidt, who was taking me on an indoctrination tour. After showing me the various rooms, we ended up in the dining room. Like the others, it was devoid of furnishings, except for half-drawn heavy brocade drapes.

"They used to have big lunches here every day," Fred said. "Twenty or thirty guests at a throw."

It was all interesting but I was still new enough to want to get back to work.

"Relax," he said, "we've got time." He looked at his watch and offering me a cigarette asked, "Do you believe in ghosts?" I laughed.

"Just wait," he said. "You'll see."

We lit up and again he looked at his watch. I noticed it was about 4:10.

"It usually starts about this time," he added cryptically.

We stood there in silence for about 30 seconds, puffing away as the pale winter sunlight slowly started retreating across the parquet floor. Then the drapes started to ripple, and with that I heard *it* and my scalp began to tingle.

It was the gentle whisper of voices—men's, women's, even the high-pitched whine of a cranky, tired child. I stared at Fred and he grinned.

"What in hell—" He silenced me with a gesture. The drapes were billowing, and the whispers became louder, more insistent, as if we were surrounded by invisible beings. Frozen in place, I strained my hearing, trying to pick out phrases, even words, but they were indistinguishable. It lasted perhaps 60 seconds, building to a climax of frenzied, billowing drapes. Now there were some isolated words I could make out. "Wait . . . weary . . . weird . . . world.' '

By then, the sunlight was gone, and in the encroaching gloom, I discovered I was shivering. Gradually, the whispers died away and the drapes became motionless.

It was after we left the building that my sense of logic returned. "That was a pretty good trick," I said deprecatingly.

"Yeah, that's what everyone says." Fred replied. "But tell me something. Outside of the voices, wasn't there something else? Something you actually *felt*?

I professed not to know what he was talking about, but he pressed on. "Something was happening in that room and you damn well know it."

I told him he was nuts and we dropped the subject.

It wasn't until late that night, just before I fell asleep, that I reluctantly admitted it to myself. I had experienced more than whispered voices in that great bare room. *I had actually felt the physical presence of invisible people moving around me.*

The following day, picking up a sandwich and Coke from the commissary, I hurried back to the bungalow and spent my lunch hour in the dining room. There were no whispers, no movement of the drapes, no ghostly presences. Nothing. The only thing I accomplished was to disprove my first theory, that the sound of the voices was coming from an amplifier. There were no hidden loudspeakers. The half-draped window was slightly open, and I was unable to close it, but it seemed impossible for a wind to have caused that much billowing through a mere five inches of open window.

During the ensuing week I dropped by three more times on route detours, twice only to be disappointed again. Then I suddenly remembered that Fred had said: "It usually starts about this time." In my stupidity my visits had been made at the wrong time.

The third time came at 4:05, when I took a temporary respite from a rush call and headed for the bungalow. The room was as before. Silent, gloomy. Then, as I waited, it happened again. The whispers . . . the billowing drapes . . . the feeling of people moving around me. The voices were different this time. As were the words. Listening intently, I could make out some of them more easily than before. "Sweet . . . summer . . . sail . . . south . . . slow . . . silly . . . silly . . . south . . ."

I knew it was an all-female gathering, not merely by the voices but—No, it was not just my vivid imagination!—I could detect the faint aroma of perfume.

It ended and I returned to my interrupted errand. This time, I reflected later, I had not experienced a feeling of apprehension; this was a lighthearted occasion, possibly a shower of some kind. When I got back to our department, I wrote down the words I had overheard, thinking that eventually some pattern might emerge that could lead to coherent sentences.

During the next week my afternoon chores all kept me on the other side of the lot and I didn't have the chance to return at the right hour. It was during that week that Dick Binder joined us.

Handsome, personable, our senior by two or three years, Dick immediately got off on the wrong foot with some of us by being able to date waitresses, secretaries and actresses who had always spurned our advances. True, the actresses were really only extras, but that was of small solace. The galling fact was that this new, charming sonofabitch was making out with broads who rightfully belonged to us.

A group of us were sitting around the back room when Dick mentioned that he had a date the following afternoon—his day off—with a certain sexy young extra, and did we know of any good, secret place on the lot where he could take her? Almost everybody came up with the same suggestion: the ocean liner on the back lot. Originally built for *One Way Passage* in 1932, it was a partial, full-scale replica of a luxury steamer, complete with pier and gangplank. Long before, it had become our favorite romantic rendezvous when someone came up with the statistic that more girls willingly surrendered their virtue on cruises than anywhere else.

Having exchanged a knowing glance with Schmidt when Dick broached his question, we immediately dissented, pointing out that not only would it mean a long, tiring walk for the young lady, but that since the aft promenade deck provided the only suitable privacy, the March chilliness could easily put a damper on her ardor. Fred casually said he had a better place.

"You know the Davies bungalow? Nobody would bother you there, and it's real classy, the kind of romantic joint that impresses a dame."

It was my turn to administer the *coup de grace*.

"Funny you should mention it, Fred," I said. "It so happens I used it only a few days ago. The broad went out of her mind!" I snapped my fingers. "Hey, I just remembered. I left a couple of nice thick blankets on the floor in the dining room"

The fact that I had never used it, and that there were no blankets, was unimportant. If Binder approved, there would be.

The next morning, 15 minutes before I was due to check in, I went on a blanket quest. I was still learning something new every day. Today it was that the Wardrobe Department did not handle blankets; they were under the jurisdiction of Property. Once there, I was sent upstairs to a sub-department, Drapery. There was no problem checking out three deep-pile luxurious blankets. I had only asked for two, but when I mentioned tha they were for the purpose of protecting two supine bodies from the hardness of a bare floor, the middle-aged secretary smiled knowingly and said in that case I'd better take three.

Early that afternoon, spiffy-looking in his best suit, Binder dropped by the back room to say that he had checked out the rendezvous, found it highly acceptable and was now waiting for his girl. As part of a crowd scene for *Torchy Blaine in Panama,* she expected to be dismissed in the next hour or so. Fred and I kept our fingers crossed that the seduction would take place before 4:10.

Luck was on our side. They were seen entering the bungalow at 3:45.

The next morning, we were confronted by an enraged colleague with mayhem in his eye. What kind of a goddam lowdown trick had we played on him?

Schmidt and I swore we didn't know what he was talking about.

Binder's misadventure turned out to be even better than we had hoped. It must have been just about 4:10 when foreplay ceased and impregnation was about to be achieved. First, the drapes started moving, Dick said, then they heard laughter and derisive whispers. Certain that they were being spied on, the girl jumped to her feet, then screamed as she felt her bottom being pinched, and grabbing her clothes, fled in a panic.

It was only after Binder consulted our records that he was finally, reluctantly, convinced of our innocence. At that hour, I had been relieving in Music Reception, and Schmidt, on a rush to the Executive Dining Room, had been on the other side of the lot.

We weren't the only ones who knew the room was haunted. The next time I had the opportunity to enter, notebook in hand so that I could immediately transcribe whatever new words I heard, I was dismayed to find two men already waiting. One I recognized as Burton Conway, an engineering expert in the Sound Department; the other was a stranger. Conway asked me if I was here "For the show?" I didn't have time to answer. It was 4:10 and the phantom voices arrived on schedule. Too embarrassed in the presence of others to write anything down, I could only listen.

The voices were different—predominantly male—their whispers strident. I could make out such words as "No . . . never . . . night . . . " and for the first time there were actual phrases: "No deal . . . dare not squeal . . . damn the New Deal . . . "

The intruders exchanged smug smiles, which irritated me. One minute later it was over and the stranger nodded.

"Interesting phenomenon," he said to Conway. "Very much like something we tracked down in an English castle."

They went over to the window and looked out. Conway pointed to the distant mountain top overlooking the studio.

"That's where the thermal breeze originates," he said. "I've measured it at 20-25 decibels. This was a bit louder than usual."

I didn't know what they were talking about, but again I resented the fact that they seemed so unimpressed. They turned back to me.

"What do you make of it?" Conway asked.

Unwilling to tell them the truth, I stammered that I really didn't know. He persisted. "Ghosts, perhaps?"

I reluctantly nodded. They both smiled.

"Ah, the innocence of youth," the other man said. "No, son, I'm afraid it's nothing as romantic as that. I'm with Western Electric; we check out things like this all the time. It really has a simple explanation. You see, when a certain kind of breeze comes down from that mountaintop, it sets up a series of sound vibrations. The acoustics in this room happen, quite by accident, to turn those vibrations into what seems to be whispering voices."

"But I've made out *words*," I blurted. "And this time there were actual phrases. You must've heard them."

"I guess we lack your imagination," Conway said.

I still refused to believe them. "Even if what you say is true," I insisted, "there's more to it than that. I've actually felt physical presences around me."

With their patronizing, closed scientific minds, it was only too obvious that they considered me nothing more than an impressionable juvenile. Which made me all the more determined to disprove their cold logic.

I was off the following day, and though I originally had other plans, I gave them up in order to be back in the Davies dining room at the appointed hour.

This time I was alone. The drapes started to move, swaying gently at first, then billowing. And I heard a female voice. Only one, whispering in my ear: "Believe . . . believe in what you believe . . . " (A funny thing, she said it while sniffling, as if she had a cold. But weren't ghosts impervious to such mortal ailments?)

With that, something icy-cold and moist pressed itself against my lips and I involuntarily gasped. There was a tinkling laugh, a sniffle, then silence. The drapes became motionless.

It took me a long time to admit the truth: I had been kissed by a (beautiful, of course) phantom. Even if it was nothing I could prove—let alone talk about—I gloried in the belief that I had refuted their damn scientific, smart-ass theories. I had made a breakthrough to another world, and I knew that by my believing, I had made a friend who would give me further, provable manifestations of spiritual existence.

I awakened early the next morning with a cold and 102-degree fever, causing me to stay in bed for the next three days.

When I returned to work, the Davies bungalow was gone, the engineers again having performed their magical feat. Then the studio gardeners sowed the naked ground with seed. By late Spring, the young grass took possession of the land and soon there was no trace of the haunted bungalow that had once stood there. The wind still came down from the mountaintop but the whispers and ghostly presences were no more. I knew they had departed with their mansion and I wished them well.

Most especially, the beautiful ghost who kissed me. Even if she had given me her cold.

8

Louella Parsons Made a Lasting Impression

TRIVIA QUESTION FOR MOVIE BUFFS: Whose name appeared the most on the credit titles of our movies?

Would you believe . . . Leo Forbstein.

From the time of his arrival in 1931 until his death in '48, the ubiquitous title "Musical Director Leo F. Forbstein" appeared on more than 700 features and shorts.

A pear-shaped, bespectacled, shrill little man, always a bit breathless, "Forby" gave the impression of being the busiest person on the lot, forever scurrying between his office, Projection Room 12 and Stage 9, the music recording stage. According to a member of his staff, the reason he always ran was that in case he ever encountered J. L., he would give the impression of being extremely efficient.

121

It was an unnecessary activity; he was. Unlike musical directors at other studios, who were also composers and arrangers, Forbstein's only musical claim to fame was as a conductor, though he was far surpassed in that respect by such as Ray Heindorf, Max Steiner and Erich Wolfgang Korngold. Mainly, he was an administrator, and as such was without peer, hiring the best arrangers, copyists, composers and musicians. It was during his tenure that our movies were usually praised for the excellence—if somewhat over-lushness—of their musical scores.

Often putting in a grueling six-and-a-half-day week as probably our hardest-working department head, Forbstein was also, by way of relaxation, an inveterate gambler. Nightly, it was either cards with cronies or a session at the tables of The Clover Club, Hollywood's most popular illegal gambling casino. During his work day, he confined his gambling activities to playing the horses, an officially prohibited pastime which was indulged in by many of our executives.

In order to conceal their forbidden pursuit, they used a telephone code when placing their bets. If the track was, say, Santa Anita, it might be called "Charlotte's theme." The first race would be "Reel one," and so on. The particular horse would be called "Scene one," or whatever post position number it bore. The amount of the bets would be in "Frames." Finally, the betting, win, place, show, or across the board, were accorded orchestral designations: brass, strings, percussion and woodwinds.

It wasn't as complicated as it might appear. A phone call to the studio bookie would sound like this: "Charley? Listen, kid, in Charlotte's theme, reel two, scene five, gimme brass for 200 frames." (Translation: "At Santa Anita, second race, number five, $200 to win.")

Since such esoteric conversations were an actual part of the technical jargon used in scoring a film, if the phone should happen to be tapped by Security—always a possibility—the call appeared to be strictly business. The only trouble was "Forby" had a mental block concerning part of the code. He constantly referred to "races" instead of "reels," a habit which drove his gambling crony, producer Sam Bischoff, up the wall.

"Goddam it," Bischoff would whisper over the phone as they exchanged tips every morning, "can't you remember? It's reel— r-e-e-l—REEL!"

"Yeah, yeah, I know," Forbstein would answer. "Now, what do you think of brass, 500 frames, scene eight, the fifth *race*?"

Music occupied most of the Music Building, which is what everybody called it, though that was not its official name. It had originally been named "The Warner Building," in consideration of the fact that it was our first new edifice after we had acquired what was originally the First National Studios in 1929. At its dedication, J. L.—ever the would-be comedian—called it, "Our first Burbank erection."

It contained the only other reception room on the lot, presided over by Al Yallen. Although of our department, Al ranked a step above the rest of us by reason of a slightly higher salary and, more important, the fact that he didn't have to wear a uniform. His desk also served as the message center for incoming calls to the stages. A few years previously, having determined that too much time was being wasted by actors receiving personal phone calls during shooting, our operators were ordered to put through all such calls to Yallen. He would then type up the messages, which we would, in due course, deliver. It was the kind of job that allowed for a good deal of leisure time and we were especially envious of the fact that Yallen didn't have to do any walking. Unless Pappmeier came prowling around, as he did infrequently, Al was practically his own boss.

Like clockwork, every three months Music Reception could depend on the arrival of a certain visitor, who would then settle in for a week-long vigil. He was Forbstein's older brother, Sam, retired, in poor health, and the principal of a large insurance policy, which he could no longer afford to carry. According to Sam, in return for being included as one of the policy's beneficiaries, Leo had agreed to pay the quarterly premiums.

It seemed, on the surface, to be a simple act of brotherly concern; in actuality, it was an embarrassing ordeal. He would arrive on a Monday, and Yallen would phone, "Mr. Sam Forbstein to see Mr. Leo Forbstein."

Secretary Peggy Willard's reply was unvarying. "He's on Stage 9 in a recording session. I don't know when he'll be back in the office."

Sam would wait out the day without complaint, go home at closing time, then return the next day.

Once, barely seconds after Yallen had phoned, receiving the usual response, Leo's booming voice was heard from the inside hallway, greeting Max Steiner. Though Sam obviously heard him, he pretended otherwise, the fixed, patient smile never leaving his face.

The charade usually continued right up until the last day of the policy's grace period, at which time, without seeing him, Leo would send out a check and Sam would gratefully go home for another three months.

Ironically, Leo never collected his share of the insurance. Sam was still alive when his younger brother suddenly died of a heart attack in 1948.

If we had had our druthers, most of us would have preferred relieving Yallen to any other relief job on the lot. Main Reception was always a beehive of activity, and J. L.'s office relief, notable as it was for acquiring the choicest inside information, meant maintaining a strict protocol and formality. Music Reception, on the other hand, had relatively few visitors, and outside of the phone messages, the complete lack of pressure made it a comfortable oasis where we could relax and do our own thing.

The hardest part was answering the phone and typing up the messages. There was the time one of us took a call for a certain featured actress. The terse message, from an obstetrician: "Tell her the rabbit died."

The messenger, naive and tenderhearted, typed it up as, "I'm sorry to report that the vet phoned to say your rabbit died."

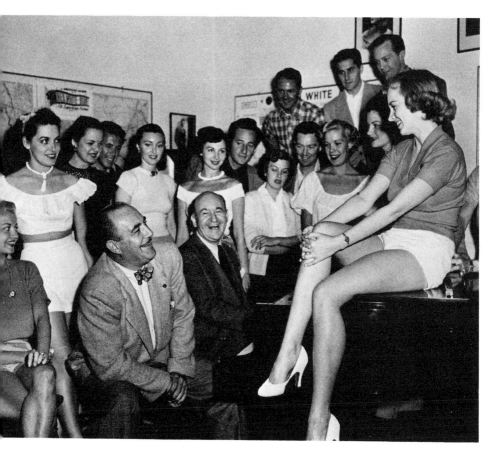

Was there ever a songwriting team that didn't enjoy being surrounded by lovely young chorines? In this publicity still from *The Hard Way*, take a look at my Dad, at the piano, and his partner, lyricist Jack School. (Mom complained that Dad never looked like that at home.)

Considering that she was unmarried, the actress must have been sorry, too.

Most of the calls were legitimate, but sometimes we suspected pranksters were at work, as was the case when I received a call from someone claiming to be Herbert Marshall. Would I please give a message to Miss Bette Davis? He and Mrs. Marshall were giving a little soiree tomorrow night and they hoped Miss Davis and her husband could attend. Then kew. Cheerio.

Which is when I began wondering about the legitimacy of the call. The phoner had the clipped, cultured accent down pat— perhaps a mite too much so. And wouldn't the real Marshall, I reasoned, have his wife phone Davis at home? The more I thought about it, the more I smelled a hoax. Finally, there was no question in my mind but that if I forwarded the message, Davis and her husband might show up for a nonexistent party, with ensuing embarrassments for all concerned. Most especially me. I threw it in the waste basket.

A few days later, Davis personally phoned Yallen, demanding to know why a certain message from her dear friend Bart Marshall had failed to reach her? Al said he knew nothing about it, but would check into the matter. With those damn records that we kept, the date and time of the call was traced to my relief hour. Rather than admit the truth, which might not have set too well with Pappmeier, I readily admitted having received and typed the message. What happened to it afterwards was not my responsibility. After all, I pointed out, even the famed U.S. Mails were known to once in a great while lose a letter or two.

Often, after three p.m. on week days, Music Reception would be visited by a coterie of what today are called "groupies." They were local high school girls, giggling and silly, who asked the usual questions about the stars. We welcomed these little diversions; it gave us a chance to hold court and some of the girls were quite cute. Invariably, there would be one or two during the week who would confidentially confide that they "would give *anything*" if they could tour the studio.

One, a bit more sophisticated and aggressive than the others, in confiding this to Stan Frazen, added with a wink, "If you'll take me around, and introduce me to some stars, I'll give you one of these." She dropped a metal object on the desk. A little screw.

Stan admitted that if her complexion had been half as clear as her intent—the fact that she was San Quentin Quail notwithstanding— he'd have jumped at her offer.

There were always those legitimate movie fans who, lacking the necessary credentials to enter as visitors through Main Reception, sought us out with under-the-table cash if we would allow them to tour the lot. Much as we coveted bribes, their offers were always summarily rejected. Some of us did so because of studio rules and personal scruples; others, like me, reluctantly said no because of a more basic emotion: fear. The trouble, as we were well aware, was that there was just no way of differentiating between the real fans and the potentially dangerous lunatic fringe.

Such as the grey-haired, well-dressed banker type who offered Yallen $10 if he could just walk around the lot for a few minutes. Al politely turned him down and the man left. Late that same day one of our cops apprehended him, trying to break through a wire fence at the end of the back lot. He had a hunting knife in his possession and a history of mental disorder. Turned over to the Burbank police on a trespassing charge, that was the end of it. No harm done. But some members of Mailing ended up with cold shivers at the thought of what might have happened had the offer been made to us.

If we, in our ubiquitous green uniforms, were often faceless and nameless, the janitors were the original invisible men. Toiling away at their never-ending cleaning chores, they seldom spoke or were spoken to. One of them, Rose (we never knew if that was his first, last or nickname), was assigned to the Music

Building, where for eight hours daily he polished brass, washed windows and generally cleaned. Always in silence. I had known him for about a year, during which time my attempts at conversation were limited to his response of "yeah" or "no." Then, one day when I was relieving Yallen, and Rose was mopping the floor, I idly said something that apparently hit a raw nerve.

Louis Armstrong had just arrived to do the "Jeepers Creepers" number in *Going Places,* and I mentioned that of all the colored musicians, he was my favorite.

"We ain't colored," Rose said. "You's colored. We's black."

His statement surprised me. I had always thought his race considered the word "black" as being derogatory. I asked what he meant.

"Go take a look in the mirror sometime," he said, continuing his mopping. "When you folks gets cold, you turns blue. When you get sickly, you turns green. And when you gets mad, you gets red in the face."

Laughingly, I agreed that it was true. He joined in, then added, "See, the good Lord made us black for a reason. So's no matter what happens to us, nobody knows what we feels inside. We's always the same . . . always black."

His voice was mild as always; it was the statement itself that conveyed a sad bitterness.

Once, Louella Parsons, escorted by fawning minions of the Publicity Department, entered the building to visit the office of songwriters Scholl and Jerome, where she was to meet a rising young starlet named Jane Wyman. Parsons listened as Wyman sang a piece of special material that Dad and Jack had written for her, made the pronouncement that the child had talent and that she'd keep an eye on her. Then, with other appointments to keep, she swept out.

It was then they noticed the state of the cushion of the chair Parsons had been sitting on. It was wet. Soaking, dripping wet. It was a well-known "secret" that she had bladder trouble, and was incontinent to the point of leaving her trademark anywhere, at any time. The funny thing was that everybody pretended not to notice. As the number one movie critic and columnist for the

It must have been the soothing music that did it, because director Mike Curtiz was in a rare gentle mood when he came over to listen to my father play one of his songs for Jimmy Cagney.

powerful Hearst newspaper chain, so great was her power that, as one wag put it, "She could pee on Louis Mayer's head and he'd swear it was raining."

With the dripping pool now making an enlarging blotch on the carpet, Rose was hastily, apologetically summoned.

"Could be worse," he said. "Always figured youse folks was fulla shit."

They tried cleaning it, but the stain never did come out of the cushion. Just as certain inns acquired reputations because "George Washington Slept Here," so that chair became famous. When visitors sat in it, Dad or Jack would proudly point out, "Louella Parsons peed in that chair." Its fame was short-lived, however; Parsons had decorated so many other chairs, sofas and couches that theirs soon became only one of scores.

It was the era of Shirley Temple, and every once in a while there would be a mother, curly-haired moppet in tow, who, having been turned away from the Auto Gate, Main Reception, Casting, Publicity and even Purchasing, ended up on Yallen's doorstep. One such woman, claiming to be the head of a religious sect, caused us an inordinate amount of suffering for something that wasn't our fault.

Arriving early one morning, she announced that she had had a visitation from God, who told her to come here and wait, that somebody in authority would discover her baby, who was destined to become the greatest child star of all time. (The fact that her "baby" was of pubescent age, and totally devoid of looks or charm, was seemingly unimportant.)

In this kind of fruit-cake circumstance, we were supposed to notify Security, and a cop would arrive who usually had no trouble convincing the intruder to leave. It was a procedure which most of us would have followed. Yallen, however, was on the desk. Kindhearted and respectful, he rejected that drastic tactic as being unnecessary. It was true that they weren't causing any trouble, merely sitting on the bench, meek and quiet, and there was something rather pathetic about the drabness of the girl and her fanatical mother.

During the lunch hours there was always a good deal of traffic through the reception room, with film editors, sound men and music personnel going back and forth. As each one passed by, the mother would look at him hopefully. No one paid any attention to them.

The afternoon wore on, and realizing that they hadn't eaten all day, Al bought them candy bars, which they hungrily devoured. Finally, it was time to lock up. Apologetically, he told them they'd have to leave. They got up from the bench.

"Something went wrong," the woman said. "I don't know what. But I do know the Lord is unhappy about this. He just told me that your studio has incurred His holy wrath and ye shall all suffer."

They went to the door, then she stopped and looked at Yallen.

"All except you," she added. "The Lord says you're a good person."

The following day, it started to rain, gradually turning into a malevolent deluge that all but inundated the studio. It continued for 72 hours without let-up. Other personnel, unable to make it to the studio, were granted permission to stay home until the storm abated. But not us. As the glue that kept the lot together and functioning, we somehow had to keep to our appointed rounds.

All during those three miserable, drenching days, we hated Yallen's guts. Cozily seated behind his desk, an electric heater warming his feet, and an ample supply of edibles and reading material stashed in the drawers, he was the picture of a contented man. Worst of all, he brought his lunch from home, even robbing us of our usual relief.

Bedraggled, like half-drowned rats, some of us demanded to know, "Why should you have it so goddam good? Why shouldn't you suffer along with the rest of us?"

Al's expression can only be described as *beatific* as he replied, "Because the Lord said *I'm* a good person."

9

"What Do I Have to Do to Get Into Your Panties?"

WOULD YOU BELIEVE we possessed the prescience that made us aware that Davis, Cagney and de Havilland would become legends in their own lifetimes?

—That we knew Bogart, Flynn and Robinson were destined for screen immortality?

—That it was obvious to us that many of our assembly-line movies would become objects of cult adoration . . . to be studied and revered as classics by future generations of film makers?

Well . . . ?

But then, neither did anybody else.

As far as our movies were concerned, once a film had completed its run, and its profit or loss entered on our ledgers, its useful life was considered over. Its only ancillary value lay in the reclamation of the silver from the nitrate stock. There wasn't much silver content, just enough to make it worthwhile destroying most of the prints, which otherwise would only take up space in the vaults. In fact, even the *negatives* of much of our B product met this fate, indicating what we thought of their historical value.

Being human (more or less) and thus unsalable for mineral value, an actor's value was even less. Who could possibly have thought that *any* of our players would still be remembered decades after they had shuffled off this mortal coil? Their longevity was considered to be about on a par with any other canned product, such as ham: "After five years, do not use."

There were exceptions, of course. Not many; but even in our callow youth we could detect more than ephemeral "stardom" qualities in a few. Humphrey Bogart was one.

In the years since his death, his legend has continued to grow. Deservedly so. At a time when studios forced their actors to fit into well-defined categories, Bogart was truly an original. Ugly, skinny, balding, in person he was a totally forgettable little man—a beige presence. But when he appeared on the screen—POW!—there was this enormity that made him almost three-dimensional. The camera has always had a natural craving for faces. Bogart had a *face*.

There was something else, too, an undefined quality that he brought to each role, no matter how unimportant or poorly written. The word that fitted this then-undefinable quality came into usage too late to be applied to him during his lifetime, but it could easily serve as the epitaph for his personal, as well as professional, life: the anti-hero.

We approved of his honesty and lack of pomposity. Unlike some actors, who objected to our usual lack of servile formality, he didn't mind being called "Bogie." Except possibly once, but that involved something more than merely the gratuitous use of his nickname.

One of us, eager to gain points with some visiting exhibitors, once called to him from a slight distance across a stage, "Hey,

Bogie, commere, I've got some important people you ought to meet."

He did so, spent a few amiable minutes with them, then excused himself and took the messenger aside.

"Listen, pal," he said. "I don't mind you calling me 'Bogie' and acting like you and I are buddies. If it makes you to be a big shot and gets you a few bucks, fine. But I draw the line at your yelling at me to come over. Suppose I'm not in the mood to meet strangers? In their eyes, I end up being a louse. So next time, you better ask me privately and respectfully, or so help me, I'll personally kick your ass off my set."

We also approved of his dislike of having to give fan magazine interviews. He always claimed that the writers were morons and their readers cretins. It was especially refreshing since so many of the other actors engaged in a not-so-friendly rivalry as to who had the most interviews each month. Two of us were fascinated eavesdroppers at one Bogart set-side interview. The first question, predictably, was, "How do you like being a movie star?"

He tugged thoughtfully at his ear lobe. "Well, I'll tell you," he said, trying to conceal the sarcasm in his voice. "Outside of the money, the best part is knowing I don't have to waste time going to the toilet anymore."

Since it was obviously a joke, the interviewer started to giggle. That was another of his pet hates, middle-aged women who giggled.

"I'm dead serious," he said. "Everybody knows that Garbo and all us other movie stars aren't like you ordinary people. You have to go to the can every morning, don't you? Well, we're above all that."

Changing the subject, the lady asked him what kind of a drinker he was.

"Strictly social."

Not, she pressed on—disregarding the danger signals of narrowed eyes and taut facial muscles—according to the rumors going around.

After an early morning encounter with Bogie during the making of
Across the Pacific, we were never quite able ever again to believe him
as a heroic figure.

"I can't help the rumors," he snarled. "All I know is, everytime I feel like having a drink, I round up a pal, which makes it a social event, right? Maybe I socialize like that ten or twenty times a day, which might make me the world's champion social drinker. But a social drinker isn't a drunk."

End of interview; he had had enough.

When Publicity Director Bob Taplinger reprimanded him, insisting that his career would suffer unless he got along with the press on their terms, Bogey replied, "I'll make a deal with you. If your guys can find somebody who can ask intelligent questions—something besides what do I eat for breakfast and how much do I drink—I'll be glad to give them a *real* interview."

Taplinger might have considered his offer, but very briefly. No star ever gave real interviews, it was too dangerous. Anyway, it wasn't important. No less a star-maker than J.L. himself was certain that Bogie would never be more than a character actor. He was too old, too ugly and certainly too cyniical to ever be a romantic lead.

Then there is this personal recollection:

Eight-thirty a.m. on a bleak Monday. I'm sent on a rush to Mimeo to pick up script changes on *Across the Pacific* and deliver them to Bogart in his dressing room. I knock three times. No response. I unlock the door and start to enter, then freeze as I come face-to-face with Bogart. He is wild-eyed, his upraised arm brandishing an empty liquor bottle. Sinking into a chair, he mutters an apology; he thought someone was breaking in. He seems to be hung-over, and his unshaven, disheveled appearance suggests that he's been up all night. Dropping the envelope on the table, I beat a hasty retreat.

Later, upon learning that Security had been alerted not to allow Mayo Methot—Mrs. Bogart—on the lot, his actions became understandable. The Battling Bogarts had been at it again. Most accounts of their tumultuous marriage gave Bogie credit for handling those imbroglios with a sense of humor. But on that morning he seemed desperate, even frightened. It was a side of him we had never seen before.

Dick Powell was another one some of us thought of as interesting. Not as the dimpled, fatuous crooner, but as a case study. Behind that exuberant, boyish-charmer facade was a cold, calculating, extremely shrewd manipulator. In short, our kind of guy.

During his years with us, with his weekly salary reaching $3,500, and his total income considerably augmented by record royalties and earnings from his popular radio show, *Hollywood Hotel*, Powell could have indulged himself with all the usual trappings of success: the show-off estate, Rolls-Royces, gambling. Instead, he lived modestly, carefully investing his money. More than a decade before the post-war boom skyrocketed the value of San Fernando Valley acreage, he envisioned the time when it would become Los Angeles' most populous suburb. Against the advice of real estate experts, who said it would never be more than a wasteland, he bought up or optioned large tracts at $50 an acre. That was a long-term investment. In other parts of the city, to provide current income, he built supermarkets, which he then leased on long-term contracts to market chains.

By 1940, with his career seemingly coming to an end, Powell had put his fiscal affairs in such good order that he was assured of an income for the rest of his life.

He turned out to be a far more versatile actor than he was ever allowed to be at our studio. Aware of his dramatic aspirations, some months before he left I dropped off a copy of James Cain's new novella, *Double Indemnity*, in his dressing room, with a note saying I thought he would be perfect for the lead role of Walter Neff, the insurance agent who becomes involved in murder. I offered to do an adaptation on spec if he was interested.

About a week later, he sent it back with a letter saying he appreciated my interest. It was exactly the kind of story he wanted to do, he wrote. But he had learned that Paramount owned the film rights and he doubted if they would consider him.

When he turned down the script of *Garden of the Moon*, he made a counter-proposal to J.L.

"Look," he said,"I've had it with these idiotic singing parts and Bogie's always griping about the gangster crap you make him do. Why not give me a picture that he's turned down and let him do this one?"

The Boss laughed. Hollowly.

Powell carefully cultivated the impression of seeming to be just another happy-go-lucky actor, but he had an interesting philosophy which seemed to govern his life.

"Never allow yourself to become too happy or too sad," he often said. "That way you can ride the highs and lows a lot easier."

He was a prize freeloader, taking advantage of everything the lot had to offer in the way of freebies, from office supplies requisitioned from Secretarial to items of clothing "borrowed" from Wardrobe. Seemingly every important purchase he ever made was with the thought of eventual resale for profit. Certainly that was so with all the houses he ever owned; none were *homes* in the sense of any permanency, but merely investments which would appreciate in value and then be sold.

He had an unusual, flamboyant way of ending personal letters. Instead of the customary "Sincerely," his concluded, "With love and kisses." Yet he was considered cold and unemotional. Except with children. He seemed to delight in their company, and when he married Joan Blondell, he legally adopted the boy and girl born during her marriage to cameraman George Barnes.

Only once did I ever hear Powell openly confess to something that made him seem humanly vulnerable. In his whole life, he said, he had never received any kind of award or honor.

"That's not important," he added. "I think that what I really miss is that nobody ever gave me a party. Not even a birthday party . . . "

For a second or two, he had the wistful look of a little kid, nose pressed against the window, hungrily eyeing all the goodies in a bakery.

Then he laughed deprecatingly, adding, "Now why did I say a dumb thing like that? Forget it."

"What do I have to do to get into your panties?"

It was not the kind of question that Errol Flynn usually had to plaintively ask of a lovely young lady. More often than not, they were only too willing to supply the answer before he could voice the question. But in this case, it was directed to Olivia de Havilland who, despite having a crush on him, was well known as Miss Prim & Proper.

She fixed him with a steely glance.

"Why, it's the easiest thing in the world, Mr. Flynn," she replied. "The same as you with with yours—you know, one leg at a time."

De Havilland was far and away the most lady-like actress on the lot. No obscenities were ever heard issuing from her kissable lips, she didn't drink and we would have staked our lives that she was our one certifiable virgin.

Very much like Davis in one respect, she could be a tough fighter for any cause she believed in. There was one good example that we knew of.

One noontime, with one of us relieving in J.L.'s outer office, she burst in, in costume from the set of *My Love Came Back*, and with those enormous root beer-brown eys flashing, demanded to see Mr. Warner at once. Refusing to be dissuaded by the fact that he wasn't in, she sat down, declaring that until such time as she was granted an audience, she had no intention of returning to work.

Executive secretary Bill Schaefer always left word where he would be lunching, but it was a rule that he was never to be disturbed except in the case of a dire emergency. Quickly and correctly, the messenger decided that the threat of holding up production certainly fitted that category and Schaefer came running. De Havilland, however, was in no mood to accept an intermediary, insisting, "I want to talk to Mr. Warner personally about our *babies!*"

It was a most provocative, fascinating demand, made even more so by Schaefer's abrupt dismissal of our informant. For the next few hours our back room buzzed with speculation. Was it possible that we were wrong about her lack of a sex life? Could she, somehow, be J.L.'s secret mistress? Had he fathered her illegitimate child—no, more than one, she had said "babies"—without anyone knowing?

The answer came late that day, and what it might have lacked in sensational drama was more than compensated for by romance. It seemed that the studio's cat population had exploded, with the latest addition, a litter of five newly born kittens, found with their mother that morning on the bed of a set which was intended for the first shot of the day.

Production was delayed while the crew sought another suitable nest for the family, causing Production Manager Tenny Wright to scream, "What're we running here, a goddam cat house?" and ordering traps set to bring the number of felines down to the barest minimum necessary for their job of rat-catching.

Learning of this, and knowing that the captured animals would be destroyed, de Havilland presented her demand to J.L., and in that light, "What is Mr. Warner going to do about our babies?" made endearing sense.

Ordinarily, when a department head issued an order, especially one having to do with improved efficiency, The Boss refused to intervene. But somehow, in this case, de Havilland persuaded him to accept her solution. The traps would be used for the purpose of catching all the male cats, who would then be neutered. With normal attrition, in due course, the population would then be brought under control.

She finally reported back to her set only 90 minutes late and J.L. was able to focus his attention on other matters. It's probable, though, that this must have been one of the many times he envied Walt Disney's ability to punish recalcitrant actors by ripping them to shreds.

If the cats could never know how a warm-hearted movie star had fought to save their lives, *we* knew. It was a story we enjoyed retelling.

Actually, a much better cat story—as far as we were concerned— came about because of this. With missionary zeal, de Havilland went about finding homes for the kittens, one of them being adopted by Jane Wyman.

Often, when a newcomer joined us in the back room, a couple of us would matter-of-factly launch into something like this:

"When I dropped off her mail yesterday, Jane Wyman showed me her little pussy. It's adorable."

"You telling me. It's about the prettiest I've ever seen."

His mouth would fall open and he would glance from one of us to the other. We never bothered to elucidate.

Once, Pappmeier happened to overhear us and I think it gave him the vapors. He confided to Haldeman that we were the weirdest bunch of sex maniacs he had ever known.

But it might have been our boss who had the evil mind. All we were talking about was a lovable little kitten.

Since sex (actually, for most of us, the lack of it) was our favorite topic, if a poll had been taken as to which of our actresses we most desired, the overwhelming favorite might have been very surprising.

Obviously, it wasn't Davis. Only little Eddie Hammond claimed she was sexy. By way of defending himself against our ridicule, he once added the qualification, "What I mean is, I wouldn't crawl over her naked body to go jack-off in a corner." But then, even as androgynous as we considered her, neither would we have.

As noted, de Havilland was believed to be saving it for marriage, which made her both unattainable and ineligible. Annie Sheridan? Joan Blondell? Delightful as we envisioned them being as bed partners, they tied a distant second.

No, our collective erections—pointing like so many bird dogs— were aimed at an auburn-haired, fair-skinned, middle-aged lady with the face of a madonna and the allegedly insatiable demands of a nymphomaniac. Her name was Mary Astor.

The first time we saw her was in 1940, when she was signed to co-star in *The Great Lie.* Perhaps it was the whispered details of her notorious "Diary Case" that originally prompted our inter-

When we took a departmental poll of the actress we'd most like to make out with, lovely titian-haired Mary Astor topped the list.

est; or it may have been due to the personal assurance of a leading man that she was at her happiest beneath a virile male. Whatever the initial reason, our sexual appetites were soon well whetted. Yet, interestingly enough, she did not openly exude sex the way Priscilla Lane, Marie Wilson, or many of the others did. Judging from appearances, the whispers, rumors, and allegations which had preceded her were more than exaggerations, they were dastardly lies! She was charming, intelligent, with a wonderful sense of humor and friendly with just the slightest touch of the aloofness of a lady to the manor born.

It wasn't difficult for actresses to *pretend* gentility, but usually only up to a certain point. One member of our stock company, a girl who later surprised us by eloping with a rival studio tycoon, acted the role of Great Lady at a studio reception honoring Britain's young Lord Mountbatten. Her performance, right down to a "finishing school" accent was exemplary until, asked the name of her current picture, replied, "I'm not quite sure, Your Lordship. They keep changing the fucking title."

We knew that Astor's cool outward demeanor was not a pose, that the lady required a superior, hot-blooded lover to bring forth the sensuality smoldering beneath her fragile exterior. Each of us, in our inexperienced youth, hoped that by some kind of miracle, *he* would be the chosen one.

To which end we spent as much time as possible on her set. Then, in hopes of a more private meeting, we went out of our way to "accidentally" encounter her elsewhere in the studio, trying desperately to appear charming and urbane, a difficult task when our opening gambit was limited to a "Good morning, Miss Astor," or "How are you, Miss Astor?"

The closest any of us came to our unrealized fantasies was when our Johnny Hickman happened to come along as she was taking a stack of books out of her car, prompting her to ask if he would mind carrying some of them to her dressing room. *Would he mind!*

He followed her inside, stacked the books on a table and turned to her with a hopeful smile.

"Thank you very much," Astor said, handing him a dollar. It was one of the very few times when *money* was not the hoped-for reward.

When he returned to our back room, Johnny mentioned that he had just had intercourse with Mary Astor in her dressing room. Though considered to be generally truthful, in this case our response was that he was the dirtiest, filthiest liar of all time!

"Listen, you idiots," he responded. "You're all such ignorant degenerate scumbags you don't even know there's another four-letter word ending in "K" that means intercourse. T-A-L-K!"

I'm sure that Astor was well aware of what was behind our smiles, courtly manners and hungry eyes. She might have been flattered, but she was both experienced and wise enough to know that we were, sadly enough for us, only children trying to play at an adult game.

Shortly afterwards, we had another kind of love affair with a beautiful lady. This time it was reciprocated.

It was with Dame May Whitty, the marvelous old English character actress, who all but stole the Robert Montgomery version of *Night Must Fall.*

Upon her arrival for *The Constant Nymph*, Pete Poulton was sent to Casting to escort her to her dressing room. As they walked across the lot, Pete ventured that he didn't know what to call her, since in the American vernacular "Dame" had a lower-class connotation. Nor did he want to address her as "Miss," since that would ignore the fact that she had been granted a title by her king.

She solved his dilemma with a laugh. "In that case," she said, "why don't you just call me *Auntie May?*"

Which we did, right down to the broad "A." It gained us a lot of respect from visitors when we said, "Auntie May, these folks would love to meet you."

They would ask if we were really related? Of course we were.

Auntie May was a charming, delightful lady and we enjoyed the brief pleasure of her company. On her last day, some of us

Dame May Whitty became our favorite actress when she suggested we drop the "Dame" and simply call her "Auntie May."

chipped in and presented her with a bouquet of roses. It was the only presentation of its kind we ever made.

When David Niven came our way to do *The Dawn Patrol*, I immediately knew what to give my kid sister for her approaching birthday. With Niven being her current hearthrob, what could be a more thrilling gift to a teenager than her love's personally autographed photo? I left a polite request to that effect in his dressing room.

A week went by, and with no response, and my sister's birthday only one day away, I unhappily concluded that he had ignored my request. Then, about five that afternoon, he strode into our outer office, still in makeup and attired in his World War aviator's costume, manila envelope tucked under his arm.

"Good afternoon," he said to Pappmeier." May I see Mr. Jerome please?"

Fred gaped. "Who?"

Niven consulted the front of the envelope. "Don't you have a Mr. Stuart Jerome?"

It was the hour when we were always rushing to meet the deadline for the pickup of our outgoing mail and Fred was not too happy to take the time to summon me from the back room. Especially for what obviously was not company business.

"Mr. Jerome?" Niven said, extending his hand. "How do you do? I'm David Niven."

It was the *only* time, while in uniform, that anyone ever called me "Mister," and it was a heady experience.

"I hope your sister likes this one," he said, handing me the envelope. Again shaking hands, he left.

Of all her presents that year, mine was my sister's favorite. An 11 × 14, it was inscribed, "To my dear friend June. Happy Birthday. Love, David."

The only discordant note came from Pappmeier. He complained that I made him look like he was my secretary.

Fresh from the set of *The Dawn Patrol*, this is the way David Niven looked when he paid a surprise visit to our department. Our boss was not amused.

10

Sydney Greenstreet, Alan Hale & Other Troubles

As ONE OF OUR MOST IMPORTANT "epics" of 1939, *The Private Lives of Elizabeth & Essex* was not only the most expensive production of the year (along with half a dozen other specials, it would provide the leverage of our Sales Department to pre-sell our entire slate of features and shorts), it also started out as the most difficult to make.

From the very beginning, it seemed to be one of those films that are jinxed. Within the first week of shooting, two accidents foretold a troubled schedule that lay ahead. The first occurred in a scene in which Bette Davis, as Queen Elizabeth, was attending a meeting of her Privy Council. Taking her place on the throne, which was mounted on a dais, Davis's heavy, cumbersome costume caused the high chair to slide back to the

148

unprotected edge. It teetered for a second, then started to go over backwards. Fortunately, her fall was cushioned by the quick thinking of a nearby gaffer, who caught the back of the chair as it hit the floor. It was only a four-foot drop, but as everyone shudderingly noted, if it hadn't been for him, David's head, adorned with a metal crown, could have come in contact with an open electrical conduit.

Very little more was accomplished for the balance of the day.

The second accident involved Errol Flynn and supporting player Ralph Forbes. It was a simple scene in which Flynn, as Lord Essex, had a confrontation with Forbes, ending in his threateningly drawing his rapier. Two rehearsals went off without a hitch and director Mike Curtiz called for a take. This time, as Flynn drew, Forbes inexplicably lunged forward and the upraised tip of the rapier penetrated his eye. He was rushed to an opthalmologist, who at first feared the cornea had been pierced, which would have resulted in blindness. Fortunately, it turned out that the injury wasn't that serious, but an unnerved company closed down production four hours earlier than planned.

When they resumed, it was grimly noted that the most dangerous scenes were still to come. With the superstitious certainty that accidents always come in threes, some of the crew entered into the gallows-humor game of making daily bets on when the inevitable third would occur and who it would involve.

The answers to both questions came only a few days later. While waiting for a shot to be set up, Alan Hale felt the need to relieve himself, necessitating a short walk down the street to the nearest men's room. En route, he happened to encounter a group of visitors being escorted by Mike Sloan, who said that Hale charmingly obliged them with autographs and a moment's chat. Later, Mike claimed he might have been the last person who saw Hale *intact*.

The accident happened in the men's room. When Hale started to zip up his costume, the recalcitrant zipper jammed on a length of his foreskin, and as the blood started flowing, he became panicky. The more he tried to free himself, the more tenaciously the device gripped his manhood. Undoubtedly it hurt; more likely, though, it was the emotional shock that caused him to run out to the street dripping blood and howling, "Help! I've amputated my cock!"

Continuing thusly, he ran all the way to First Aid. Our medic, Doc McWilliams, although supposedly a specialist at curing hangovers, venereal diseases and other occupational ailments, apparently was not up to the surgical skills of extricating a torn foreskin. A car was swiftly dispatched from Transportation and Hale was rushed to a local hospital where the required emergency surgery was performed. Since he was needed for the rest of the day's scenes, again shooting was suspended.

"Fucking ektors!" Director Curtiz was heard to complain. "Kent even drust dem to dake a louzy piss!"

With that, the jinx came to an end. During the ensuing ten weeks of shooting, much of which involved dangerous battle scenes using hundreds of extras, horses, and stunt men, there were no further accidents.

When Hale returned to work, he took some kidding from his co-workers. Davis suggested that perhaps he should hire a nurse to take him to the toidy. One more accident, said Flynn, would mean the end of his sex life.

It was one of the more-challenging questions we used to put to newcomers to our department: "Betcha two-bits you can't name the movie in which Alan Hale got himself circumcised."

Among our many bad habits, we seemed to take a perverse delight in deliberately mispronouncing names. As previously noted, writer Aeneas MacKenzie forever afterwards became "Penis" MacKenzie thanks to us. Then there was actor Paul Henreid, who logically ended up as Paul Hemorrhoid. We even reached the point where we referred to our hierarchy as the *Warnout* Brothers. (In this case, however, we quickly put an end to it; we could imagine the kind of impression we would give visitors if we greeted them with the ringing phrase, "Welcome to the Warnout Bros. Studios!")

As with most bad habits, though, our other mispronunciations became ingrained. Thus, when the script of a new production,

Alan Hale was one of the greatest scene-stealers on our lot. But according to co-workers, during the filming of *The Private Lives of Elizabeth and Essex*, he went a little too far, even if it was by accident.

The Amazing Dr. Clitterhouse, came out of Mimeo, it was natural for us to immediately refer to it as *Dr. Clitoris*. It was by use of this title that our Bill Hoback inadvertently got the studio in a bit of trouble.

Escorting three church officials, Bill unthinkingly said that he would try to get them on the set of Edward G. Robinson's new film, *The Amazing Dr. Clitoris*. Their strange expressions instantly and eloquently told him that he had committed a gaffe, but deciding it might be better not to go into explanations, he let it go at that. The dignitaries visited the set, thoughtfully watched one scene being shot, then left the lot. (When Bill complained that there was no forthcoming tip, one wag suggested that the least they could have done was to have blessed him.)

The fallout came about a week later. In a letter to J.L. from the head of the group—an Episcopal Bishop—there was an ominous warning that " . . . our church will not condone the release of a certain film of yours, the brazen title of which is a moral affront to every decent American."

The studio was accustomed to receiving all kinds of complaints and threats; usually they were the work of the lunatic fringe. This was different. Written by an important religious leader, it was potentially very serious. The concerted efforts of religious groups had in the past prevented many pictures from going into general release, and under the threat of a boycott studios had been known to even shelve, or re-shoot, the offending movie.

The letter was brought to J.L.'s attention about 10:30 a.m., embroiling some of our top echelon for the next hour in trying to solve the mystery of the morally offensive title. It was Charlie Einfeld who finally resolved the matter by the simple expedient of placing a long-distance phone call to the Bishop.

Upon learning the misapprehensive source of their indignation, Einfeld quickly corrected him, spelling out the correct title. He also said he would mail a copy of the script, so that the church officials could determine for themselves the high ideals we strove for in this and every movie we produced. Concluding, he said that since the bishop had been put to some trouble by this matter, the studio would like to make a donation to his diocese.

When Einfeld laughingly told J.L. what the bishop had thought the title was, The Boss was not amused, somehow placing the blame on cast member Humphrey Bogart.

"Bogart was probably introduced to this guy," he opined, "and told him that was the title. It's exactly the kind of trouble-making joke that that sonofabitch would pull!!"

J.L. remained worried about the title right up to release time, noting in a memo to Einfeld that " . . . if a goddam pope (or whatever that guy was) can mispronounce it, what about all the ordinary moviegoers? Let's make sure we don't run into any censorship problems."

We didn't. *The Amazing Dr. Clitoris*—excuse me, *Clitterhouse*—became one of our top-grossing pictures of the year. But imagine, all that brouhaha just because our Wild Bill Hoback thoughtlessly used one wrong word. And they thought we weren't important! Ha!

In the context of today's films, it seems inconceivable that the censorship code once prohibited any scenes showing a married couple in bed together. Some of the little independents ignored this edict, but woe unto any major studio that attempted such stark reality! As fascinated witnesses to one such attempt, we mention it here as perhaps a museum piece.

One morning Stan Lefcourt burst into the back room with the breathless announcement: "Hey! You guys wanna see something terrific? Stage 11—they're shooting a sex scene with a *couple* in bed!"

We knew he was putting us on. If he had said there were two people actually copulating on the sidelines we would have accepted it without surprise. But a *filmed* scene? No way! Impossible! Merely to verify our certainty that the story was a hoax, a few of us later journeyed over to the set of *International Squadron*.

Incredibly, it was true! Occupying *one* twin bed, portraying newlyweds in a hotel room, were Olympe Bradna and William

Lundigan. She was wearing a long, heavy nightgown and he was in pajamas. There was nothing even faintly suggestive, either in their actions or the dialogue. Yet the sight of them in bed together *was* sexually exciting. We asked the script clerk how come it was being shot this way?

"That's the way the director wants it," he shrugged. "The script calls for them to be in separate beds, but he says it's unrealistic that way. The dummy must still think he's in Europe."

Director Lothar Mendes was new to our lot and possibly labored under the misapprehension that he could make script changes without prior Front Office approval. He quickly learned otherwise. When producer Edmund Grainger saw the rushes, he hit the ceiling.

"Are you outta your mind?" he said to Mendes. "My God, even if we were able to get that scene past the Breen office, we'd have every local censorship board in the country on our necks!"

He was probably right. As staged, the scene had a charming intimacy, but the fact remained that it was considered prurient because in the movies newlyweds did not occupy the same bed. It was, of course, re-shot, and when it was previewed no one commented on the strange sight of a young couple waking up in separate beds after their first night together.

So much for our handling of that nasty word s-e-x, circa 1941.

Just as any suggestion of overt sex was taboo, the same applied to normal bodily functions.

Escorting a family on The Tour, Dick Rawlings' first stop happened to be the set of *Daughters Courageous*. The company was just breaking for lunch, and ordinarily Dick would have moved them to another stage but they were fascinated by the layout of rooms depicting Claude Rains' turn-of-the-century home. Enthusiastically noting the authenticity of the period furnishings, right down to the newspapers and magazines of that time, they moved from room to room until they reached the bathroom. There the man's face clouded.

"Well, I'll be damned," he muttered.

Dick looked at him wonderingly. Only a moment before he had obviously been enjoying himself. Something had suddenly gone wrong.

"What in hell kind of a bathroom is this?" the man demanded.

His 12-year-old son laughed. "Yeah. Where's the toilet?"

We had become so conditioned to "movie realism" that we had long before ceased to notice that this one indispensible piece of equipment was never shown in bathroom scenes. Such as this, which contained a tub and wash basin, both of which our Plumbing Department had made usable. But there was no toilet.

Dick attempted to explain that the fixture, even with the lid down, was considered objectionable. This only served to further anger the man.

"Well, then, what do they use to relieve themselves?" he snapped. "The sink?"

With the discouraging feeling that he had a nut on his hands, Dick quickly suggested that perhaps they'd like to visit another stage. They did, and he was grateful that there were no more bathrooms to aggravate the visitor. But the rest of The Tour was not a complete success; the man kept grousing about the lies that movie people perpetrate on the public.

When Dick finally returned the family to Main Reception, the man shook his hand.

"I didn't mean to take it out on you," he apologized. "It just got me sore to think how they can show an honest-to-God bathroom without a toilet in it."

He handed Dick a business card.

"You ever need anything in my line, I'll give you the wholesale price."

At the time, Dick probably would have been more appreciative of a little cash. Some years later, after he had become a top-flight cameraman, Rawlings' new home contained three custom-designed commodes. Purchased, as he proudly pointed out, at a wholesale price.

Back in the early 1930's, after a ravaging fire, we installed our own Fire Department. Headed by Chief George Kitchen, his intrepid crew of three had their own fire house and, naturally, their own shiny red fire engine. Since there wasn't even one tiny blaze during our time, the Chief and his men spent most of their days polishing their engine, checking their equipment, and waiting—perhaps hopefully—for the alarm that would give them the opportunity to demonstrate their expertise and valor. It finally happened one afternoon.

With some time to spare between set-ups, Sydney Greenstreet left the set of *Across the Pacific* to make a phone call from a nearby booth. It turned out to be a serious error in logistics. A tall, immense man, weighing over 300 pounds, it forever remained a puzzle how he was able to get his bulk into the booth in the first place. But that became academic in light of the more important question: How to get him out?

It was when he completed his call that he discovered, much to his chargin, that he was stuck. No matter how he twisted and turned, he was solidly wedged inside. A little while later an assistant came out looking for him. Apprised of Greenstreet's predicament, he summoned some of the crew to try and unbudge him. To no avail. The fat man was securely trapped. By then, some of us had gathered to watch and laugh, though it was far from being a humorous situation. Greenstreet was a very dignified, reserved gentleman and anybody with any sense of compassion would have realized he was becoming terribly uncomfortable. Moreover, he was now holding up production and it was axiomatic that anything that unnecessarily cost the studio money was not funny.

Someone pulled the fire alarm. Within seconds, siren wailing, the fire engine hove into sight, Chief Kitchen at the wheel, he and his men in full battle regalia. With the sound of the siren having penetrated even the noiseproof stages, a small crowd of extras and employees started to gather, offering all sorts of suggestions for Greenstreet's removal. The Chief ignored them. If this wasn't exactly a fire, it was at least an emer-

Sydney Greenstreet, our favorite fat man, customarily enjoyed a "snack" between lunch and dinner.

gency, and as such it presented his department with the opportunity they had long awaited.

A man of action, Kitchen surveyed the situation and came up with a swift decision. The only possible way to get Greenstreet out was to hose him down. When he and the glass walls of the booth became equally slippery, he would then slide out, like a banana ejected from its skin.

It sounded simple and logical. A line was made fast around the actor's girth, and the hose was turned on and aimed inside. It took only seconds to note that what had seemed workable in theory had, in practice, a fatal flaw. Even at its lowest pressure, the fire hose carried such tremendous power that had it been directed against Greenstreet for another moment, it could easily have maimed him.

A garden hose was substituted, and when the water was combined with soap powder, the combination proved to be slippery enough so that, an hour after his ordeal began, and somewhat the worse for bruises and a thorough dousing, Greenstreet was finally freed, to the accompaniment of cheers from the spectators.

It was then that one of them, a grip, laconically declared that they had done it the hard way. He pointed to the four corner bolts by which the booth was secured to its concrete flooring.

"Didn't need the fire department," he said. "All we had to do was remove the bolts. Four of us could've easily lifted the booth over his head."

Probably. But it would have lacked drama. More important, it would have robbed Chief Kitchen and his brave crew of their *Moment of Glory*. Just as we had our own legends, this certainly must have become one of theirs.

11

Writers: Integrity and How to Rise Above It

Oυτ OF A MYRIAD of fascinating departments, my favorite was the Writers Building. Situated in a shady, quiet corner of the studio, far removed from the distracting turmoil of production, it was deliberately planned to give its occupants the solitude and serenity necessary for wooing the creative muse.

In actual fact, it was a boisterous madhouse, exemplified by two office sections officially named the Upper and Lower Wards. Herein at any given time dwelt some 40 to 60 writers, among them such budding lumineries as John Huston, Robert Rossen, Jerry Wald, and the Epstein twins, Philip and Julius. To the rat-a-tat-tat background accompaniment of the secretaries' continuous typing, raised voices would be heard as collaborators discussed and argued story points and scenes.

159

It was an unusual day when Jerry Wald's high-pitched, enthusiastic voice was not echoing through the second floor hallway as he lobbed cliché after cliché at his partner, Dick Macaulay, in hopes of coming up with something new for one of the musicals they were constantly churning out.

"In the dream sequence, we have these little babies, see? Ten, twenty of the cutest little bastards you ever saw. They're all in their layettes crying, until the dame starts singing to them. Then they start laughing and you know what? My God, this bit alone could win us an Oscar!—the babies start dancing! We'll get Buzz Berkeley to work up a routine and—"

"Wait a second, Jerry! Where in hell are we gonna find little babies who can *dance?*"

"That's Casting's problem, not ours. Boy-oh-boy, is this gonna be great! Let's see if we can get Wallis on the phone."

Alleged by some of his colleagues to be the model for the unscrupulous and untalented Sammy Glick in Budd Schulberg's famed Hollywood novel *What Makes Sammy Run*, Wald was highly thought of by the Front Office. A prolific idea man, he was a master at switching old plots around and *telling* a story. His detractors, however, pointed out that he needed a *writer* collaborator to make it work on paper. They may have been right; during his years with us, he never received a solo screenplay credit.

Wald got his start in New York as the youthful radio critic for *The Graphic*. At a time when radio stars were beginning to rival movie stars in terms of public adulation, he saw the opportunity to make a name for himself by starting a feud with a top personality, selecting as the target of his ridicule reigning idol Rudy Vallee. It was the kind of thing that sold newspapers and caused talk in the trade, but after a while Wald aspired to higher things and more money than the paper was willing to pay him. Selling some story ideas to our New York office, and convincing them that this was only the tip of his creative iceberg, he was given a contract and embarked for the Coast.

Interestingly, his first assignment was working on a movie called *Sweet Music*, starring . . . Rudy Vallee.

Writers was the one building where a country-club atmosphere of conviviality was, if not encouraged, at least tolerated.
The theory being that, since writers were a little bit crazy to begin with, the same disciplinary rules that applied to other employees could not be enforced with them. However, as with
other seemingly pressureless departments, appearances could
be deceiving. Despite the informality and on-going fun and
games, there were certain rigid rules that had to be observed.

First and foremost, writers were expected to check in by nine
a.m. and leave no earlier than 5:30. Second, once into screenplay, they were expected to turn out no less than 30 pages of
script per week. Every Friday afternoon, an assistant from the
Story Department would visit each writer and pick up copies of
his output. This was both to ensure the fact that they were actually working and also to determine their contributions to the production they were assigned to. Often, with three or four writers
working independently on the same script, it became a hassle
figuring out who had contributed enough to the final screenplay
to warrant receiving the all-important screen credit.

Coming up with 30 pages in the space of a five-and-a-half-
day week posed no great problem for the more experienced
hands. Like John Huston. Carrying on a torrid affair with an actress who happened to be an insomniac, and needing the night
hours to meet her romantic requirements, he dictated 40 pages
of script for *The Story of Dr. Ehrlich's Magic Bullet* in one
marathon-paced 14-hour day, exhausting a corps of secretaries.

The pages were doled out to his producer, Wolfgang
Reinhardt, at the rate of eight a day, and for the duration of that
week, Huston would blearily stagger into his office at nine, collapse on the couch and fall asleep.

During that time, as his normally emaciated frame started to
become skeletal, Reinhardt happened to run into him as he was
leaving the lot one night, observing that although the script
pages were excellent, maybe he was pushing too hard. Truer
words were never spoken.

The romance came to an end on the seventh night when, like
God, Huston rested. Inadvertently, he ruefully admitted, by

committing the unpardonable sin of falling asleep atop his lady love.

If rule number two could be met with equinimity, it was the first, with its inflexibility, that was most hated. And evaded. It had long been an industry-wide feeling that writers could not be trusted to work at home. Never mind the fact that they might send in the required number of pages; it was dangerous to allow any employee that much liberty. Besides, it would set a bad example for the other slaves. No, the only way writers could be fully trusted was to herd them together where they could be under Big Brother's watchful eye, and make them put in regular working hours, the same as everybody else.

They *were* permitted the luxury of occasional tardiness. Such provable excuses as, say, a terrible toothache necessitating an emergency dental appointment, having to attend the funeral of a close relative, or being involved in a head-on collision coming over Cahuenga Pass were, reluctantly, ruled as being legitimate reasons for late check-ins or early departures. But if it became habitual to check in after 9:30, or to leave by five, danger loomed on the horizon. A memo from our Legal Department would coldly refer to a certain contract clause which gave the studio the right to terminate employment for due cause.

There were two entrance routes used by our writers. Some drove on the lot and were checked in by the cop at the Auto Gate. Others went through Main Reception where the receptionist, with her freshly typed list of names, would note the exact time of their arrivals and departures. Every morning at 10:15 we would pick up both lists and deliver them on a rush to J.L.'s office where, it was claimed, he took them with him to the bathroom, devoting as much time to them as he did to perusing the Sales Department's teletyped figures of yesterday's national grosses.

As with all restrictive edicts, the system of check-ins and check-outs led to any number of schemes to try and circumvent the eight-hour workday. The most obvious, of course, was simple bribery. It was known that one cop on the Auto Gate received five dollars a week from each of half a dozen writers, all of whom were always marked on the time sheet as arriving a few minutes before nine. It worked for a long time, until someone in the Front Office became curious about their mass punctuality. Did they all arrive in one car? Or did they assemble at 8:56 outside the gate and form a caravan? Apparently, the spy took enough interest to investigate. The cop was replaced by another who, regrettably, didn't accept bribes. Thus forcing some of our best writer-carousers to curtail their nightly activities in order to actually meet the morning deadline.

With those who entered through Main Reception, it was a different matter. The entrance was presided over by a tall, blond young woman named Grant Donley, a firm believer in the old-fashioned maxims of honesty and truth, and writers were hard pressed to come up with ways of convincing her of their early arrivals, when, in fact, they would check in an hour later than required.

A dashing young newcomer named Niven Busch, who habitually arrived around ten every morning, would explain to Donley that he had actually arrived at eight, put in time at his desk and then had gone across to the drug store for breakfast. Accompanied by a Danish, which he always presented to her, his explanation seemed believable, especially since he always showed up in shirt sleeves and loosened tie. Since a cop opened up at seven and remained until she took over at nine, Donley saw no reason to doubt his word and for some months Busch had the honor of being listed as the earliest writer-arrivee on the lot. His happy scheme came to an ignoble ending one day when Donley herself arrived before eight, and with no sign of Busch before his usual entrance, unhappily concluded she had been lied to.

With the subsequent warning memo from Legal, Busch was forced to change his life style. But never again did he speak to Donley, much less present her with a daily pastry.

Then there were the Epsteins, Philip and Julius. Identical twins, right up to their bald and slightly-pointed heads, they worked out a deceptively simple plot. As a team, they decided it was ridiculous and unnecessary for *both* of them to show up every day; all they had to do was take turns, with one relaxing at home while the other came to work as himself and his brother.

It worked like this: Phil, let's say, would enter and give Donley his name—she never knew which twin was which—and tell her that Julie was parking his car. Once inside, he would hurry down the hall to Purchasing, which had an outside entrance, go out to the street and within seconds reappear as his brother.

It was an ideal situation, one that might have gone on forever had not Hal Wallis, suddenly and unexpectedly, called for a conference on the script of *Saturday's Children*. With two hours' advance notice, Phil would have had ample time to summon Julie from Malibu. The only trouble was that he wasn't there, he had spent the weekend in San Francisco and wouldn't be back until evening.

Phil attended the meeting solo, claiming his brother had gone to keep a doctor's appointment. But apparently suspicions were aroused that perhaps the twins were up to something, because thereafter Donley was instructed always to make certain she was seeing double before she checked in either one.

As would be expected, writers had their fair share of idiosyncracies. One of producer Bryan Foy's stable, George Bricker, had a quirk about using the name "Tess Tickle" in each of his scripts. Never noticing the play on words, Foy would complain that it was too silly a name to use and the character would be re-named. This went on for several years, and a dozen scripts, with Bricker invariably coming up with a minor female role named "Tess Tickle" and Foy re-naming her.

At long last one day, Bricker's patience and perseverance paid off. Summoned to the set of *The Kid Comes Back*, he was told by director Breezy Eason that he needed a quick re-write of a scene. Within ten minutes, Bricker turned out the new pages. If, when he saw the rushes the following day, Foy was surprised to hear Wayne Morris tell Barton MacLane, "I had dinner last night with my old girl friend, Tess Tickle," he never mentioned it.

A tough, former crime reporter named A.I. Bezzerides once inadvertently shocked his middle-aged, prim, spinster secretary into near hysteria while dictating a scene for *Juke Girl*.

"Interior bar, night," he started, his eyes hovering toward the ceiling for inspiration. "Charley comes forward and faces the foreman ominously. Charley, quote, Listen, you dirty prick, I'll break your fucking balls before I—"

With a terrible shriek, the lady dropped her pad and fled to the bathroom. When she finally regained her composure, she tearfully begged her boss for re-assignment to another, far less realistic, writer.

Bezzerides' producer pointed out that he was wasting his time and the company's money by writing that kind of dialogue for a movie.

"I know that," he shrugged. "But shit, it's only a first draft. I gotta get the feel of the character before I have to water the fucking dialogue down to, 'Listen, you louse, I'm not taking anymore of your guff.'"

He was a good 35 years ahead of his time.

Robert Rossen was considered one of the best of our young writers. A brooding iconoclast who constantly fought against the idiocies of the censorship code, Rossen was even willing to do battle with J.L. or Wallis if necessary. He often used the word "integrity" in connection with his scripts, this at a time when most writers were reconciled to playing it safe by maintaining the status quo. Even though he lost more wars than he won, Rossen's scripts for such films as *Dust Be My Destiny* and *The Sea Wolf* were models of the hard-hitting, socially conscious melodramas that we were noted for.

In a story conference with Wallis on *Out of the Fog*, he violently objected to the executive producer's decision to omit a certain scene.

"Damn it, Hal," he said, "you're violating my whole sense of integrity."

"Integrity, integrity," Wallis chided. "That's all I keep hearing from you. Isn't it about time you *rose* above it?"

There was an old joke about an author who was brought out to Hollywood under long-term contract to write screenplays. Ashamed of his work—despite a $2000 weekly salary—he and his wife let it be known to their neighbors that he was in the fertilizer business.

It might not have been apocryphal. There was no question that many book writers considered movie writing to be a demeaning prostitution of their talents. Yet in spite of this (or perhaps because of it?) the studios constantly clamored for their services. Even the best screenwriters were looked down upon in comparison to their august brethren, "Authors."

One such who came to work for us in 1939 was James Hilton. Already famed for *Goodbye, Mr. Chips* and *Lost Horizon*, he had been eagerly sought after by other studios and we had achieved a coup by acquiring his services when we bought the film rights to his newest best-seller, *We Are Not Alone*.

Assigned an office in the Writers Building, Hilton got off to a dismal start with his colleagues. First, by being tendered a luncheon by The Brothers in the Executive Dining Room and then by being the subject of a series of publicity interviews.

None of this was his own doing; indeed, it was only too evident that he hated being put on display. Still, many of his fellow writers who had never even met J.L., much less been invited to a free lunch, smarted under the realization that, despite top movie credits, they remained anonymous while a man unproven at writing scripts was, according to a publicity release, considered ". . . one of the greatest writers since Shakespeare."

Their dislike was compounded by his seeming aloofness. Drab-looking, short, with close-cropped graying hair parted in the center, and given to wearing bow ties and out-of-style suits, Hilton would have been perfectly cast as an English valet or butler. He rarely ventured more than a muttered, "Good morn-

James Hilton was already famous as the author of *Lost Horizon* and *Goodbye, Mr. Chips* when he came to work for us on the screenplay of his newest book, *We Are Not Alone*. A shy, well-mannered Englishman, when he completed his assignment, he did something to Jack Warner that was unheard of.

ing," always with averted eyes, and never socialized during the afternoon coffee break. The overwhelming consensus was that he considered himself superior to all the others.

As a long-time fan, when I learned that we had signed him, I brought from home my copies of *Goodbye, Mr. Chips* and *Lost Horizon*, keeping them in my locker against the time when I could summon up the courage to ask him to autograph them. During his first week he was too busy being feted and publicized to be further annoyed. It was on Friday afternoon of his second week that, summoned to take the west route, I noticed a manila envelope from Research addressed to him. I added my two volumes to the other mail.

It was an opportune time. Hilton was alone, his door ajar, seated at his desk, scribbling on a yellow legal pad. Spread out in front of him were three or four open scripts. Apologizing for my intrusion, I told him he was one of my favorite authors and asked if he would autograph his books for me. He did so, asking my name, which in turn prompted me to say that I hoped to become a writer; certainly not one of his calibre, but a screenplay writer.

"No, no," he said, "you mustn't denigrate it in comparison to other forms of writing. I find screenplay construction quite fascinating. Also elusive." He sighed, pointing to the open scripts. "I've been studying these to try and learn the art of telling a story visually. It's most difficult. At my age, one doesn't learn new tricks so easily. . . ."

His voice trailed off embarrassedly. I stood there for a moment, hoping he would continue, but he didn't. Nor did he once lift his eyes to look at me; they remained glued to the desk. Feeling I had intruded long enough, I awkwardly said it was an honor to have met him. He offered his hand.

"Thank you," he said, "and good luck with your screenwriting."

The fact that his handshake was limp, and that his eyes remained averted were not due, I suddenly realized, to unfriendliness, much less a feeling of superiority. To the contrary, he seemed so terribly diffident that it was obvious he was incapable of initiating a friendship or even a mere conversation.

If the screenplay form of writing continued to be of fascination to him, it apparently remained equally elusive. He subsequently returned to the craft he knew best, novels, and his screenplay of *We Are Not Alone* was rewritten by our skilled Milton Krims, who shared credit.

On his last day, Hilton committed an act of heresy that would have further alienated him from his fellow writers, had they known about it. In longhand, he wrote a bread-and-butter note to J.L., thanking him for the opportunity of turning his book into a film, but regretting that, as a raw apprentice, he wasn't experienced enough to have done a better job.

It might have been the first letter of its kind that The Boss ever received. After recovering from his initial shock, he instructed Bill Schaefer to find out when Hilton would be available again.

"I want that sonofabitch back here," J.L. said.

Hilton never did return. But there is an historical footnote based on his departure. Some years later, when a young writer came to the studio to do a rewrite on a Flynn western, remembering the well-mannered Englishman's note of thanks, and especially J.L.'s reaction, on his last day he sent a similar letter.

A week later, he received a response from Bill Schaefer.

"Mr. Warner has asked me to convey his thanks for your letter," it read. "He wishes you well in your new career."

But he didn't ask me to come back.

Just as production could not have functioned without the services of the anonymous workers in the crafts departments, so the writers were totally dependent on their secretaries. The good ones knew how to cover for their boss's absence when he got a sudden call from his producer; how to mix a martini to his specifications; how to subtly remind him that he had used his favorite original line in his last two screenplays; and how to make sure he had peaceful contemplation (translation: a nap on the couch) when courting the creative muse.

Their department head was Sadie Fryer, a plump Jewish-mother type of about 60, who took a close interest in the personal lives of her girls. Whenever Sadie hired a new secretary, there was a set admonition that accompanied her welcome.

"There's a certain informality in a studio that doesn't exist elsewhere," she would say. "Working for a writer or producer involves the kind of close personal relationship which could easily lead to a romantic attachment on your part. Just bear in mind that as far as these men are concerned, sex is nothing more than a harmless little game. Don't allow yourself to get involved."

Most of them heeded her advice. Secretarial jobs at a glamorous studio, and especially with a starting wage of $30 a week, were always sought after and they knew that any sexual transgression would mean termination. Most . . . but not all.

Dixie, as I'll call her, was an exceptionally cute little redhead, whose skills went beyond typing and shorthand. Assigned to a new writer, she soon obliquely let it be know that she was not averse to play for pay. Since her boss enjoyed relaxing at the end of a workday with a drink or two, the idea of a little sexual diversion seemed like a delightful capper. They struck a bargain: Dixie would gladly provide the diversion at $10 per. The deal was consummated that night.

Thereafter, almost every evening about six, the writer would put aside his old business, call Dixie into his office, lock the door, break out the scotch, and get down to new business. If it was only a little relaxation to him, it meant a good deal more to her. Another $30 to $40 a week. The arrangement lasted for over a month, during which time J.L. must have been pleased to learn from the time sheets that he had at least one writer dedicated enough to remain at work until seven p.m. many nights.

Unfortunately, the amount of time spent in the office was not the sole criterion for continued employment. The writer's producer decided that the project they were developing had no future, and late one Tuesday we delivered the dreaded memo from

Legal, terminating him at the end of the week. It was a hard blow and that day there were no more fun and games. The blown tens and twenties were now needed as eating money, if necessary, until his agent could come up with another assignment.

On Wednesday, no longer in need of even a secretary, he sent Dixie back to the steno pool with sincere thanks for services rendered, as well as for her fast shorthand and accurate typing. As far as he was concerned, that was the end of it. But that was only his opinion.

Friday afternoon, as he was packing the last of the studio's typing paper, carbons, pencils, pads and paper clips into his brief case, Dixie came in. Not with a final, "So long and good luck," but with the news that she was pregnant and required an immediate abortion.

The writer was a happily married man, with two kids and another on the way. A veteran screenwriter with an established salary of $750 a week, he had been around long enough to know blackmail when he saw it.

"How much?"

She mentioned a nice round figure. Five grand. It was $4000 more than he had in the bank, and though he knew she was prepared to negotiate, the cold meanness of her demand infuriated him. He shook his head.

"Sorry, kid. No dice. You were well paid for your overtime. Now get outta here before I forget we used to be good friends."

She shrugged. "If that's the way you want it, OK by me. I just thought I'd give you the chance to pay off instead of getting in touch with your wife."

He eyed her in silence. She stared back defiantly. Picking up the phone, he dialed the three digits of a studio extension.

"Security?" he said, mentioning his name. "I want to talk to Chief Matthews. It's important."

For the moment he waited, he detected a touch of uneasiness in Dixie's eyes.

"Chief Matthews? I think this is a matter that might concern you. The girl who used to be my secretary is here in my office.

She's trying to blackmail me. I'm willing to file a complaint against her if you want to send for the vice squad."

He listened for a few seconds, nodding. "Yeah, I know how the studio feels about this kind of publicity, but I don't care what happens to me. I want this bitch arrested! Yeah, I'll be waiting."

Hanging up, he looked at Dixie grimly. His expression was unnecessary; the phone conversation had already altered her plan.

"Wait a minute," she said. "I don't want any trouble—let's just forget the whole thing, huh?"

He glanced at his watch. "You've got maybe five minutes before the cops get here." Adding, "You know what'll happen if you ever try to get in touch with my wife."

Her running footsteps were echoing down the hallway before he finished speaking.

At the desk in the front office of our department, Ed Haldeman shook his head wonderingly as he spoke to Bates Bowers, who was feeding the outgoing mail into the mailing machine.

"I think these writers are all nuts," he said. "This guy calls me, asks for Security, and when I tell him he's got the wrong extension, keeps on talking—some gibberish about his secretary blackmailing him and he wants her arrested."

"Maybe it was a scene he was writing," Bates suggested, "and he was trying it out on you."

"If so," said Haldeman, "it stank."

Ed was wrong. It might have been the best scene he ever dreamed up. Dixie quit her job that night. The writer got an assignment at MGM, then later came back to us at double his former salary.

Perhaps best of all, Sadie Fryer was spared the anguish of finding out that one of her girls was a hooker.

12

The Unmaking of One Star & the Non-Making of Another

Some of the funniest lines we ever read were not in scripts, or even the fan mail, but rather in the memos which we constantly distributed.

One, from head of Publicity's Bob Taplinger, addressed "To All Departments," observed disapprovingly, "In recent weeks a number of important visitors have been subjected to overhearing employees using coarse and sometimes even obscene lanaguage. Moreover, they were witness to the gross spectacle of adult set personnel. goosing each other. Such displays reflect badly on our studio as well as ourselves.

173

"Next Thursday we are going to host the Prince and Princess of Denmark. As they tour the lot, please be sure to be on your very best behavior, so that we can make certain this will be an occasion they will never forget, in a happy sense."

It would be nice to report that Taplinger's plea was heeded by all. Unfortunately, there is no historical record of whether there was less goosing than usual that day.

A number of memos were concerned with the problem of malingering. "To All Assistant Directors," from Tenny Wright's Production Department, noted: "It has been brought to my attention that a lot of valuable time is being wasted in the afternoons by people leaving their sets to use the rest rooms. It is important that you try to get them to watch their food and drink intake at lunch so that this practice will cease."

We could visualize a certain tough assistant director named Jack Sullivan, who had been a Marine Drill Instructor in his youth, addressing his people before the noon dismissal:

"Now hear this, you crumb-bums! There will be no time off this afternoon for anybody to dally in the can, so when you go to the commissary, you damn well better not drink a lot of coffee, or eat their goddam chili and beans!"

Occasionally, there would be memos of cryptic or mysterious nature and of course these warranted our further investigation. Such as one from Legal, copies of which we distributed only to Security, the Auto Gate and our two reception rooms. It merely stated that an actor whom I will call Jimmy Burns was barred from the studio.

It was far from being the first of its kind that we delivered during our time. Such injunctions, usually temporary, had concerned a drunken director, a few rebellious writers and a number of agents. Even our local trade paper, *The Hollywood Reporter*, was once barred from sale in the commissary because of what the Front Office considered to be an overly adverse criticism of one of our more important pictures.

This was far different. Jimmy Burns was by way of being one of our up-and-coming stars. A few years previously, starring in a

Broadway comedy, he had been put under contract when we acquired his play and turned it into a hit movie. From then on, equally versatile at comedy or drama, his rise was fairly spectacular and it was known that the Front Office had big plans for his future. Burns was well liked by the rank-and-file people, and as we disseminated the stunning news, we were implored, as always, to find out the real lowdown.

There were an ample supply of rumors to draw on, such as:

—that he had gotten into a fist fight with Hal Wallis . . .

—that because of his German ancestry, he was secretly the head of the California Nazi bund . . .

—that he had been caught in the schoolhouse smoking opium with a certain child actress . . .

In our continuing role of Cassandras, any of these would have been believed had we chosen to use them, but to our credit we always tried to dig up the actual facts first. (If we failed, as will be noted in one or two isolated cases, then we would be forced to resort to whatever made-up story sounded best.)

With the Burns story, however, we got all the dirt, and when we finally put it all together, it turned out to be far more sensational than even the wildest rumors.

It seems that a top executive, pining for his lovely new bride, who was vacationing in Mexico City, early one morning put in a surprise long-distance phone call to tell her how much he loved and missed her. Apparently having been up—or down—all night, she was now in deep, sweet slumber. Her phone was answered by a sleepyvoiced Jimmy Burns. Freeze-frame!

There might have been some harsh words delivered later by husband to wife, but eventually the bride was forgiven her transgression. Not so with Burns. His injunction was permanent. After his layoff time was used up, a weekly salary check was mailed to his agent until, at option time, he was dropped.

Even if there wasn't an acknowledged blacklist in those days, there certainly was at least a tacit one among our moguls. Burns soon found himself *persona non grata* at the other major studios. Eventually, with the success of a TV series, he made a comeback as a character actor, but never again did he ever set foot in our studio.

Then there was the equally mysterious memo sent out by Brynie Foy, addressed to "All Directors and Script Clerks" in his B unit.

"I realize you normally have enough to do without having to concern yourself with this," he wrote, "but since we can't depend on the actors to always do it, you're going to have to be responsible for each and every actor having his fly fully zipped up before shooting a scene. Remember, this is *your* responsibility."

Who, we wondered, was the exhibitionist who had incurred Foy's displeasure by acting with an unzipped zipper? Since it sounded interesting, again we pursued the answer.

It turned out that the directive was the result of a scene in a recently completed melodrama, *Broadway Musketeers*, featuring Margaret Lindsay, Ann Sheridan and Marie Wilson. Taken out for its first preview, it was well received by the audience until, during one tense scene toward the end between Wilson, John Litel and character heavy Dewey Robinson, there were some scattered titters and laughter. It probably didn't involve more than half a dozen people, but that was enough to cause Foy and director John Farrow to wonder what those few found to be so incongrously laughable?

Previewed the second time, the same thing happened. Again the laughter was widely scattered, as though only a tiny fraction of the audience had noticed any inadvertent humor in the scene. Nor did the reaction cards, which were filled out by members of the audience, provide any clue.

Holding the usual sidewalk conference afterwards, the executives admitted to being completely baffled. Up until that point, the picture had been received even better than at its first preview. Although a typical B in terms of budget, Farrow had kept it fast-moving and suspenseful and had hoped that its success would serve as a stepping-stone to more prestigious assignments. Now, in its most dramatic moment, it seemed he had somehow slipped up. They decided against taking it out a third time.

"Whatever the hell is wrong with that scene," Foy declared, "it's obviously such a little thing that most of the audience doesn't spot it. Well, we're gonna have to run it for ourselves until we find out what it is."

The following morning, Foy, Farrow and film editor Frank Magee, met in Projection Room 3. Since they had all seen the film many times from the first rushes on without noticing anything wrong, Foy included one outsider, producer Bill Jacobs, in hopes that his fresh viewpoint might spot the cause of the laughter.

Reel 6 flashed on the screen and a moment later the scene in question began. Their eyes glued to the action, the original trio saw nothing they hadn't seen before. Then Jacobs chuckled. Instantly, Foy ordered the projectionist to stop the film.

"OK," he demanded. "What is it?"

"Do you really mean," said Jacobs, "that none of you saw it?"

"Please, Bill," Farrow said wearily. "Saw *what?*"

Jacobs was genuinely surprised. "The guy with Wilson and Litel, what's his name—Dewey Robinson? Run it again, but be sure and keep your eyes on him."

The scene started over again. Now, suddenly, it seemed so glaringly obvious.

"Oh, my God!" Foy whispered, sinking down in his seat.

Incredibly, it had gone unnoticed in all their previous viewings. At the climax of the scene, after a few lines from Litel, Dewey Robinson lashed out at Wilson, slapping her hard across the face. In his sudden lunge, there was a flash of him with his fly fully open, gaping like an entrance to a cave. It was only visible for a second, but they all wondered how they could have missed seeing it before.

Jacobs said the explanation was simple. "It's a helluva scene for Marie. It comes as a shock when he suddenly hits her and your audience blinks in reaction—which is exactly what you guys must've done every time you ran it. All you need is that blink and you miss it."

Jacobs was right. It was only those few insensitive people not caught up in the intensity of Wilson's reaction who had noticed the gaffe. But now, of course, there was a new problem. Since they couldn't release the film in its present censorable state, they had no alternative but to reshoot the scene. The picture had been completed two months previously, the sets struck and the actors now on new assignments. The set had to be re-built, Wilson and Litel borrowed from their present pictures and free-lancer Dewey Robinson rehired at one day's pay.

Foy came down to Stage 2 the morning Farrow set up for the retake. Gloweringly, he personally checked Robinson's zipper. But being a busy executive, with two or three pictures always in production, post-production, or preparation, zipper-checking was not the sort of continuing chore that he could be expected to handle himself. Thus the mysterious memo.

The one envelope that could strike fear into the hearts of any contract employee bore the notation, "Legal Department." Over the signature of attorney Roy Obringer, a tall, saturnine man known as "The Executioner," were the memos that announced in cold legalese the lay-offs, suspensions and—most dreaded of all—terminations of employment.

Within my first month, I was sent to Legal on a rush at five one afternoon and loaded down with a batch of envelopes, among them one each for songwriters Scholl and Jerome. Naturally giving them priority, I tracked them down to Stage 9, where they were in a recording session with Ann Sheridan. The memo notified them that as of six p.m. that date, they were being put on six weeks' lay-off.

"I had to go and get you a job here for *this?*" Dad said. "Thanks a lot." He laughed, but somehow I had the feeling he didn't really find it humorous.

Then there was the Legal memo addressed to a writer who had arrived the year before from a playwriting career in New York, and who had subsquently, almost every day without fail, complained bitterly about his stupid assignments, the lousy climate, his moronic producers and the confining atmosphere of the stu-

Adorable Jane Bryan might have been confiding to director Edmund Goulding the reason why she suddenly abandoned a most promising career shortly after she co-starred in *We Are Not Alone*.

dio. We thought he would surely be happy returning to the more literate world of the legitimate theater. But when he was presented with the envelope he turned pale.

"Listen, kid," he said, looking at the messenger pleadingly, "what's it worth for a little favor? I mean, like telling them you couldn't find me?"

He started to reach for his wallet, but the boy regretfully shook his head. In any case, it wouldn't have mattered. If the writer counted on the fact that, as with a summons, he would be safe if he could evade being served, it wasn't so. Agents were notified at the same time, and if the recipient had no agent, a registered copy of the memo was mailed to his home address.

One happy remembrance of a delivery from Legal: the addressee was a lovely young stock actress named Jane Bryan. It was delivered to her on the set of *The Old Maid* and after reading it she started yelling with joy. Her option had been renewed for a year with a substantial raise in salary.

"I'm gonna be a star!" she whooped. "Hey, everybody, look at me—I'm gonna be a big star!"

A few more pictures and she was well on her way. The fact that it never happened was her own doing. She fell in love with a young business executive named Justin Dart and got married. When she told J.L. of her decision to give up her career, he said she was crazy. Fully expecting her to return to the studio after her fill of the dull routine of married life, he ordered her put on suspension. It turned out that she wasn't crazy after all. A happy family home life, it seemed, was more to her liking than the ephemeral pleasures of stardom. As the wife of the head of Dart Industries, and a grandmother, a recent newspaper photo showed our little Janie Bryan to be still a beautiful lady.

Knowing the machinations of the studio as we did, it's entirely possible that even today, more than 40 years after the fact, some long-forgotten dusty file still holds her contract, with the attached dated notation, "On Suspension."

In a long series of memos, there was one humorous example of The Boss's efforts to transform a talentless parasite into a box-office commodity. Or at the very least, to get her off his back. Her name was Elsa Maxwell. A fat, middle-aged professional partygiver and hanger-on, with the mien of a doberman and features of a bulldog, for some reason she had acquired a reputation as one of the pets of Café Society. A dear friend of Ann (Mrs. Jack) Warner's, her chronic financial problems had apparently caused her to put the bite on him for substantial sums. Hoping to get off the hook, J.L. instructed Legal to draw up a contract for her starting at $600 a week. At the same time he told Gordon Hollingshead of our Shorts Department to develop a series of two-reelers in which she would star. Taking note of her appearance, his memo ended:

"Obviously, Maxwell can only play comedy. I don't know if she can act, although she's put on a helluva good act with her friends for years. But give it a try."

"Holly's" efforts resulted in a series co-starring her with a former prize fighter named Slapsie Maxie Rosenbloom. If the shorts had been only half as hilarious as the conditions under which they were made, she might have ended up as another Marie Dressler.

With delusions of already being a star, Maxwell decided that the dialogue written for her was not to her liking and would have to be rewritten. By herself. Her *bon mots* were laughable all right, but not in the context for which they were intended.

Then in keeping with her reputation as a hostess, her socialite and titled friends were invited to visit the set every afternoon. Between three and four p.m. production would often come to a standstill as tea and watercress sandwiches were served. It was a memorable sight to see her flouncing around the stage, welcoming her guests and exchanging all the latest gossip, meanwhile driving veteran director Bill McGann half out of his mind with her endless delays. Ordinarily, as would all of our directors, he would have given short shrift to any actor who held up shooting, but with her mentor being The Boss himself, McGann could do little more than grit his teeth and bear it.

It was noted, however, that on more than one occasion, by late afternoon, with half a dozen unshot scenes still remaining

The pickle-puss in the middle belongs to Elsa Maxwell. The studio set out to make her a comedy star. The results were laughable.

on his schedule, his normally florid Irish complexion would turn dangerously purple. Like most of our boozers, he tried to resist temptation until the end of his working day, but after a period of putting up with Lords, Ladies, Counts and No-Accounts, McGann gave up and joined in the festivities. Seated far away from the Maxwell group, he kept his dainty tea cup filled to the rim with straight gin.

Rosenbloom who didn't exactly have to *act* the part of a punch-drunk fighter, could never quite understand why his co-star was accorded so many special privileges. Having tried, without success, to explain many times previously, McGann decided that a brand-new explanation might be in order.

"Didn't you know, Maxie?" he confided. "She's J.L.'s secret love. He claims she's the best lay in town."

This was something, finally, that Rosenbloom could understand. "Oh, now I get it," he said. "I was wonderin' how she got dis. Listen, just between you and I, I t'ink Mr. Warner's got lousy taste."

Whatever talents Maxwell did possess—if any—were not evident on the silver screen. The series was short-lived, but by then, with whatever money she had saved, plus eight weeks' salary still due before her contract expired, she was content to return to Europe. Just before she left, she dropped by J.L.'s office one noontime. A relief messenger explained that Mr. Warner was at lunch.

"Well, tell the dear boy goodbye," she said. "And say that I'll be looking forward to seeing him in Cannes."

Upon his return, a mystified Bill Schaefer read this message: "12:50: Miss Elsa Maxwell came by to say goodbye to Mr. Warner and that she was looking forward to seeing him in the can."

13

How to Steal Almost Anything

THE MOST MISERABLE of all our chores, although occurring only once a year, was once too often for me. It was the delivery of the Pacific Telephone Company's new directories. Their crew only lugged the bundled books into our department; the inter-studio distribution to each of our 350 offices was up to us. The job was always given to someone at the top of Pappmeier's goof-off list. It was a distinction that I achieved three years in a row.

The first time was only six weeks after I started and was, I felt, undeserved. True, I had displayed a proclivity for taking 25 minutes to cover the west route, a trip which normally was done in ten. But since it included my favorite haunt, the Writers Building, I didn't see how any aspiring screenwriter could pass up the chance to chat with the likes of Norman Reilly Raine,

Ring Lardner, Jr., or my special idol, John Huston. It was an argument that went down in defeat under Fred's cold reminder that I had been hired as a messenger, not a writer.

His smile was ear-to-ear as he informed me of the directory distribution. However, I would have a partner, a newcomer named Dick Selzer. A one-time kid actor, whose previous claim to fame had been as a second-string Dead End Kid in a road company of the play *Dead End,* Dick wasn't a goof-off as yet; this was to serve as part of his indoctrination.

With the aid of a small cart into which we crammed our first 100 directories, we set off to the accompaniment of Pappmeier's warning that we were expected to complete the job in the allotted three and a half days or else!

It was backbreaking labor, and in order to maintain our schedule, we barely had time for two hideout smokes an hour. But at the end of our first day, we returned with an empty cart, causing our boss to faintly compliment us. No matter how faint, it was the first praise I received, and I basked in it overnight with not a twinge of conscience that, in our exhausted state, we had dumped the last 15 books in the incinerator.

The second day we ran into bad luck when it started to rain. We protected the books with a tarpaulin, but by noon, despite the slickers and rainhats provided by Wardrobe, we were soaked to the skin. By then we had reached Stage 5, a huge building which housed the Research and Art Departments on the second and third floors. Here, I pointed out to my partner, we would have at least an hour's sanctuary and that he'd better enjoy it. Beyond, on the front lot, with its dozen technical departments, we would encounter the lowland into which the run-off rainfall treacherously accumulated, in many sections becoming knee deep.

For some reason, Selzer was becoming increasingly unhappy. "Screw that!" he snarled. "I'm getting outta this chicken-shit deal!"

I momentarily envisioned him returning to the department and telling Fred what he could do with his phone books. It turned out that he had a better idea.

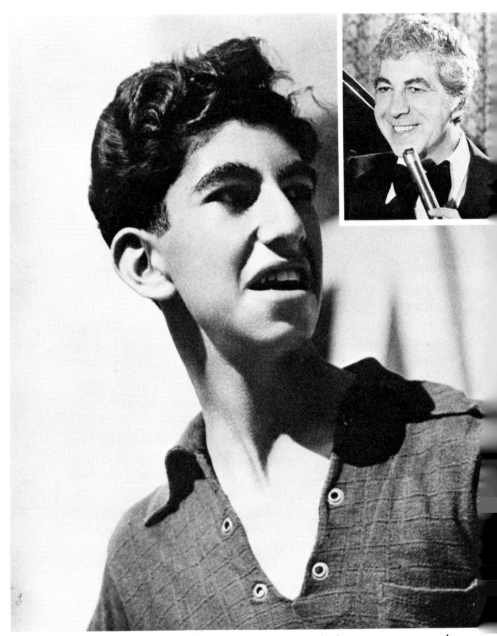

Who would have ever thought that a scrawny little messenger named Dickie Selzer would one day become the world-famed Mr. Blackwell?

Laden down with a bundle of five directories—by now each individual book felt as if it weighed ten pounds—we started up the narrow wooden staircase, continuing until we reached the third floor landing. There Dick paused, seemingly out of breath and staring down the steep staircase thoughtfully. As I passed him and headed down the hallway, I heard a hair-raising scream, accompanied by a series of bone-crunching crashes. Rushing back to the balustrade, I saw Selzer somersaulting backwards down the stairs, his agonized shrieks echoing within the stillness of the stairwell.

By the time his body came to rest on the second-floor landing, the hallway was filling with unnerved art directors, assistants and secretaries. I was the first to reach Dick's side. Miraculously, he wasn't dead. Not even unconscious. Though he appeared to be relatively uninjured, between moans he whispered he was certain he had broken his neck and was dying.

Whisked to a hospital, it turned out that nothing had been broken. He was kept on salary while he recuperated at home and when he finally returned to work, our sympathetic boss relieved him of having to undertake any of the more physically demanding errands.

I kept my suspicions of Dick's "accident" to myself, until one day, alone with him in the back room, I voiced the opinion that he was crazy to have risked his life merely to get out of completing the deliveries.

He laughed. "Don't be so stupid. That's an old acrobatic vaudeville routine. Looks great, but there's nothing to it."

That day in the rain might have been Selzer's best acting. He never made it as a movie actor, but many years later, under the new name of *Mr. Blackwell*, he became a prominent dress designer and TV personality. Annually, he now makes headlines with his acerbic list of the ten worst-dressed women.

On the few occasions when I've run into Dick since our messenger days, I've always developed a backache. I know it's psychosomatic, but I can't help remembering. We were short-handed that week; I had to finish delivering the phone books all by myself.

Every three months the phone company sent one of their men to collect the coins from the 22 booths scattered around the lot. Since many of the booths were in out-of-the-way locations, one of us would always escort the collector to make sure he didn't miss any of them.

Mostly in proximity to the sound stages, the booths were used by the extras and bit players who, every afternoon between set-ups, would line up to start calling Central Casting to find out whether there was any work for them the following day.

It really wasn't worth the phone company's time and trouble to collect the nickels. There rarely were any. The extras used slugs, which they bought 20 for a dime. After constant complaints to our business manager, the phone company finally threatened to remove their equipment unless the cheating was stopped. Security then placed notices in each booth, warning that anyone caught using slugs would be prosecuted to the fullest extent of the law.

The next time a collector came on the lot, instead of the usual 60-70 percent slugs, he found the ratio was now closer to 90 percent. The notices had, of course, alerted regular employees to the practice and they, too, became customers of an entrepreneur in our machine shop who stamped them out by the thousands. With no practical way to stop the cheating, the studio finally had to guarantee a monthly minimum payment for each of the booths.

An actor then earning $1,000 a week bought a paper from the newsboy who toured the lot every afternoon, absentmindedly handing him a coin.

"Hey, mister," the kid complained, "this ain't no nickel, it's a slug."

Embarrassed, the actor hunted through a pocketful of change without being able to come up with one legitimate coin, finally handing him a dollar bill.

"I don't know where that slug came from," he said to some of the crew who were standing around. He was lying. They knew that he knew. He bought them from the same source they did.

A good part of the pleasure of working in a huge studio involved, at least for some, the purloining of anything of personal interest—or sometimes resale value—that one could manage to remove from the lot without being caught in the act.

One of our male stars had a habit of borrowing expensive bric-a-brac from Property, explaining that it gave his dressing room a "homey" touch. What he should have said was that it gave his *home* a "homey" touch, since that is where it ended up. Permanently.

An assistant in a minor department, by reason of being able to drive his station wagon inside, was able to add a whole new room to his house by way of slow but steady theft. Lumber, concrete, paint, nails, plaster, wallpaper, etc., were all freely taken from our various craft departments.

Some contract players, perhaps out of a haunting memory of past poverty, took the towels, rolls of toilet paper and bars of soap from their bathrooms. Others kept various items from Wardrobe which they took a liking to. One elderly wardrobe man, who was responsible for returning them to his department, once heatedly accused John Garfield of stealing six expensive silk shirts that he had been wearing for a movie.

"OK, so I swiped them," Garfield admitted. "But I'll swear up and down that I gave them back to you. Now whose word do you think they're gonna take?"

When the wardrobe man took his complaint to his department head, *he* was blamed for the loss.

"You know these goddam actors," he was told. "They'll steal anything. It's your fault for leaving all six in his dressing room. You should've given him no more than one at a time."

One expensive piece of studio property turned up in a flea market iin Glendale. It was an antique desk lamp which had graced the office of one of our executives. By coincidence, a secretary browsing in the store happened to pick up the lamp and noticed our inventory Department's number on the base. Whitey Wilson, head of Property, was told about it and we had to buy it back.

When the executive was politely asked how come his lamp had ended up in an antique store, he became irate. Damn it, were they accusing him of being a crook? All he knew was that it had disappeared from his office some time ago and he assumed it had been returned to Property. The matter was dropped, though the store owner remembered the man who had brought it in one Saturday afternoon. His description bore a close resemblance to our executive.

In our department—naturally one of the leaders in the finer points of pilferage—an aspiring artist spent his spare time prowling around the Art Department, eventually accumulating a complete assortment of the materials necessary to pursue his career professionally.

Another swiped copies of discarded scripts en route to the incinerator, selling them to second-hand bookstores for a dime each. On a good week, he would make only about $4, but as he pointed out, that was one-fourth of his pay check.

Possibly the one who possessed the most *chutzpah* was the colleague who took stacks of glossy fan mail photos from the Still Department. Placing inexpensive classified ads in various movie magazines, he advertised: "Personally autographed photos of the stars, $1 each. Write out whatever *personal* inscription you want and the star of your choice will copy it. Do you want him/her to say they love you? That you are their best friend? That you gave them their start? Whatever you want them to say will be handwritten on a beautiful 8 × 10 glossy photo! Impress your friends, your family, your boss! Mail in $1 for each photo today!"

As the writer of the copy, for which I received ten cents royalty on each $1 order, I was proud of the fact that it proved amazingly effective. Within two months, my friend's post office box was overflowing, with fresh orders arriving daily from all over the world. I put in long stretches with him on many nights helping pen the special inscriptions. Strangely, as if they were unable to release their inhibitions, most of the requests were as innocuous and unimaginative as the "Sincerely yours," and "Best Wishes," that were printed on the free fan photos.

One order I vividly remember, from a man in Cleveland, *was* different. Following his instructions, I wrote: "For Lester, in memory of the love we shared together that beautiful night. Forever, Basil."

It was penned on the bottom of a picture of . . . *Basil Rathbone.* (Lester might have been a pervert, but he did have imagination.)

Although my friend kept no business records, we estimated that in less than nine months he took in over $3,000. All of which, outside of the negligable expense of the ads, was clear profit. Even mailing the photos was free, courtesy of our mailing machine when Pappmeier wasn't around.

It came to an end only because he was drafted. I could have continued the business, but somehow my heart wasn't in it. I still wanted to be a writer, and toward that end, I stole only the things that I needed. Stationery supplies. I didn't intend to be greedy, but it did reach the point where a large closet in my bedroom was crammed with enough reams of typing paper, boxes of carbon paper, manila envelopes, typewriter ribbons, pads, pencils and paper clips to have stocked a small stationery supplies store.

For a whole decade afterwards, whenever I sat down at my typewriter, I was reminded of the studio's largess and was properly grateful. Like everybody else, I rationalized my thievery: it would never be missed, and in any case wasn't I trying to come up with Academy Award-caliber scripts, which I would offer them for first acceptance?

Not all stealing was for personal gain. In one particular case it seemed to be the result of a personal idiosyncracy. Or, perhaps, kleptomania.

Checking through his files one day in search of a number of borrowed portables, Frank Martin of our Typewriter Department made an interesting discovery. Typing out a note, he called upon us to deliver it on a rush to Errol Flynn on the *Santa Fe Trail* set.

"Dear Mr. Flynn," it said. "According to our records, you checked out two Royal portable typewriters on the following dates. Since we are in urgent need of these machines for script clerks who are working on location, we would be most appreciative of your returning them to us at your earliest convenience. Sincerely yours."

Flynn glanced at the note, crumpled it into a ball and dropped it on the floor. The machines were not returned.

More reminders were sent; all were ignored. A week went by in this manner, and with the Production Department pressuring him, Martin decided he would have to see Flynn personally. His timing was bad, the *Santa Fe Trail* company having departed that morning for three weeks of location shooting. With no further alternative, Martin went to our business manager and explained his predicament.

The latter, after years of being an officious assistant director and having recently been promoted, was determined to prove his worth.

"Whaddaya mean, if we don't get these back we'll have to buy new ones," he stormed. Picking up his phone, he added, "I know exactly how to handle this."

Glen Roswell, the third of my Valentine's Day cohorts, was next up when the buzzer sounded. Handing him the master key to the dressing rooms, Haldeman told him to go to Flynn's suite and see if he could find the missing portables. It was after four. Glen had put in a rough day since eight and the mercury and humidity were stuck in the torrid zone. Understandably, he was somewhat less than thrilled at the prospect of having to bike two heavy machines halfaway across the burning Sahara of the lot.

Cleverly resorting to a legal argument, he pointed out that even if he found them, their removal without Flynn's permission could constitute a burglary. Somehow, Haldeman was not impressed with his faultless logic.

"What the hell do you mean, 'burglary'?" he demanded. "How can we burglarize our own property? Get outta here!"

Entering the coolness of Flynn's living room, Glen sank into the comfort of a leather lounging chair while he tried to think where, if he were Flynn, he would stash two typewriters? Drawing a blank, he decided that perhaps refreshment was needed to stimulate the thinking process.

The fridge yielded nothing more interesting than a wedge of cheese, half a tin of caviar and a bottle of Chablis. With more of a desire for tuna-fish sandwiches and cold milk, he ate and drank without much enthusiasm.

With the repast out of the way, Glen decided it was time to play detective, reasoning that if the machines were here at all, obviously Flynn would have hidden them cleverly. He gazed around for a tell-tale sign of a secret partition, or at least a locked cabinet. There was neither.

Well then, he grimly decided, if that's the way it's gonna be, I'll just have to check every nook and cranny, even if it takes the rest of my shift.

Directly in front of him was closet, much too obvious a hiding place. But it was close and at least demanded a quick look. Yawning, he opened the door. And froze.

The closet was empty . . . except for typewriters. He had uncovered a treasure trove! Two portables. *Plus three standard-size Royals.*

Glen was a hero in Martin's eyes when he delivered the portables. As he turned to leave, he idly asked if any other machines were missing?

"Damn right there are," Martin said. "Three big ones. Some of those thieving writers must've swiped 'em right outta the Writers Building. Why?"

"Oh, no reason," Glen quickly answered. "No reason at all. Just wondering."

As honorable a young man as Roswell was, he saw no reason to blow the whistle on Flynn. He had accomplished his mission. If the guy was queer for typewriters, it wasn't any of his business.

Besides, he still had half an hour to go before his shift ended, and if more typewriters were to be transported, he had a pretty good idea who would have to schlepp them.

Despite a well-deserved reputation for keeping the studio crime free, Security couldn't be expected to stop the continuing problem of petty theft; there was nothing else to do but add the cost of this thievery to our regular overhead.

There was, however, one strange, isolated caper that was different. In that case, the value of the stolen material was so great that Chief Matthews himself was called upon to play Sherlock Holmes.

It involved Research, one of our more fascinating departments. A warren of small, cluttered rooms on the second floor of Stage 5, its untidy profusion of books, magazines and newspapers, fragranced by the musty aroma of old paper, gave it the ambiance of an old English book store.

Staffed by Dr. Herman Lissauer, Ph.D., and six assistants, all of whom peered with owlish myopia through thick glasses, and who customarily spoke in whispers, it was indispensible to production.

No question but that Lissauer and his experts were exceptional, each hired for his or her specialized knowledge in one or more fields. It was proudly claimed that collectively they probably came as close to knowing, or at least having access to, the sum total of mankind's knowledge as was humanly possible. And if there was a need for something they didn't already have in their files, they quickly acquired it.

Since on every project the script was where it all began, their special favorites were, of course, the writers. Assigned to, say, a western of the 1870's, or a gangster story of the twenties, or a modern-day story in a foreign setting, a writer had only to dial 701-2-3 for information relating to his particular subject matter, and within minutes a mass of salient material would be gathered from Research's files and shelves, and if the request was urgent, delivered on a rush by one of us.

Well, one day a middle-aged, nattily dressed man entered the department, introducing himself as a newly hired writer. He was working, he said, on a gambling story and needed to know about various gambling systems. Since few writers ever bothered to make personal visits, the staff was flattered by his presence, inviting him to sit down and have a cup of coffee while they combed through their files. In a few minutes, they came up with half a dozen books and an assortment of articles. He signed a receipt, thanked them and departed.

Discovering some additional material the next day, they dispatched it to their new friend. We were unable to locate him; his name was not included among the writers on payroll, nor did the Story Department have any knowledge of him. Finally, an embarrassed Dr. Lissauer was forced to contact Security with the bad news that an apparent impostor had made off with books which we valued at over $5000.

Chief Matthews personally took over the investigation, but it led nowhere. Not even turning up the answer to how an outsider could gain access to the studio itself, let alone the out-of-the-way Research Department. With our insurance only providing payment in case of fire, we were finally reconciled to taking our loss. But as Lissauer pointed out, it wasn't the money that was important, the books themselves were virtually irreplaceable.

Who, we wondered, was the crook, and what did he want with such arcane subject matter?

The answer came out of the blue some months later, in the form of two packages addressed to Research. Postmarked Reno, Nevada, one of them contained the books and articles that had been checked out; the other was a five pound box of stuffed fruit. Accompanying the latter was a note from the "writer" thanking the staff for the loan of their material.

He explained that he had been on the lot that day as an extra. After many years of being an unsuccessful actor, and unhappy with his dull existence, he decided to fulfill a life-long ambition as a professional gambler. Thanks to the knowledge he had acquired through their information, he was now several thousand dollars ahead of the casinos and intended to remain in Reno permanently.

Grateful that it had received its property back, the studio was happy to forget the whole matter. Lissauer and his people were appreciative of the stuffed fruit and that seemed to be the end of it.

Not quite.

About a year later, one of the Research staff happened to encounter the very same extra-cum-gambler in the commissary. The systems had finally turned against him and eventually he lost everything. Now he was back as a $12.50 a day extra. But his face lit up as he said he had realized his dream.

Not everyone could say that.

14

George Raft-Peter Lorre & Other Aberrations

THE PROMISE that each new day held was always the most pleasant time at our studio. Later, inevitably, there would be the usual crises, displays of temperament and internecine warfare. But in those early hours after dawn, with the sun glinting off the arched silvered roofs of the towering sound stages, there was an atmosphere of gentle tranquillity that belied the true-life dramas yet to come.

By seven a.m. with the night construction crews checking off the lot, day crews and actors checking in, the mingled "so longs" and "good mornings" were friendly and subdued.

At that hour, there was only one department fully manned and wide awake. Makeup. With the aroma of coffee and donuts permeating the building, a dozen or more makeup and hairdressing experts would be busily engaged in trying to get their charges ready for the usual nine a.m. shooting call.

The rows of little private cubicles gave it the outward appearance of a large, luxurious beauty salon, but there the resemblance ended. On one side, tilted back in a barber's chair, Bette Davis might be found while the boss, Perc Westmore, created the delicate and time-consuming magic that would turn her into an aging Queen Elizabeth. Across the aisle, Clay Campbell would be fitting Bogart with one of the hairpieces he so devoutly hated. Down the hall, Maggie Donovan might be working over a fat and jowly Eddie Robinson, tightening his chin line with an ingenious web of invisible rubber bands. Hair stylists would be fussing over James Cagney, engrossed in *The Law Review* while receiving his usual soft permanent. Nearby, George Brent would impatiently be submitting to the dyeing process that concealed his prematurely white hair. Incongruously, our male stars sometimes ended up looking prettier than the females.

Gradually, as the hands of the big clock in the entrance hall moved on, the actors' cross-conversations—sleepily monosyllabic at first—became more animated and louder as cup after cup of black coffee was consumed. By 8:30, the voices reached a cacophonic din as last night's gossip was eagerly exchanged.

It was business as usual one Monday morning when Kenny Shuttleworth entered with script changes for Sylvia Sidney. Except that this time Kenny noted an important difference: *All* the gossip was concerned with one particular happening, a delightfully juicy sex scandal! With the typical awareness that made us so efficient in these matters, he lingered long enough to pick up the salient particulars.

It concerned two of Hollywood's most prestigious celebrities, our own director Anatole Litvak and a certain reigning Queen at Paramount. It had happened Sunday night at Ciro's, which by way of then being the town's most popular night club, made it an All Star Scandal. (A few days later, everybody seemed to have their own version of *exactly* what had transpired, which, if all were to be believed as eyewitnesses, would have necessitated the seating capacity of the Rose Bowl.) Nonetheless, at our studio there were those who had actually been present, and though accounts varied in some particularly intimate details, in essence it boiled down to this:

Seated with different groups, sometime late in the evening Litvak and the Lady Star joined company and became increasingly friendly. To the point, ultimately, where they ended up underneath a table. Which is where the versions differed. According to Version A, Litvak performed a certain unlawful sex act called cunnilingus on the Lady; Version B had it that she performed a certain unlawful sex act called fellatio on him; then there was still Version C, which claimed that the pair merely engaged in an old-fashioned act of sexual intercourse. Being the least intriguing of the three, this last was of course generally ignored.

There was one trouble with Kenny's story when he breathlessly returned to our back room. Most of us were not quite certain of the *exact* meanings of cunnilingus and fellatio, and although explained in conflicting ways by a few of our better-educated colleagues, it became essential for us to know the true definitions. In our sudden quest for knowledge, probably never before did so many of us journey all the way to Research as we did that morning. After the fifth or sixth request for a certain legal-sex dictionary, a member of the staff typed up simplified but satisfying definitions and tacked them to the bulletin board, where our later arrivals—even before stating their business—were directed.

By early afternoon, at least partially thanks to us, the story had spread like wildfire throughout the studio. By nightfall it became the prime topic of conversation within the entire industry. More than merely being titillating, it was the first genuine sex gossip since Thelma Todd's mysterious death a few years previously, and in her case most of the lurid details were only unproven rumors.

Within a few days both reigning movie columnists, Parsons and Hedda Hopper, alluded to it, but because celebrities' sex lives could only be hinted at, and barely so at that, it must have been frustrating for their readers to learn that the Lady and

Litvak were a shocking disgrace to the industry and not know what they had done to deserve such condemnation.

The incident reportedly reached the proportions of an inquiry by the Breen office. It was rumored that the morals clause in their contracts would have been invoked, ousting them from their respective studios, but for the intercession of Harry Warner, who recommended they be given the chance to atone.

It was great fun while it lasted. Especially during those first few days, when we gladly translated into street-jargon detail the meaning of those two strange words for secretaries, waitresses and others of their ilk who lacked our vast knowledge.

Then there was the shamelessly brazen display of homosexual love between two of our male stars. It wouldn't have been so bad if their affair had been conducted in private, but the disgusting fact is that one of them got his kicks out of doing it in public with as many spectators as possible. In this case, the spectators were a form of visitors.

Not all outsiders who entered our domain were privileged to see at least something of how a studio functioned. The very lowliest—we called them "peasants"—had to make do with a ten minute tour viewed through the window of a bus. We had a deal with the Tanner Bus Company whereby, at regularly scheduled intevals each day, busloads of tourists were slowly driven around the lot as part of an all-day sightseeing tour. Outside of viewing row upon row of sound stages and the permanent sets on the back lot, there was seldom anything else they could talk about when they returned home and were asked, Tell us all about what you saw.

Rarely did they even get to see a familiar face, and when a bus did happen to pass a costumed actor walking down the street, the excited pantomime inside clearly indicated they were asking each other, "Who's that? . . . Hey, I know, that's— uh—what's-his-name . . . Sure, I saw him in that movie— uh—whatayacall it. . ." Nine times out of ten, "What's-his-name" turned out to be an anonymous extra.

Irrepressible Peter Lorre loved to play practical jokes. Probably nothing ever topped the spontaneous act he put on for a busload of
gawking, shocked tourists.

We tried to give the "peasants" a thrill by waving and calling "No autographs please," but the only reaction we ever got was a few vague stares. We just weren't movie star types.

Though most of the busloads of gawkers went home disappointed, there was one group who experienced the vicarious thrill of seeing the Sodom and Gomorrha of "The Real Hollywood." It was something that must have remained a prime topic of conversation for the rest of their lives.

Peter Lorre and George Raft, working on adjoining sets, happened to be engaged in conversation outside of Stage 18 when a Tanner bus lumbered into view. On a sudden impulse, prankster Lorre took Raft into his arms in a tight embrace. As the bus slowly moved past, forty pairs of staring eyes, set in shocked, incredulous, middle-America faces, witnessed the two stars engaged in a passionate mouth-to-mouth kiss.

The bus turned the corner before Raft was able to extricate himself from Lorre's embrace.

"My God!" he cried, gagging. "What the hell was that for?"

Lorre shrugged sadly. "I just thought we should give those poor creeps a little fun."

So if you happen to know someone who visited Hollywood in 1940, and who claims to know that George Raft and Peter Lorre were lovers, don't laugh.

Across from our mail-sorting outer office and sharing the same hallway, was Blayney Matthews' office. Head of Security , he was a hulking, sharp-eyed man in his forties with an enormous belly and a deceptively mild manner. If he had been an actor, he would have been typecast as a detective, which is what he had been, establishing a reputation as the D.A.'s top investigator before we hired him away from downtown. An important part of his job was protecting the more important members of our studio family from exposure to unwanted publicity and/or confrontations with the law.

Both of these were under consideration when he summoned Ward Bond from the set of *Sergeant York* one Saturday afternoon. Matthews' door remained slightly ajar and those of us pretending to be busily engaged in sorting mail were treated to the following colloquy:

MATTHEWS: Ward, the reason I wanted to see you is because of a complaint made against you by a waitress at the Elite Café. She claims you were in there the other day and insulted her.

BOND: Aw, come on, Blayney, this is a gag, huh?

MATTHEWS: No, this is serious, Ward. The D.A.'s office says she's already gone to them and wants to press charges.

BOND: Charges? Christ, Blayney, I don't know what in hell you're talking about.

MATTHEWS: OK, lemme be specific. Last Wednesday. Blond girl named Ellie. Says you ordered four straight scotches and a hamburger steak. Remember any of that?

BOND: Yeah, I think so. Yeah, that's right. That's what I did. So how did I insult her?

MATTHEWS: Well, she ways you bit into the hamburger and then spat it out in her face, saying it was overcooked. Right?

BOND: Goddam right it was overcooked! Sure, I told her to take it back to the chef and have him cook me up a new one. Rare.

MATTHEWS: Yeah, go on. That what happened?

BOND: Christ, I dunno. (LONG PAUSE) That was three days ago.

MATTHEWS: Did she come back and tell you the chef said it *was* rare? That if it was any rarer, it'd be raw?

BOND: Yeah, that's right! And the lousy bitch said she agreed with him.

MATTHEWS: And then what'd you say?

BOND: I dunno. Nothing much, I guess.

MATTHEWS: She claims she's got a witness who heard you threaten her by saying something to the effect that you were gonna stick it up her ass. Is that true?

BOND: Sweet Christ no! She's a fucking goddam liar! A dirty, cocksucking piece of whoring shit liar! That's what she is! (CONTINUES INCOHERENTLY FOR A MOMENT; NOT UNDERSTANDABLE)

MATTHEWS: OK, take it easy, Ward, take it easy. Here. (SOUND OF LIQUID POURED INTO GLASS) Now relax and think hard. Did you say *anything at all* to her after she came back and told you it was rare?

BOND: Lemme think. (LONG PAUSE) Hey, wait a minute, I think I remember! Yeah! (LAUGHS) I told her if she thought it was a good piece of meat, why didn't she stick it up her fucking twat!

MATTHEWS: (GROANS) Oh, for crissake, Ward, you don't want her making that kind of complaint.

BOND: Huh? Whaddaya mean? You trying to tell me that little cunt could cause me trouble?

MATTHEWS: Goddam right she could. If she hauls you into court, you're liable to get some nasty publicity, not to mention what the judge might fine you. Take my word for it, there's only one thing to do.

BOND: Yeah? What's that?

MATTHEWS: First, here's a note that I had the boys in Publicity write, telling her how sorry you are about the way you acted. Rewrite it in your own handwriting.

BOND: Okay, I'll do that, I sure will.

MATTHEWS: Wait, that's not all. I want you to buy her a box of candy. A big one—two or three pounds. And slip a twenty inside the box.

BOND: Twenty? *Twenty bucks?*

MATTHEWS: That's getting off dirt cheap. I guarantee, you do that, she'll forget the whole goddam thing.

BOND: (LONG PAUSE) Well, OK, Blayney, sure, if you think so. OK. (LONG PAUSE) But shit, Blayney, tell me one thing, huh?

MATTHEWS: Yeah?

BOND: Well, how the fuck did I insult her?

Matthews was the silent custodian of more studio secrets than even The Brothers. He knew *everything* that went on in the private—and sometimes not-so-secret—lives of the more valuable of our human commodities. There was talk about certain

It all started with a few drinks, an inedible hamburger steak, and a snippy waitress. It ended up spelling trouble. No wonder Ward Bond has blood in his eyes.

things he was involved in: obtaining illegal drugs for an addicted star; putting an end to the blackmail of a homosexual director; saving the career of an up-and-coming young actor whose sadistic sex desires manifested themselves in beating and torturing young girls. But these were only rumors.

What was *known* was that he had important connections downtown, both with the press and the law. He was, we all agreed, a damn important guy to have on your side in any kind of trouble.

Some years later, after Matthews' retirement, I went to see him with the idea of doing a book based on his experiences at the studio.

Hoping to get off on a good footing, I told him—truthfully— that I had used him as a model for the lead in the pilot script of a new TV series called *Highway Patrol,* adding that I had even named the character Dan *Matthews.*

He seemed flattered, asking who was playing the role?

"Broderick Crawford," I said.

He winced. "I remember Brod when he was a kid . . . " His voice trailed off in some less-than-happy remembrance.

The book never happened. Matthews rejected the idea out of hand, saying that he had been well paid for his services and that he didn't want to capitalize on other people's miseries. He might well have been the most loyal employee we ever had.

Two years later, when he died, he took his secrets with him to the grave.

15

Seasons Greetings to Ida Lupino & John Garfield

Has there ever been a factual account of Hollywood that has failed to include *The Legendary Tale of Christmas Eve at the Studios?*

I doubt it.

As obligatory as the kinky sex in a Harold Robbins novel, as mandatory as the bloody violence in a Sam Peckinpah movie, it has always been depicted as a bacchanalian orgy—a combination of Mardis Gras, the first Armistice and Bastille Day.

According to such eyewitness authorities as F. Scott Fitzgerald, Budd Schulberg and Adela Rogers St. John, the day before Christmas was the once-a-year occasion when all the barriers were lowered. The caste system was laid aside, the mailroom crew could hoist a few with the top brass and—best of

all—sex abounded, free for the taking, with every female hedo-
nistically inclined.

Ah, what a day to remember!

Except that it never quite happened that way during our time.
Which is not to say that it was not a remarkable day; it's merely
that never once did any of us participate in, or even observe,
anything faintly resembling an orgy. But other than that one
great disappointment, it *was* an unforgettable time of celebration.

After the early mail deliveries, business gradually ground to a
halt, and by noon even Pappmeier would be in so benevolent a
mood that such normally reprehensible acts as drinking on the
job, becoming insulting and obstreperous, even passing out,
would be overlooked and afterwards there would be no recriminations. Incredibly, we could even hide out for an hour at a
time, touring the lot at will, without fear of being denounced as
goof-offs.

The pictures in production were always among our first stops.
They usually wrapped up early, and there would be set parties,
during which even the "fucking Hungarians" would become
halfway human. With the assist of a sprig of mistletoe, we were
often able to get bussed by some of our actresses. Nothing exciting enough to lead us to believe they were willing to go further,
but for once we were more than anonymous faces in green uniforms.

The Writers Building would be awash in liquor, but then every department was accorded that same one-day's privilege.
New, temporary liaisons were formed, and there was more forni-
cation than usual, but the secretaries we coveted were usually
paired off with their respective or prospective bosses, and we
were lucky if we ended up with waitresses from the commissary,
or some of the less attractive girls from the Steno pool.

But even without one measly little orgy to look forward to,
there were certain compensations to gladden our greedy little
hearts. The producers contributed cash to a pool which we
evenly divided, amounting to about $10 each. The writers did

the same, with their division coming to another $7-8, adding up t., a full week's pay. This, though, was only the beginning. The two top talent agencies, MCA and William Morris, sent booze and wine, and some of the smaller agents hand-delivered boxes of cigars and cartons of cigarettes. Then the actors, or their functionaries, started to arrive, and soon the large sorting table in our outer office would be stacked three feet high with boxes of candy, assortments of delicacies, and enough fruit cakes to stock a bakery, all addressed to "Our pals, the messengers."

Once, Pat O'Brien paid us a visit, handing out 24 gift-wrapped boxes containing cuff links. A little while later, a messenger from Bullock's Wilshire delivered an equal number of more boxes, individually addressed, each containing a tie, courtesy of Jimmy Cagney.

"Hey, this is great!" a newcomer exulted. "Now if somebody else'll only send us some underwear!"

That was the year Bette Davis came to call. Flanked by her chauffeur carrying it on a platter, she proudly presented us with a 20-pound roast turkey. We weren't quite certain how she expected us to divide it; perhaps, like the patroness of an orphanage, she wanted to make sure we all had a Christmas Eve dinner.

Those of us who were around the office fell silent and gaped when she swept in, and in her usual brittle manner called out, "Hello!" She looked around smilingly. "Well, so this is where my favorite guys hang out. Merry Christmas, boys!"

It was the first and perhaps the only time that our Queen paid us a personal visit and it took Pappmeier a long moment before he partially recovered sufficiently from his shock to return her greeting.

"Oh, thank you," he finally said. "Welcome and Merry Christmas to you, too, Miss—uh—uh—" in his shock, as he ruefully admitted later, he had momentarily forgotten her name.

Having done her good deed, she was about to leave when Eddie Hammond, having imbibed enough to overcome his natural shyness, pressed a glass of champagne into her hand.

"Here you are, *Bet*," he said, "have a drink with us."

It could have been embarrassing. First our boss couldn't remember who she was, then one of the messengers mispronounced her name. But to her credit, Davis didn't even flinch at the "Bet," a common error which she usually sharply corrected.

She took a sip of the bubbly, shook hands all around and made a quick exit. Eddie, who had long admitted a sexual interest in her—"If you think she's pop-eyed now, ain't nothin' to what she'll be once I get through ridin' her"—looked after her dazedly.

"Oh, wow," he whispered, almost to himself. "Wait'll I write my folks that Bet Davis and I had champagne together. . . ."

There were always a few awkward occurrences to liven the day, things that we would laugh about afterwards. Such as the time one of us, unaccustomed to mixing three straight scotches with rum cake for breakfast, staggered on a set and proceeded to throw up in front of the camera, not alone ruining what was supposed to have been the final shot of the day, but causing a 40-minutes delay while the crew cleaned up the mess.

Another drunken colleague, being led to an unused dressing room to sleep it off, happened to encounter Ida Lupino, prompting him to give voice to something that had apparently long been on his mind.

"Ida, jus' wanna tell you somethin', honey," he confided. "You got the' prettiest damn tits on the whole damn lot. An' tha's not all, I'll bet that your—"

Dave Beck, who was escorting him, said that Lupino reacted like a lady. Murmuring a quick "Thanks," she rushed away, unfortunately forestalling further compliments on her anatomy. Why'd she rush away, the kid later wondered? He thought actors always enjoyed getting compliments.

Not all of our mischief was committed out of drunkenness; sometimes it was soberly premeditated. One of us went so far as to journey all the way to our Western Street to collect a load of horse manure, which he then boxed, gift-wrapped and delivered to Miriam Hopkins' dressing room. Holding a grudge against

Anatole Litvak, who was then embroiled in a romance with Hopkins, he thought this would be a good way to get even.

The card, which he thoughtfully placed on top, read: "To my dearest, with love. Merry Xmas. Tola."

Unfortunately, Hopkins had already gone home, and the package—starting to exude a remarkable aroma—remained unopened until after the holiday. We never did find out whether she opened it. Chances are, her suite was so redolent by then that the contents of the prettily wrapped box was only too obvious.

If some of our behavior was sophomoric, the actions of older, wiser employees weren't any better. The cast party on *Flowing Gold* was just getting underway when one of us delivered a rush memo to John Garfield. He started to read it, then turned pale.

"Dear Julie," it said. "Have just seen your first week's rushes and never, in all the years I've been in this business, have I ever witnessed such incredibly hammy acting. Who do you think you are, another goddam Muni? I'm afraid you're going to have to be replaced. Maybe by a good actor like Ronnie Reagan. Season's greetings." It was signed, "J.L. Warner."

An intense, gifted actor, Garfield was an original "angry young man" decades before playwright John Osborne coined the phrase. Fast becoming one of our more popular stars, he was conceited, surly and humorless. Shaking, he handed the memo to director Alfred Green.

"My God, this is awful," Green said. "I'm the director—it puts me in a very bad light."

Garfield pulled it back and incredulously read it again.

"*Ronald Reagan!*" He suddenly became infuriated. "Why, that dirty sonofabitch! Wait'll I tell Warner what he can do with his fucking contract!"

He raced across the lot. In front of the entrance to Main Administration were two writers. They looked at him sorrowfully.

"You heard about it, huh, Julie?" said the first.

"J.L. wants us to rewrite for Reagan, give him more love scenes, make him a more ballsy character," the other added. "By the way, his office's locked. They've all gone home."

Garfield checked for himself. When he returned, he found the writers convulsed with laughter. It was only then that it dawned on him that he had been the victim of a hoary practical joke.

"Very funny," he muttered, weakly joining in their laughter. "I knew it was a gag all the time."

Comedy was not one of his stronger points.

As a matter of fact, J.L. usually did not set foot inside the studio on the day before Christmas. According to producer Robert Lord, it was strictly out of consideration.

"You see," he explained, "with everybody boozing it up, too many employees might lose their inhibitions and tell him what they really think of him."

"Ah," we said understandingly, "out of consideration for them."

Lord shook his head. "No, out of consideration for himself. He'd have to fire half the studio. Think what that would do to the budgets of the pictures in production."

His explanation *did* make sense.

The only gift we received from the studio was the offer of a free lunch. But by noon, having eaten and drunk our way through most of the more festive departments, the thought of a commissary meal was somewhat less than appealing. However, with consideration of the inevitable lean days ahead, we once asked Connie if we could get rain checks. Her answer was a resounding "No!"

So, offically, The Boss never gave us anything. But then, so far as we knew, he never gave any Christmas presents to other employees either. Except once.

J.L. had been on an extended European holiday, and on the day he returned to the studio, Warren Wever was sent to his office and loaded down with some 40 lightweight, gift-wrapped boxes, each addressed to an executive or department head.

Warren had delivered about half, leaving them with secretaries, before he finally learned what they contained. At his next stop, Perc Westmore opened the gift in his presence. Inside were three white handkerchiefs, along with a handwritten card:

> Dear Perc,
> Ann and I were thinking of you while we
> were in Italy.
>
> J.L.
>
> P.S. This is also your Xmas present.

Westmore's only comment was a whispered, "That cheap bastard."

Possibly some of the other recipients expressed the same sentiments. It was then early September.

By official decree, the studio shut down early on Christmas Eve, with all employees notified to be off the lot by five. Long before, the last of the set parties would have ended,the writers would have left, and the fun and games would be over for another year.

By four, we would draw lots for the numerous gifts which had been addressed to "The Mailing Department." By acclamation, the year of Davis's turkey, it *was* donated to a church orphanage.

Then we drank one more toast to each other, cursed the cheap actors and directors who had failed to include us in their gifting and prepared for the last ritual. This came with Fred, waxing sentimental, shaking hands with each of us. There was a genuine warm feeling of mutual affection, which would last until the next working day.

Laden down with our loot, we would head for home. And if the stories we told our families and friends of our adventures on that marvelous day were more fantasy than fact, who could blame us?

I often wondered: In that letter Eddie Hammond was going to write to his folks about having a drink with Davis, what flights of imagination did *he* indulge in?

Could it have been something like, ". . . and 'Bet' and I clinked glasses, and as she drank she looked straight into my eyes, and I could see a sudden longing and I knew that before the night was over . . ."

Why not?

16

*Build-ups, Let-downs
& a Social Disease*

IF THERE WAS ONE EMPLOYEE who could be said to outrank The Brothers in certain respects, it had to be a dynamic, handsome Irishman named Gradwell Sears. As our V.P. in charge of Sales, it was his job to sell our yearly slate of 50 features. In those days of block booking, exhibitors would be promised, for example, two Muni specials, three Flynn and Cagney specials, and an assortment from Davis, Robinson and Powell. In return for which they also had to buy 30 or more B's, plus our shorts and cartoons.

On Sears' frequent trips to the Coast, his was the final word on what kind of pictures we were to make and who would star in them. Davis was big box office in the genre of weepy, women's-type stories. Flynn was smasheroo in swashbucklers and high-budget westerns. Cagney and Robinson were continuing to fill theaters with their gangster films. On the debit side, Paul Muni wasn't able to draw flies in the smaller towns, the Dick Powell musicals were becoming difficult to sell everywhere, and some of our sophisticated comedies were being laughed at . . . but not by the audiences.

More than relying on fan mail as the barometer of an actor's popularity, it was the exhibitors' knowledge of who and what enticed paying customers that Sears was interested in, and his word was The Holy Writ.

The story cycles that were so common then were largely based on decisions made in the New York Office. As long as gangster movies were still selling, we would schedule at least eight for the new season. Since the hicks enjoyed breezy, fast-moving comedy-dramas, our B unit would be instructed to come up with several low-budget series. Double-billing them with whodunits and Karloff thrillers was a winning combination. When, as eventually happened, the public became surfeited with these, Sears would proclaim that it was time to concentrate on something else. Usually this was whatever had recently turned out to be surprise b.o. from another studio.

Over at a little independent called Republic, a singing cowboy named Gene Autry was starting to coin money for them. Foreseeing a new cycle, Sears decided this was something we should take advantage of. We had abandoned the classical B westerns several years previously when a short-lived series starring an unknown named John Wayne had failed to make the grade. But this was a new twist to an old idea—a *romantic* cowboy.

Brynie Foy was given the go-ahead for three 60-minute musical westerns, to be produced on budgets only slightly higher than some of our two-reel shorts. We had a handsome young redhead named Nick Foran under contract. He possessed a good singing voice, and a virile appearance, and he was, with one slight change, Foy's immediate choice as our singing cowboy. Deciding that Nick sounded too foreign, Publicity changed his first name to the more American-sounding "Dick."

For a brief time, our answer to Gene Autry was singing cowboy Dick Foran. Popular with hick audiences (as well as his horse) he was riding high until our Sales Dept. made an unhappy discovery.

Six months later, with the release of his second picture, Foran was on his way to becoming one of the top western stars. His fan mail doubled, then doubled again, causing us to serve notice on our competitor that Autry's days as King of the Singing Cowboys were numbered. It turned out that it was Foran whose days were numbered.

Twelve pictures and less than 18 months later, it was all over, purely a pragmatic case of economics. The musical westerns were unsalable in the large cities, and although the small-town exhibitors clamored for them, we couldn't compete on rental terms with Republic, or another indie, Monogram, which had recently got into the act. Miniscule as they were, our western budgets had the usual heavy studio overhead tacked on, making them far more expensive than the others. It was too bad, because their popularity continued to grow, making millionaires out of Autry and his successor, Roy Rogers.

Foran remained at the studio a few years longer, playing leads in B's and second or third leads in A's. What was always surprising to us was that when we took small-town visitors on The Tour, one of the stars they most wanted to meet was Dick Foran.

He was not the only victim of Sears' fiscal decisions. The great Muni was another. While his specials were considered important to us in terms of prestige, they seldom ended up in the profit column of our ledgers. After *Juarez*, Sears said that he needed another *Scarface*, the gangster film that had originally boosted Muni to fame. But when presented with the script of *High Sierra*, Muni screamed "No!"—he had already gone that route! By mutual consent, he left us soon afterwards.

It was no wonder that Grad Sears' visits were known to certain stars as "nervous time." Options would be lifted or dropped and contracts rewritten according to what his sales records showed. It was cold-blooded business in an industry that dwelt in dreams . . . which sometimes turned into nightmares.

There was always a demand for new faces, and because of it some of our lesser players found themselves elevated to stardom, even though it took a long time before this elevation showed up in their pay checks. Ronald Reagan was one of them.

It was in 1939 that he emerged from the obscurity of our stock company with his portrayal of "The Gipper" in *Knute Rockne— All American,* but then almost two years elapsed before *King's Row* established him as potential star material. We were pleasantly surprised when the critics singled out "Dutch," as everybody called him, as the most praiseworthy of an excellent cast. He was unassuming and un-actorish, with the friendliness of a puppy. But he was also a bit dull, with a rather humorless, one-track mind. In our expert opions he totally lacked the qualities so necessary for stardom.

His sole avocation seemed to be politics, but not politics per se, only constant espousal of FDR's New Deal. Most of us who were growing up during the Depression agreed with him that Roosevelt was our greatest president since Lincoln. But then we were content to change the subject to something more interesting, like sex or money. Not so with Reagan. If one of us encountered him and idly asked, "How are you?" his response was liable to be a 15-minute diatribe against the Hearst press for its latest attack on the administration.

Looking back, it is certainly not an exaggeration to say—but, oh, how hard now to remember—that in those days he was a *left-wing radical!*

Between scenes, his favorite set pastime was engaging in political debate with any adversary he could find, an activity that eventually withered and died for lack of opponents. This wasn't because his co-workers were always in agreement, indeed many were rabidly anti-FDR. It was mostly due to his fanaticism, which gave them little opportunity for rebuttal. Once, Donald Crisp, who considered Herbert Hoover a liberal, enraged by one of Reagan's remarks, delivered what he considered the ultimate insult.

"You goddam *communist!*" he shouted. (Happily, the old man lived long enough to see Reagan not only recant his youthful political views, but to end up even further to the right than he was.)

Was Ronnie Reagan extolling the virtues of FDR's New Deal while courting pert little Jane Wyman in this Commissary luncheon photo? It was his favorite subject at the time.

"Dutch" apparently carried on his proselytizing even during moments of passion, thus ruining a rumor we were about to start. With his low hairline and beardless face with its strange skin texture, we thought he might well be a eunuch. A secretary who had a yen for him got her wish one Christmas Eve, assuring us we were wrong. Her only complaint was that in-between two quickies, he lectured her on why it was essential that Roosevelt be elected to a third term.

It was shortly after the release of *King's Row* that a fan sent him an intricately charted astrological forecast. Mailed as an over-sized postal card on a shirt cardboard, it depicted in various crayonned colors the planetary positions at the moment of his birth. On the bottom half of the card, a precise hand had printed the course he was to follow if his destiny was to be realized. Without question, it was one of the most hilarious things we ever read.

According to the astrologer, he should give up acting and concentrate on political life. This course, if assiduously pursued, would result in important recognition by the time he reached his early fifties. But this would merely be the prelude of a greatness yet to come. All signs in his horoscope indicated the realization of the highest possible achievement by the year 1980.

"Oh, wow!" cried Billy Naylor. "He'll be 110 years old by then. It's gotta mean he's gonna be dead and come back as one of The Brothers."

"He won't be that fucking old," Lou Ferguson dissented. "Anyway, you know who's more important than them? The Pope. He's gonna be the first American Pope!"

Some of us actually rolled on the floor before Fred was able to restore order.

We were going to include it with the rest of the fan mail, but then we debated whether the zealous guardians of that department would forward anything so blatantly ridiculous, since it was either a put-on or the work of a nut. The consensus was that Reagan's "pre-ordained destiny" would never reach him through official channels. Still, it was just too delightful a hoax to be disposed of so lightly.

Al Steele put it in its right perspective. "Look, we all know Reagan's never gonna make it big as an actor. So why don't we make the poor shmuck feel good for a little while and deliver it to him ourselves?"

I drew the delivery that afternoon of the manila envelopes from Fan Mail. As usual, Flynn and Davis had the fattest envelopes. Compared with most of the others, Reagan's was pretty skinny. I opened it, slipped in the shirt cardboard and left it on top of his bureau.

As far as we were concerned, that was the end of it.

Whenever we encountered him afterwards, we never mentioned it, not out of any embarassment for him, but for fear that it might trigger another attack of hysteria. Anyway, we decided, "Dutch" probably read it, laughed as hard as we did, then tore it up. To quote a famous line from one of our films, it was only "the stuff that dreams are made of."

Obviously, it's sheer coincidence that he eventually gave up acting and turned his attention to politics, becoming our Governor when he was in his mid-fifties. That horoscope couldn't possibly have had anything to do with it. I mean, who could believe what some jokester had written on a shirt cardboard? It's just not possible that our destinies are pre-ordained, is it? *Que sera, sera?*

I can't believe that he kept it . . . and that by the dark of night removed it from its secret hiding place, poring over every long ago memorized symbol as he waited and bided his time until 1980. And yet . . . and yet . . .

Hey, "Dutch"—excuse me, I mean President Reagan, sir—remember me? I never called you an amiable zero like the other guys did. I was the messenger who delivered that prophetic message to you. I was the one who believed in you all along. Remember?

Ann Sheridan had been with us for four years before her growing popularity was recognized by the Front Office. Lacking the ruthless ambition of others, she seldom complained about her unimportant, thankless roles and it came as a surprise when Publicity launched her on the Big Buildup as America's

Ann Sheridan, in her pre-"Oomph Girl" days. She had a beautiful face, but the figure of a skinny boy. We soon changed that.

"Oomph Girl." Though beautiful of face (cameraman Jimmy Wong Howe claimed she was the most photogenic female in Hollywood) and possessing a wonderfully sexy husky voice, Sheridan sorely lacked the mammary endowments deemed necessary to fit her new title. No problem. Wardrobe was instructed to have one of its experts design a lovely pair of 38's to compensate for nature's mistake.

The female breast had, of course, been a delightful part of the scene ever since the movies first began. In the early silents they were heaved to show emotion. Later they were cleaved for the same purpose, except by then the emotions came from the males in the audience. By the early 1930's breasts were a big thing. Jean Harlow made a name for herself by discarding her bra and applying ice to her nipples to make them stand out. Others followed her example as decolletage became the fashion and necklines plunged to the navel. Which is when the industry's arbiter of morals, the Breen office, stepped in and in effect issued the ultimatum: "No more tits!"—an edict that remained in force until, in 1937, we made a picture titled *They Won't Forget*.

Well aware that the Code forbade the slightest display of the female breast, director Mervyn LeRoy pulled a clever switch. He hid them so completely—yet so tantalizingly—that today the prophetically titled movie is remembered solely for the brief scene in which a nubile Lana Turner walks down the street, her magnificent young boobs enclosed in a tight sweater, and bobbing in rhythm with each step.

No question but that this was far sexier and more provocative than the half-visible breasts ever were. But since the Code wasn't being violated, the Breen office had to reluctantly accept this new vogue. So it was that in 1939 pin-up photos of Sheridan began appearing in all the fan magazines. It was always pretty much the same pose; the only things that changed were the sweater and the breasts. The one got tighter, the others bigger.

Always outspoken and disdainful of Front Office mentality, Sheridan bitterly resented the deception. As far as she was concerned, "Oomph" was the sound a fat man made when he bent

1720-P12

When Ann Sheridan complained about how ridiculous she felt as America's "Oomph Girl," the advice Pat O'Brien gave her might have been the reason that one day she got rid of the ever-growing, built-in bosoms.

over to tie his shoelaces. Co-starring with Cagney and O'Brien in *Torrid Zone* when the campaign reached its zenith, she complained about her newest photos, which gave her the chest proportions of a wet nurse.

"You're absolutely right, Annie," said O'Brien. "Tell 'em you're through with all this crap." He paused and grinned. "Better yet—give 'em *tat for tit.*"

One departmental remembrance of Sheridan: Delivering fan mail, one of us found her in her dressing room, reclining on the couch, her milk-scotch glass beside her, listening to a Samba record on her phonograph. She greeted the messenger with her usual friendly smile and a "thanks" as he handed her the bulging envelope. Turning to leave, his eyes fell on something. In a waste basket was the manufactured symbol of her "Oomph," a harness with a built-in pair of huge foam-rubber half globes. Noticing his startled reaction, she laughed. "Too big to flush down the john," she said.

Adored by her co-workers as a regular guy, she was that most unique of actresses, totally without guile or pretense, completely honest. When asked by Louella Parsons what caused the end of her short-lived marriage to George Brent, Sheridan succinctly replied, "Brent bent."

Marie Wilson, of the procelain complexion, white-gold hair and possessor of the longest natural eyelashes in Hollywood, reached stardom by playing dumb blondes. If it wasn't completely true-to-life casting, it was close enough. Not that she was stupid, merely the most child-like innocent on the lot.

When the staid, elderly head of an important midwest theater chain was introduced to her, Wilson politely begged off accepting his outstretched hand on the grounds that she was suffering from "a social disease" and didn't want to expose him to it. Shocked, the old man quickly excused himself and left. Upon learning of her remark, Vice President Charlie Einfeld called her on the carpet.

"Don't you have any better sense," he yelled, "then to go around talking about your sex life?"

When Louella Parsons asked Ann Sheridan what had caused the breakup in her short-lived marriage to George Brent, her succinct reply couldn't be printed in Parsons' column.

She didn't know what he was talking about. He told her. "Oh, that," she said, brightening. "Well, you know how you and the fellers in publicity are always telling me to watch what I say when I meet important people? I didn't wanna tell him I caught a cold at a party."

Einfeld slowly began to understand. "The . . . social disease? That's what it was?"

"Well, of course," she said. "I caught it at a social event, and a cold *is* a disease, isn't it? I don't know why you're bawling me out, I thought it sounded a lot nicer."

For once, Einfeld had no comeback.

It was during the filming of *Boy Meets Girl* that she casually made a remark (later to become an underground legend) that epitomized her ingenuousness. In a scene with Jimmy Cagney in which she sat on his lap, he kept fluffing his two lines, something that was most unusual for him. It took a dozen takes before he got it right. Afterwards, Wilson said to her makeup woman, "Sitting on Jimmy's lap was like being on top of a flagpole." She honestly had no idea why the woman suddenly broke up.

We always had a lot of respect for Cagney as an actor. After that, he gained considerable personal stature in our eyes.

For all of the measure of fame and glory bestowed on them at our studio during our time, it seemed that The Fates decreed that our greatest stars must pay a price.

Busby Berkeley, Joan Blondell, Humphrey Bogart, Jack Carson, Gary Cooper, Donald Crisp, Michael Curtiz, Glenda Farrell, Dick Foran, Kay Francis, Hugh Herbert . . .

Allen   Jenkins,   Orry-Kelly,   Rosemary   Lane,   Barton MacLane, Paul Muni, Dick Powell, Claude Rains, Edward G. Robinson,   Rosalind   Russell,   Ann   Sheridan,   Marie Wilson . . .

They all died of cancer.

Marie Wilson said it in total innocence, but her comment about sitting on Jimmy Cagney's lap, during the filming of *Boy Meets Girl*, instantly became an underground classic.

17

Farewell, John Barrymore; Welcome, Alexis Smith

ONE Wednesday afternoon in the Spring of 1941, the Call Sheets for the following day's shooting listed this cryptic information:

STAGE 4. KEIGHLEY. "DINNER"
TEST: J. BARRYMORE, 1 FEMALE (BIT)
9 A.M. SHOOTING

Spelled out, it indicated that on the morrow director William Keighley would be shooting a test of John Barrymore for the role of Sheridan Whiteside in *The Man Who Came to Dinner*.

For those who knew the fabled Barrymore only by reputation—his name uttered with reverence by other actors—this was an event not to be missed. We were aware that for

229

months past Bette Davis had been using all of her not-inconsiderable clout trying to persuade the Front Office to use Barrymore in place of the stage originator, Monty Woolley, for what was considered to be one of the plum roles of the year. Now she had at least won a partial victory; the rest would depend on whether, in his waning career, he could measure up to it.

My day off was on Saturday. Knowing the only way I could watch the test being shot was on my own private time, I tried desperately to persuade one of my colleagues to switch from Thursday to Saturday for their day off, but even with the inducement of two bucks cold cash, there were no takers.

Overnight, I managed to come up with a scheme.

On Thursday morning, working the nine to six shift, I reported for my first call promptly at nine, aware that because of my known avid interest in Barrymore, Pappmeier would be keeping an eagle eye on me. I was given the front lot, a route which would take me past Stage 4, where I knew I was expected to stop off. At which point Fred would pounce.

I blithely ignored the Keighley stage as I hurried on my appointed rounds, returning to the department 16 minutes later, record time for me. Fred looked at his watch and frowned, obviously wondering why I had suddenly become so efficient.

I waited on tenterhooks in the back room for an important phone call. It was a busy morning, and a few minutes later I was summoned for another mail route, this time the West. For possibly the only time, there was no stopping to chat with any of the occupants of the Writers Building. Six minutes later I was back and Pappmeier was becoming worried. It was unnatural for me to work this hard, and why was I so obviously steering clear of Stage 4?

My third summons came at 9:30. It was, finally, the one I had been awaiting. Ed Haldeman called me out of the back room.

"Errol Flynn just phoned," he said, with some degree of hostility. "He wants some friends shown around the lot. He specifically asked for *you*. How come you? You pimping for him or something?"

I replied that it was beneath my dignity to respond to such a loathsome question and made a quick exit. But not before hearing Fred's ringing admonition, "I don't care if they are friends of Flynn's. I want you back here in an hour, understand? *One hour!*"

Outside, my fellow conspirator, Sam-the-voice-of-Flynn, was waiting for the three bucks I had been forced to promise him. He drove a hard bargain, especially considering his part only involved one lousy phone call. But I didn't begrudge the money; witnessing a Barrymore performance would be worth every penny of it.

It was almost 9:40 when I entered Stage 4. I was in luck. As was usually the case, the nine a.m. shooting call was a hoped-for-but-seldom-achieved target. The camera crew was still lighting the library set as I took my place on the sidelines. There were over a dozen other spectators, writers, secretaries and one director, Edmund Goulding, who had directed Barrymore and Garbo in *Grand Hotel*.

Time started creeping by and there was no sign of Keighley or Barrymore. They were, I was told, in a portable dressing room, probably going over the script.

Noticing how I kept eyeing my watch, one of the camera crew told me to relax.

"We probably won't be able to get a take before lunch," he said.

Damn it, I thought, am I to go to all this expense only to be deprived of seeing Barrymore? I had less than ten minutes left of my alloted hour.

With that, Keighley walked onto the set, followed by Barrymore. There were muted "oohs" from the secretaries, and Barrymore arched an eyebrow and winked at them. In person, his appearance turned out to be something of a shock to me. Much smaller than I had imagined him, he was, moreover, hardly more than a grotesque caricature of the man who had once been called the handsomest actor in the world. All too obviously, he appeared to be afflicted with a variety of ailments:

his hands were palsied, his feet and ankles swollen to the point where he could only shuffle along in open house slippers, and his sunken, bleary eyes were empty, devoid of all expression.

The test was to consist of a two-minute scene between Whiteside and his nurse, "Miss Bedpan." It was, of course, Whiteside's scene, with the bit player nurse mainly feeding him the few necessary lines. Strategically located outside of camera range, three grips held the blackboards with the heavily chalked dialogue which had long before become a necessary assist to Barrymore's failing memory.

Keighley called for a camera rehearsal. As Barrymore began to speak, it seemed to be more in the mood of a Shakespearean tragedy than Kaufman & Hart's comedy. In place of the acidulous, misanthropic Whiteside, we were being presented with a King Lear, whose sickly, shriveled presence in the wheelchair evoked, instead of laughter, a sense of pity and despair.

Halfway through, shaking his head sadly, Goulding left. For the rest of us, it seemed only too obvious that the test was a fiasco, a tragic mistake that should be abandoned before the camera recorded it.

There were no further rehearsals. With the clapboy slating the scene, "Take 1," Keighley whispered "Action."

Suddenly a remarkable transformation began to take place. Before our very eyes, a sickly old man became imbued with the vitality of a new life. With his face screwed into an expression of sour distrust, his voice alternately sarcastically falsetto and crankily bass, Barrymore proceeded to play Sheridan Whiteside in his own way, with nuances never even approached by Monty Woolley.

It was then, with skin running tight, I realized that—old pro that he was—he had been husbanding his strength for the camera. For the most part, the lines he spoke were not those chalked on the blackboard. But it didn't matter. The meaning was the same and in fact many of his ad-libbed innuendos surpassed the original lines.

The scene ended with his ordering the nurse to ". . . kindly take your loathsome hand off my . . . knee," the minute

Edmund Goulding (in white, standing below camera) directing John
Barrymore (in homburg) in *Grand Hotel*, might have been recalling
this moment as, ten years later, he watched Barrymore give his last,
best performance in a scene which the public would never see.

pause before his last word, accompanied by uplifted eyebrows, accentuating the double-entendre.

With Keighley's "Cut and print," there was amoment's total silence. We were still under the spell of his magic. Then, spontaneously, we all broke into wild applause.

Struggling out of the wheelchair, Barrymore responded with a mock bow, then suddenly grimaced in pain.

"Where in hell's the nearest loo?" he called. Advised that there was a men's room down the street, he shook his head. "The fossilized remains of my bladder doesn't travel very well."

Turning away, he went behind a flat and audibly proceeded to relieve himself.

I was only three minutes late returning to the department— *only three minutes*—but would you believe Pappmeier had noticed? Obviously aggravated that I had achieved my desire to see Barrymore, he sought revenge by telling me to go to Stage 5 and pick up ten cans of film for the Lab. It was revenge all right. But I think I got even with him when I forced a big grin, and remembering what Mel Marks had done, said, "That's OK, Fred. Boy, what an hour I had! A twenty-buck tip, and not alone that, but I actually got to see John Barrymore pee!"

When the executives gathered to look at the test the next day, there was some lively debate about signing Barrymore. He was considered a far better box office combination with Davis than the relatively unknown Woolley. Even Keighley, who was slated to direct the picture, and who had originally had some trepidations, said he was now in favor of using him.

"I guarantee you that Jack'll give the performance of his life," he told J.L. and Wallis.

When Barrymore was finally ruled out, it wasn't the studio's doing. Knowing the state of his health, the insurance company that covered the contingencies of cast illnesses refused to insure him.

POSTSCRIPT: One Friday night in the spring of 1950, visiting Errol Flynn in his Mulholland Drive home, I happened to mention that a former messenger friend of mine, Peter Brooke, later having been promoted to Casting, had come across the one existing print of the Barrymore test. It had been tossed away in a vault and, realizing its historical worth, Peter had quietly "liberated" it.

Flynn, who had been Barrymore's close friend, had never seen it. Now nothing would do until I tracked Brooke down and got him to bring it over. That very night!

The projector was set up and waiting when, long after midnight, Brooke arrived, the 200 feet of film in a can tucked under his arm. I sat back in anticipation of reliving a very fond memory. But, alas, it was not to be. As Flynn turned on the projector, the brittle nitrate stock decomposed and before our eyes John Barrymore's last great acting turned to dust.

Whenever our dramatic coach, Sophie Rosenstein, became enthused about the potential of a new member of her acting group, the Front Office usually listened. One particular enthusiasm was engendered by a handsome young man named Byron Barr. One day we dropped off a script to Rosenstein of a soon-to-be-cast production, *The Gay Sisters*. Upon reading it, she immediately felt that the second male lead opposite Barbara Stanwyck was made to order for her protégé. A screen test was arranged, which Rosenstein directed, and the unanimous opinion was that she was right.

During the picture's filming, Publicity's Bob Taplinger had an inspired idea: He thought it would be a good gimmick for Barr to legally adopt the name of the character he was playing. With the concurrence of J.L. and Charlie Einfeld—as a contract player Barr was too unimportant to be consulted—a publicity campaign got underway, and one day we delivered mass memos announcing that "The actor presently known as Byron Barr will henceforth be named Gig Young." In the best tradition of Hollywood, on that historic day Barr became a non-person and a new studio product was readied for public sampling.

He turned out to be salable, with both audiences and critics tabbing Young as a comer. To complete the fairy tale, he and his mentor fell in love, Rosenstein divorced her husband and

He began with us under his real name in bit parts. But with his featured introduction was the character named Gig Young in *The Gay Sisters*, our Publicity Dept. decided that the permanent name change would have box office appeal. So one day we delivered the studio-wide memo announcing that ". . . the actor heretofore known as Byron Barr will henceforth be known as Gig Young." We left one of the memos in his dressing room, but it wasn't until the following day, when he picked it up, that Byron learned he no longer existed.

they were married. Although Rosenstein was 20 years older than Young, their marriage seemed to be a happy one until she died of cancer a few years later.

Among the continuous flow of hopeful new talent was a stunning, leggy blonde named Alexis Smith. Although most of the youngsters never got past the audition point of reading for Rosenstein, Smith did well enough to warrant a short film test. Every few weeks a compilation of these would be run for J.L., his executive assistant Max Arnow, casting director Steve Trilling and assorted producers.

On this particular occasion they ran four tests, with the first three failing to engender any special interest. Smith's, the last, was viewed without comment, except by Rosenstein, who pointed out that she photographed well, knew how to take direction, and was the cool, poised society type of whom we were always in short supply. As an added fillip, she said that MGM had asked to see her test in the event we weren't interested.

J.L. shrugged. If the kid seemed to have potential, she also had one bad defect.

"I think she's too tall," he said.

It's true that feminine height was often the kiss of death, especially so at our studio where the roster of male stars such as Cagney, Bogart, Robinson, Garfield and Rains were decidedly on the diminutive side. Even though it was common practice to stand them on boxes when they played opposite taller actresses, some of the men, particularly Garfield and Rains, took this as a personal affront to their masculinity, often displaying the kind of tantrums that caused tensions and production delays. So, for the most part, Casting tried to provide actresses shorter than their male counterparts.

"Yeah, you're right," Steve Trilling added. "Even if she worked her way up, she'd only look good with Flynn or George Brent. Let MGM have her." (He might have been unconsciously prejudiced by the fact that he was only a little over five feet.)

Max Arnow, who was Trilling's superior (and over six feet), had a different idea. "I think maybe she's worth a six-month

Because of what J. L. considered to be a serious handicap, we came close to not putting beautiful Alexis Smith under stock contract.

stock contract. The main thing, Sophie, you gotta teach her to *slouch.*"

Which Rosenstein did. For the next few months, while her fellow neophytes were schooled in poise and graceful posture, Alexis Smith walked around the lot with rounded shoulders and lowered head. Her first few roles put an end to that nonsense, and eventually, of course, she was able to glory in her perfectly proportioned height. Even so, she never became the top star she could have been. Was it because of her height or, perhaps more likely, because we were not the right studio for the "cool, poised society type"?

It's interesting to speculate what her movie career might have been had they heeded Trilling's advice and "Let MGM have her."

During our time, a promotion to Casting was considered the *ne plus ultra* that any of us could aspire to. Far more than the salary, which for beginning assistants was only $40 a week, the main attraction was the glamor and prestige that went with the job. Each assistant casting director specialized in a certain kind of casting: ordinary extras, dress extras, bit players, stunt people, etc., and within his own realm he knew the feeling of Power. Each had business cards bearing his embossed name, and underneath was the magical phrase, "Casting Department, Warner Bros. Studios." When working as talent scouts, which entailed attending all the theatrical events, presentation of his card was all that was necessary to attract the loveliest girls, who often were only too amenable to the most outrageous propositions.

Although not openly discussed, there was one other well-known perquisite: the opportunity of added income through kickbacks from actors and agents. Despite being expressly forbidden, it was a common and nefarious practice that existed to some degree in every studio. Ours was no exception. In this case, it was a young assistant whom I'll call Smigrod, whose job was hiring the ordinary $12.50-a-day extras. Having long since made it known to his trusted group that he expected a 10 percent kickback on every day's work he gave them, there would be times at the height of production when his $50 salary would be augmented by $125 a day in under-the-table payoffs. But then would come the slow periods, during which he'd be lucky to pick up an occasional $25, an amount which didn't begin to cover his newly acquired expensive tastes.

It was during one of these production lulls that Smigrod decided it was time to come up with a more recession-proof idea. He became a pimp. Contacting a select number of the prettiest young extras he knew, he put it to them bluntly: If they made themselves available for a $20 "date," he would take care of getting the customers and they would split 50-50.

At some point each day, accompanied by two or more of his group, he would tour the stages, ostensibly for the purpose of seeing whether the girls fit the directors' requirements for any extra or bit parts that might be coming up. Since such interviews were a normal part of Casting's business, they went unquestioned.

After introducing the girl to the director, and often some of the actors, he would confidentially confide to whomever he thought was a potential customer that he had heard from a reliable source that she was a fabulous $20 lay. Most of the "dates" were arranged for after working hours, away from the studio, but Smigrod also let it be known that the girls were available right now in case they wanted a little diversion. What with the boredom of waiting interminable periods of time between setups, it was somewhat akin to asking a man dying of thirst if he would be willing to pay for a glass of water.

In short order, Smigrod's customers included most of our actors and directors. It wasn't unusual to see one of the latter, weary and troubled, disappear into a portable dressing room between setups, strictly for the purpose of "studying his script." Everybody would pretend not to notice as, a moment later, he would be joined by a young lady. For the next ten to 15 minutes it was understood that the director was not to be disturbed.

Obviously, with our ever-alert spy system, the Front Office must have known what was going on, but since these dalliances never held up production, Security was probably ordered to keep its eyes closed. As a matter of fact, harried directors and listless actors usually re-emerged rejuvenated and smiling. Or as George Raft once put it, "It sure beats sitting around and picking your nose."

"Smigrod's Movable Whorehouse," as we used to call it when we saw him crossing the lot with his entourage in tow, continued in this manner for some months, and with an average take of $40 a day for himself it seemed as if he had found the bluebird of happiness. It took a spoil-sport like Wayne Morris to put an end to it.

Enjoying a build-up as the result of his success in *Kid Galahad*, Morris got more than he bargained for when he forked over his $20. A week later, about to start a new picture, he came down with what Doc MacWilliams diagnosed as a severe case of gonorrhea. The Front Office was notified and the shamefaced actor was forced to reveal how he had contacted it.

When Blayney Matthews interviewed the offending girl, demanding to know who else on the lot she had serviced, she ran off a long list of names, then broke into tears.

"I told Smigrod I thought I had the clap and shouldn't be working," she sobbed. "But he gave me some pills and told me not to worry."

An hour later our enterprising whoremaster was handed his final pay check and escorted off the lot. Since he had always sneered at our $2 to $3.50 offers, we were delighted to see him get his comeuppance.

We never knew for certain how many other employees became infected, but for the next few months we were extra careful when using the studio's toilets.

18

Jack Warner & Other Hoary Legends

İT IS LATE NIGHT *and the studio is deserted. The rising wind carries on its moaning breath the scent of approaching rain. Overhead the storm clouds overtake the moon and an eerie darkness falls.*

A figure emerges from Main Administration, and as it comes closer the moon momentarily reappears and I recognize J.L. He's alone, preoccupied, lines of fatigue etched in his face. Then, from behind him, a man emerges from the shrubbery and I see he is holding something shiny in his upraised hand. A knife! He's stalking J.L.!

I scream a warning: "Mr. Warner—look out!" But the wind swallows my cry.

Now the assassin is almost close enough to strike. J.L. senses something and turns, startled and fearful, as the knife starts to descend toward his heart. But no! With superhuman speed, I am there first, a buffer between them.

I feel the blade tear through my uniform and into the flesh of my chest. With supreme will I wrest the weapon away with one hand while the other delivers an uppercut that renders the assassin unconscious. J.L. holds me in an embrace as I start to sink to my knees.

"You saved my life!" he cries. "How can I ever repay you?"

I never got the chance to tell him. It was always at that precise point that I awakened. How many, many times I dreamed that heroic dream? Always the same, always without an ending.

Laughing about it, I once embarrassedly mentioned it to my colleagues. Most of them admitted to having had similar ones, all right out of Steig's *Dreams of Glory*. I think mine finally came to an end after the contretemps of formally being introduced to J.L.

It was all Alan Gordon's fault. A recent addition to Publicity, he had gone to USC with Jack Warner, Jr., becoming one of his closest friends and a fixture at J.L.'s Sunday brunch-tennis tournaments. Living within a block of each other, Alan and I started sharing rides to the studio every day.

On this fateful occasion, I was waiting for him in Main Reception shortly after seven p.m. when he came out. Accompanied by Mr. Warner, who was just finishing telling a joke.

I moved back against the wall, hoping that, chameleon-like, I could blend into the wallpaper so that Gordon wouldn't have to note the embarrassment of my presence. He stopped in front of me. J.L. paused with him. Matter-of-factly, Alan said, "Mr. Warner, you know Stu Jerome."

Of course he did. That is, he must have *seen* me hundreds of times by then . . . relieving in his office, walking the halls of Main Administration, bringing him rush telegrams in the Private Barber Shop, riding a bike across the lot. I had even dared speak to him. "Good morning, Mr. Warner." And "How are you, Mr. Warner?" Once or twice he had even growled or cleared his throat in response. But on all those occasions I had always been in uniform, a faceless, nameless nonentity.

He looked at me. From Alan's remark, which was made as a statement, it was obvious that I was an employee. Further hints were provided by my sports attire, the manila envelope (filled with stolen typing paper) under my arm and the fact that I wore eyeglasses.

"Sure," he said, offering his hand. "Writer, aren't you?"

Why, dear Lord, I reproached myself a hundred times afterwards, did I choose that particular time to be truthful? Why couldn't I have had the wit to get myself and Gordon off the hook with a simple yes? Why, dear Lord, did I have to be so stupid? Why? Why?

"No, sir," I gulped, my hand in his. "Mailing department."

His hand went limp, instantly retrieving itself from the contamination of touching mine.

"Well, good night," he said lamely, addressing Alan.

Driving home, I voiced my fears that the ill-advised introduction might result in repercussions.

"Don't be silly," Alan said.

I never did hear anything more about it, but shortly afterwards Gordon was fired. Not that J.L. had anything to do with it. As one of Hollywood's most eligible and popular young bachelors, Alan spent much of his working day on the phone with girl friends, an activity that his unromantic boss frowned upon. (It turned out to be one of those blessings in disguise. He went on to become a successful independent publicist and then a millionaire distributor of photographic equipment.)

A few days later, I happened to pass J.L. on the lot. He looked right through me without a trace of recognition. For once, I was grateful for the anonymity of my uniform.

What was Jack Warner *really* like?

In our time, at the height of his power and in the prime of life, with our impartial prejudice we saw him as everything that his detractors claimed: ruthless, cruel, dogmatic, frequently vulgar. His so-called jokes belonged in a stag show. His treatment of subordinates, even top executives, could be shameful. As fashion-conscious as we were, his expensively tailored wardrobe dismayed us. His suits were always a little too sharp, his loud ties sported a diamond or pearl stickpin, a foulard handkerchief flowed from his breast pocket, all of this set off by a contrasting vest. The sum effect was that of a con man or a burlesque theater second banana.

Of course, that was only a matter of personal taste. With his pencil-thin mustache and trim physique, he was considered to be handsome and dashing. And there were even those who claimed he could be charming. (This last quality seemed to be saved exclusively for his social life.)

In any event, his was certainly a presence that commanded respect. Or, perhaps more accurately, *fear*. Yet there were times when we had reason to believe that the overwhelming opinion of him as a cold-blooded tyrant was not entirely true, that it was actually a planned public image by an employer who knew that he had no alternative but to project himself in that light.

Those of us who frequently relieved in his outer office had opportunities to get to know him as did few others. The information came from freshly typed copies of memos dictated that morning. All strictly confidential. A series of them disclosed that brother Harry had been the instigator of the campaign against Kay Francis, and that J.L., although carrying out the orders, only reluctantly approved of some of their tactics. We also learned that The Brothers often feuded with each other, sometimes going for weeks without having any communication except by terse memos.

All of which seemed to put H.M. Warner in a vastly different light. Some years older than Jack, he appeared to be the very antithesis of his flamboyant brother, quiet, gentlemanly, almost reclusive. It was widely believed that Harry left the day-to-day running of the studio to J.L. while he, as sort of an elder statesman, concerned himself with the world-wide operations of their empire. Whereas J.L.'s studio reputation was that of a bastard, H.M. was seen as the benevolent good guy.

But, we wondered, was that really so? Many of the firings and suspensions were ordered by H.M., even though it was Jack who carried them out. And there was something else for us to ponder over: through Security and the hiring of private detectives, Harry had acquired some particularly gamey evidence of sexual misdeeds on the part of some of our top talent. He instructed his brother to use this evidence whenever necessary to keep them in line. As far as we knew, this was something J.L. never resorted to.

Which is not to say that his methods were any less infuriating to those employees he personally dealt with. It was no wonder that our studio was known in the industry as "The Burbank Branch of San Quentin," with J.L. cast as "The Warden." It was particularly hard to understand his cavalier treatment of such obvious talents as Bogart, Sheridan, Marie Wilson, Dennis Morgan and many others, all of whom see-sawed for years between playing leads in B's and minor roles in A's. From picture to picture, they never knew whether they would be starring or playing a minor support.

Even after Bogart scored a major success on loan-out to Goldwyn for *Dead End,* it didn't mean a thing when he returned home. His next assignment was as the second lead in a B.

There are those "authorities" who claim that this was J.L.'s way of seeking revenge against troublemakers, and while this was true in a few cases, there were other factors that entered into it. Unlike other studios, where promising talent was rewarded by carefully planned, long-range buildups, we were mainly interested in keeping our contract people busy during their minimum 40 weeks a year, never mind the importance of their roles. If an actor didn't like playing a supporting part after having achieved critical success in a more important role, his only alternative was to go on suspension. Or if an agent sought better terms for his client and was considered too difficult in his demands, he was likely to find himself barred from the lot. At one time or another, our "barred" list included most of the top agents in town. Myron Selznick, one of the top agents at that time, called it a badge of honor.

Early on, we noticed something interesting whenever J.L. crossed the lot: There were always those important employees who, seeing him from a distance, hurriedly detoured to avoid what might have been an unpleasant confrontation. Once, one of us was in a men's room when director Lloyd Bacon ducked in, and after a moment asked the boy to see if the coast was clear. It was.

"Thanks," said Bacon. "If I had run into him, he'd have asked what I was doing, I'd have had to tell him I was waiting for a script to be finished and by the time he got back to his office, I'd be on lay-off."

On other occasions, we often saw J.L. encounter long-time employees in minor positions, and he'd greet them by name and sometimes chat for a moment. One of them was former actor Don Alvarado, Mrs. Warner's first husband. While it was alleged that J.L.'s romantic interest in Ann Alvarado, a brunette Latin-type beauty who somewhat resembled Dolores Del Rio, had caused the breakup of the marriage, it apparently wasn't so. At least there couldn't have been any bitterness on her ex-husband's part, because with the waning of his acting career, Alvarado came to work for us as an assistant director.

J.L. and his first wife had only one son, Jack Milton Warner, "Jackie Junior" as he was known to us. He came to work at the studio following graduation from college. Quiet, extremely shy and retiring, he seemed to be trying to live down his father's reputation. Well-liked, he set about learning the business, first in the cutting rooms and then as an assistant producer in the Shorts Department. His budding career was short lived.

One morning, he and his father had a meeting. At 11 a.m., Jackie drove off the lot and before the day was over his name was removed from his parking space. There were no memos in this case barring him from the lot. But perhaps it was his decision to quit. He never returned.

There were, of course, a deluge of rumors, mostly claiming that Jackie had angered J.L. by taking his mother's side in their divorce action. Although we were never able to learn the full—or true—story, we did find out that Harry, whose only son had tragically died some years previously, tried desperately to

J. L. Warner and his son, Jackie Junior, during happier times. Their bitter quarrel ended the hope for a Warner dynasty.

heal the bitter schism between father and son. Without success.

On that long-ago day, when the name "Jack M. Warner" was painted over on the asphalt, it signified more than a bitter family quarrel. Jackie Junior was the last of the male heirs. It ended a dynasty.

If The Boss we knew was sometimes not quite as harsh and tyrannical as claimed by others, was there ever any evidence of his humanity and compassion? Perhaps there was a dichotomy. We knew of a dozen old-time stars, most of them going back to the silents, who enjoyed permanent employment with us as members of our stock company. True, their present salaries were mere pittances compared with the stipends they had commanded at the height of their fame, but it was still a living in the profession they knew and loved.

This, too, was something we learned from his memos, instructing Casting to use these people as often as possible, for bits, atmosphere, even as extras if nothing else was available, but in any case to use them in preference to hiring outside actors. Most of them weren't especially appreciative of being relegated to the background, but Payroll tried to carry them for a full 52 weeks a year, for which they were indebted to a man whom many of them secretly called "The bastard."

There was another example we found out about. In Whitney Stine's excellent book on Bette Davis, *Mother Goddam*, Davis makes a brief mention of James Stephenson, a member of our stock company, who came to prominence as the second male lead in *The Letter*. Director William Wyler had wanted a more important name for the part, but Davis fought for Stephenson and her insistance paid dividends. Surprised at his sudden fan popularity, the studio cast Stephenson in several more featured roles, then six months later he was top-billed with Geraldine Fitzgerald in *Shining Victory*. It was not a prophetic title. What Davis and Stine failed to mention in their book was that his escalating career was tragically cut short by his sudden death a few weeks after the picture was completed.

As with so many of our 3000 employees, J.L. didn't know the actor personally. Yet when he learned that Stephenson had left a wife and a year-old son, he instructed Accounting to continue paying his salary for a full year. At $500 a week it was an amount that could easily be absorbed in our general overhead, but we thought it was a humane gesture. That, and a personal letter of condolence to Mrs. Stephenson, saying that if he could be of any help to let him know.

During a time when rival moguls Louis B. Mayer, Darryl Zanuck and Harry Cohn, among others, were acquiring unwanted but apparently well-deserved reputations as chasers and lechers, there was nary a hint of The Boss's sexual peccadillos. If an actress was summoned to his office, it might have been for the purpose of a stern lecture or vulgar dressing down. But she never had to *undress*. He was happy with his beautiful new bride, and though others in our top ranks considered sexual favors a normal perquisite, J.L.'s sofa never served as a casting couch. He did have one well-known vice: playing *chemin de fer* for high stakes.

Finally, it's about time that one of Hollywood's hoariest and most enduring legends is laid to its eternal rest. The one about J.L. roaming the studio at night switching off lights. Perhaps, like other legends, it had its basis in fact, but that must have been in much earlier, leaner days. During our time, none of us ever saw him reach for a light switch. Not even once.

One thing that we thought strange: Every afternoon around four, one of us would be sent to the Executive Dining Room to pick up a custard and glass of milk for him. He was suffering from stomach ulcers. But wasn't that an ailment he was supposed to *give?*

Originally, there had been four Brothers. Sam, who is credited with saving the company from bankruptcy by the introduction of sound, died at an early age. The third brother was Albert (né Abe) who had somehow acquired the military title of Major. Since he was headquartered in New York, we never knew exactly what he did, but as one of the ruling *troika,* he probably didn't have to do anything.

He customarily visited us twice a year, touring sets, lunching in the Executive Dining Room and napping in the afternoon. Once, he stopped one of us and inquired if his dear friend George Arliss was shooting that day?

"No sir, he's not on the lot," the messenger replied, diplomatically refraining from adding that Arliss had departed the studio many years previously.

Possibly because he didn't seem to make any important decisions, Major Albert was considered the most likable of The Brothers. A few of us were going to lunch one day when we passed J.L. and Albert.

"There they are," cracked our Al Silverman, "the Major and the minor."

Luckily, our backs were toward them; still, they must have heard our raucous laughter.

Before the advent of World War II caused them to endure the hardship of domestic vacations, Harry and J.L. used to separately take extended European trips each year, much to the disgust of Whitey Wilson, head of our Property Department.

It wasn't their vacations he minded, nor even the fact that in order for their trips to qualify as tax-deductible business expenses they had to enter into various business deals in behalf of the studio. Wilson, a quick-tempered, tough Irishman, who had been with the studio from its earliest days, hardly even complained about the profusion of statues, antique furniture and other assorted junk that always followed in the wake of their return. It was *pianers* that drove him mad.

For some unknown reason, every year they went abroad, they each bought one or two concert grands. By 1939 we had accumulated *twenty-two* of these monsters, most of them still in their shipping crates, taking up every available bit of space in the Prop building. That was the year when two more arrived.

"More pianers?" Wilson was heard to scream. "My God, we're gonna have to build a new Prop building just for the goddam pianers!"

But being a shrewd department head, he came up with a better, and far less-costly, solution. How would the Music Department like to acquire all the Italian pianers they could use? Forbstein was willing, and the composers were delighted with the idea of trading their rinky-dink uprights for these superlative instruments. For the first time since their arrival, Wilson was seen with a smile on his face. It was short lived.

When the first concert grand was delivered to Music, it didn't take long for the prop men to realize there was just no way they could fit any of these into the small offices. At least, not without reconstructing the entire building.

Poor Wilson. Those "goddam pianers" must have been to him what we were to Pappmeier. A constant source of irritation.

With J.L.'s departure for the long holiday, the entire studio seemed to relax a bit. Not that anything really changed for the better; it only seemed that way.

One employee who decided that The Boss's absence called for a special kind of relaxation was a producer named David Lewis. Tall, in his thirties, considered handsome despite pop eyes and twitchy mannerisms, Lewis was a pinball-machine addict, habitually spending his lunch hours hunched over the machines at the drug store. It was shortly after J.L. left town in 1938 that Lewis came up with his inspiration. Seeking out the owner, he arranged to rent a pinball machine. It was delivered to his office that evening.

Thereafter, every working day for the next four weeks, the hallowed second-floor halls of Main Administration echoed to the sound of bells and buzzers. A visitor, asking one of us what those mysterious sounds were, was blithely told, "Oh, it's just Dave Lewis playing with his balls."

We considered it to be merely one more producer's eccentricity, more innocent than most. But there was a method to his seeming madness. Lewis had started in the business as one of Irving Thalberg's proteges. As he explained to a writer who was working with him on a script, Thalberg's story conferences always included some kind of mind-limbering game away from the

Producer David Lewis's hobby might have been off-beat, but it did contribute to the success of *Dark Victory*.

problems at hand, often resulting in the solution of some vexing story point. He apparently knew whereof he spoke.

The many conferences he held with writer Casey Robinson, while they wagered quarters on high scores, resulted in one of our most acclaimed pictures: Bette Davis's *Dark Victory*.

The machine was returned just before J.L. got back. In a way, it was too bad that as a result of Lewis's theory of creativity it wasn't tried experimentally by some of the other producers. But then, to each his own. The others' inspiration stemmed from the usual wenching, boozing and gambling.

19

Miriam Hopkins & Other Enemies

In our impressionable youth, despite the cynicism and disenchantment that came from familiarity with some of our fellow employees, we still had our share of *genuine* American heroes. Tom Mix, Babe Ruth, Joe Louis, to mention a few.

There was a time when columnist Mark Hellinger was included in that exclusive roster. Indeed, Hellinger came as close to being our department's avuncular figure as any mortal could.

A beefy, slouching man, who always wore grey or blue serge suits, dark shirts and white ties, he looked like a gentle-hearted gangster. Newly arrived as a writer-producer, his warm friendliness and lack of self-importance endeared him to most of us from the start. Not to mention his generosity, which soon became legendary. For example, when leaving the commissary, he would insist on collecting the checks of even the slightest acquaintances, a fact that soon caused us to move to a section of the counter where he couldn't possibly miss our eager countenances as he came out of the Green Room.

Far better than a free lunch, he soon let it be known that if any of us happened to be in a financial bind and required a little folding money to tide us over until payday, we needed to look no further than our new-found friend. Nor did he ever mention repayment.

"Don't worry about it Pappy," he'd say. "Hell, it's only money."

He had a unique, New York-accented style of talking, and often around six when he would break open a bottle of brandy, if we had occasion to stop by his office, we would be invited in and regaled with some of his fascinating anecdotes of the people he had known and the stories he had covered as a crime reporter in the twenties.

Sometimes, tough-looking, dese-dem-and-dose Eastern cronies came to visit him and Mark would call for a messenger to show them around. It always meant a $10 tip, slipped to us in advance. That was Class!

As a kid, I marveled at his short-short stories and for years tried to emulate his style. Always unsuccessfully. I once mentioned this to him and he smiled understandingly.

"It's just a matter of experience," he said. "See, what you gotta do is first figure out your switcheroo ending. Then everything else falls into place." He spent the next ten minutes teaching me more about his kind of journalism than I had learned in four years of high school.

That night, inspired by his advice, I devoted six hours to writing a short story. I took it to him the next day and asked if he would please read it whenever he could spare the time. He shoved his own work aside, insisting that I sit down and wait while he read the eight pages then and there.

As he put down the last page, he nodded his head. "Hey, this is beautiful, Pappy. I think you've got a real story there. I love your switcheroo—it's great!"

I walked around with my head in the clouds for days afterwards, determined that I was going to write a great book and dedicate it "To my best friend, Mark Hellinger, who gave me the encouragement." The book never happened, and as for our love affair, it came to an abrupt and ignominious conclusion shortly afterwards.

Two of us stopped by his office shortly after six one evening, and hearing him on the phone, waited outside. Apparently talking with his business manager, his voice raised in anger, we heard him say he was fed up with being the patsy for all the studio parasites and free-loaders who were draining him of hundreds every week.

"I'm afraid to poke my head outta my office," he said. "Every day these friggen bloodsuckers are standing there with their hands out. Now some of these kids've got a new angle—making me read the shitty stories they've written!"

Inured as I was to the hypocrisy and deceit of so many of our betters, this, coming from my friend, hurt more than I wanted to admit. We didn't intend to take advantage of him in any way that I knew of, but why had he put himself in that position in the first place? There had certainly been no reason for him to want to buy our respect and affection. Except, perhaps, his need to be considered "A swell guy. The best."

I moved to another spot at the commissary counter where he wouldn't see me, and when I had to enter his office, I dispatched my business with the kind of swift, cold efficiency that Pappmeier would have approved of. Thereafter, whenever I encountered him, his hearty, "Hiyuh, Pappy?" elicited only a respectful and subdued, "Hello, Mr. Hellinger."

I re-read the story that he had so extravagantly praised. It wasn't very good; I tore it up.

If temper, arrogance and lack of common courtesy had been the prime requisites of stardom, Miriam Hopkins might have been The Greatest.

It was cause for celebration when she checked off the lot after *The Old Maid*. But then nine months later she returned to do *Lady With Red Hair* and we all went into mourning. It wasn't merely her attitude that rubbed us—as well as most of her co-workers—the wrong way. There were times when Davis, for example, could be very bitchy, but she was never imperious. Hopkins always commanded, demanded, complained, whined . . . about everything. Her honeysuckle-and-molasses voice would become icy, and her eyes would narrow, giving her the look of a petulant, tyrannical overage child. Edmund Goulding had the perfect word for her: the world's champion *kvetch*.

On the day of her return, our Larry Dannenberg was dispatched to the Auto Gate to show her to her dressing room. Her limousine drove her to the edge of Dressing Room Row, with Larry keeping apace on foot. But then she had to walk the rest of the way, a distance of about half a short block. She was not pleased.

"This is ridiculous," she muttered. "At Paramount, I would always be driven right up to my dressing room door."

Nor was she made happier upon entering the suite selected for her. Formerly occupied by Muni, its gloomy, old-fashioned furnishings were right out of a gothic novel.

"Lord have mercy," she whined. "They've given me the *dungeon!*"

Larry didn't bother explaining that one of the set dressers would be coming by to redecorate according to her wishes. He turned to go.

"Just a moment, boy," she ordered, opening her purse. He waited expectatntly as she fished around. "Here, this is for you."

Her outstretched hand held a quarter.

"Gee, that's so very kind of you, Miss Hopkins," he said, sarcasm dripping from each word. "But we're not allowed to accept tips."

"Good for you," she said, quickly dropping the coin back in her purse. "Personally, I think it's a very demeaning practice, don't you?"

In the long run, we made her pay dearly for her stinginess. With a gourmet's interest and a trencherman's appetite, her larder usually contained roast beef or ham, pates, fruit and cheese, plus a goodly assortment of fine wines. All of which we sampled, once perhaps going a wee bit too far.

It concerned a magnificent half of a rare prime rib roast beef. Which of us discovered it first, as it reposed so appetizingly in her refrigerator, I never did learn. But the fact is that three of our colleagues, separately, and unknown to the others, each helped themselves to a slice (or two, or three) of cold beef, until it ended up as some slivers of fat drooping from denuded bones.

When Hopkins returned to her dressing room later that day, she happened to be famished. Moments later, screaming in frustration, she phoned Security, making a great ruckus about her suite having been burglarized, with all sorts of valuables stolen.

Luckily for the culprits, they had all made social visits and this time there were no fan mail envelopes as incriminating evidence. Still, because we had access to the master keys, the entire department was under a cloud of suspicion. We sweated for an hour while Blayney Matthews personally checked out the loss of Hopkins' valuables. When he returned, his eyes were colder than usual as he beckoned Fred into his office.

Seven minutes later, calling one of his infrequent full departmental "catastrophe conferences," Pappmeier joined us in the packed back room.

"I've g-g-got g-o-ood news and b-b-bad," he started, and noting that his stammering was down to more or less the norm, we all started breathing a little easier.

"Chief Matthews had de-de-determined that no-no-nothing was st-st-stolen. Miss Hop-k-k-kins admitted that. Except for a w-whole roast be-be-beef. Now one of you ob-ob-obviously went in and to-took it. Whoever it was, I w-w-want you to be a m-m-man and own up."

A long minute went by as he eyed some of the possible thieves. His glare seemed to center on me longer than some of the others, but for once I was innocent and I stared back at him in smug satisfaction. None of the criminals was man enough to come forward, nor of course would we ever think of blowing the whistle on our colleagues. (Like the members of the U.S. Senate, we all had so much dirt on each other that we had no alternative but to obey our code.)

"OK," he said, after another 15-second wait. "Before you leave this r-r-room, I want all your lo-lo-lockers opened. And I'm t-t-telling you g-g-guys one thing. Chief Ma-Ma-Matthews says if this happens one-one-once more, he thinks I should f-f-fire the whole b-b-bunch of you! Now let that be a wa-war-warning!"

We pretended to be worried and contrite, but we really weren't. We knew it was an empty threat. Where else, especially on short notice, could he ever find a more dedicated group than us?

Fred inspected each locker personally, luckily for us. If Matthews had conducted the inspection, he undoubtedly would have noted the quantities of contraband stashed away. With ensuing questions and subsequent trouble. But all Pappmeier was looking for was a prime rare roast beef. He didn't find it.

The whole incident, of course, only served to reinforce our hatred of Hopkins. One of us came up with a good way of getting even with her.

"You know the way she likes to have some wine every afternoon," he said. "Let's piss into one of her wine bottles."

His suggestion was greeted with much enthusiasm at first, but then cooler heads prevailed, pointing out that if she became ill during production, it would cost the studio money. We were very adult when it came to fiscal matters.

As for our pilfering, it continued as before, except that from then on we ignored her.

"Fuck Hopkins," we used to say. Figuratively, that is.

Then there was Hal B. Wallis. As second-in-command and executive producer of the A pictures, he was to us the coldest, unfriendliest executive of them all. Much more so than J.L. We were on some sort of speaking terms with all of the other high echelon who dwelt in Main Administration, but in his case we soon learned that it was a waste of breath to offer even the most respectful greeting.

Once, while he was crossing the lot, a messenger was sent to intercept him with an urgent message to phone his office. Our colleague reported that Wallis seemingly didn't even hear him, though the boy repeated it. Wallis continued his pace, never changing expression, nor even acknowledging the message by nodding his head. It was a humiliating way to be treated.

We were not the only ones Wallis considered to be non-persons. Whenever he was on the lot, he kept his eyes glued to the ground, making it obvious he didn't want to be spoken to. An agent once made the mistake of approaching him while he was on his way to the Executive Dining Room.

"Don't ever talk to me when I'm on my way to lunch!" he snapped.

As well known as agents were for smilingly taking abuse, this one stopped dead in his tracks and looked after him with open disgust.

Wallis's underlings were forced to endure this inhuman treatment. We weren't. Prideful as we were, his attitude made him a charter member of our "shit list." He was married at the time to actress Louise Fazenda, so we dubbed him "The prisoner of Fazenda," and circulated stories that among his many mistresses were Lola Lane and an attractive young story editor named Irene Lee. (Actually, we never had any knowledge of Wallis's extra-marital affairs, if any, but when it came to one of our vendettas, we never let truth interfere with malicious gossip.)

Situated near our department's entrance, on the south side of Main Administration, was an ornate, heavy wooden door beyond which was a stairway leading up to J.L.'s and Wallis's private offices. They were the only ones who had keys, often using this private entrance when returning from lunch. It was on such an occasion that we witnessed an extraordinary sight.

Standing on the sidewalk in front of the door was Wallis, smilingly engaged in conversation with a . . . *messenger!* Incredulously, we noted that the kid—a newcomer from Chicago named Mickey Fields—was responding as an *equal!* We could hardly wait for him to return to our back room for a third-degree grilling.

Fields had no idea that his little tête-à-tête was of such dramatic importance to the rest of us. He explained that his father and Wallis had been close friends for many years, which is how he got hired. Whereupon it was bluntly pointed out that any friend of Wallis's was automatically an enemy of ours.

"Take your pick," he was told. "Either him or us."

It was about as childish an ultimatum as we ever issued. But of course Mickey knew that as long as he remained in the department, our good will was essential. We never again saw him speak to Wallis.

Such was the use (mis-use?) of our power.

If, from all the foregoing, it would appear that we were a bunch of irresponsible juvenile delinquents or perverted Katzenjammer kids, it really wasn't so. Not entirely. Many of the guys were honest and industrious, minded their own business, developed contacts in other departments and seriously planned their futures. Sometimes the hoped-for goal would only be as close as the Time Office or Accounting. Others aspired to the cutting rooms, directing, even producing. Jules Levy confided the latter ambition, receiving the usual hooting laughter.

"What's so funny?" I said. "Jules does have one of the prime requisites—a totally obnoxious personality."

Not too many years later, Levy became a partner in a new production company, Levy-Gardner-Laven. It fast became one of the top independents, turning out a number of highly successful movies and TV series. Since my dear friend, Jules, was in charge of hiring their writers, I couldn't understand why my agent was never able to get me an assignment with them.

Another of our group with "lofty ambitions" was a kid named Max Wilk, who came from New York where his father was our East Coast Story Editor. Spending two summer vacations with us, he immediately endeared himself to Pappmeier with his cheerful, gung-ho attitude. Nice fellow, Max, but not one of my favorites.

Like me, Max was determined to become a writer and we once exchanged manuscripts for critical comments. Neither of us much liked what the other had written. "Nothing personal," I told him, "but even with your dad's influence, you'll never make it."

Well . . .

At last count, Max Wilk had made the best seller lists . . .five or six times. (OK, so I was wrong a few times. Big deal!)

Stan Frazen, Hugh Chaloupka, Billy Naylor and Bob Swanson hoped to become film editors. Dick Rawlings' ambition was to make first cameraman. Arnold Laven and Don Weis envisioned themselves as directors. Warren Wever saw his future as an agent. Peter Brooke devoted himself to screenplay writing. Bert Dunne was interested in production. Art Wilde's dream was the Publicity Department.

In time, all of them—and there were others—achieved their goals.

I continued to pursue mine. Not with any degree of success, but with enough encouragement to chain myself to the typewriter four or five nights a week developing story ideas, which I then asked producers to read. With paternal patience, some were extremely kind and helpful. But not to the point of putting their money where their mouths were.

"You know something, kid?" Brynie Foy said, handing back the fifth story outline I had submitted to him in that many weeks. "Instead of the guy reporter, make it a dame, and maybe instead of the city locale, change it to a small town and then . . ."

My heart started pounding as he continued talking about specific scenes and character changes.

"You mean . . . you might be interested, Mr. Foy?" I asked dazedly.

"Bring it back and I'll see what it looks like."

His brusque answer was the most beautiful, inspiring sentence I had ever heard! They were all I needed to sustain me through six nights and one day of churning out a completed 100-page screenplay. The one day was my day off, when I finished the last 20 pages, proofed, corrected and sweated for 16 hours.

The next morning, my handiwork proudly enclosed in the same sky-blue cover that our other screenplays wore, I presented myself to Foy's secretary, Myrtle von Stein. She eyed me wonderingly.

"I thought you kids always knew everything, even before it happened," she said. I looked at her blankly.

"Mr. Foy isn't here anymore," she continued. "Happened yesterday. He and Mr. Warner had some kind of a whoop-te-do about a final cut."

The script ended up in my trunk. One of many. Many many.

Another opportunity of a sort came along shortly afterwards. Norman Cerf, a friend of mine who was a cutter in the Trailer Department, tipped me off that they were looking for a writer. Writing "Coming Attractions" was not what I wanted to do, but at least it would be a beginning.

Eddie Selzer was head of the department. A bespectacled sparrow with all the charm of a buzzard, he handed me a script, curtly told me to read it and write a sample 60-second trailer.

"We don't screw around with fancy writing in my department," he warned, ending the interview. "I want it on my desk by nine tomorrow morning."

A potboiler titled *Gambling on the High Seas*, our typical approach would have been:

NOW IT CAN BE TOLD!
THE DARING EXPOSE OF CROOKED GAMBLERS!
THRILL TO THE VIOLENCE, DANGER AND TERROR OF INNOCENT
VICTIMS WHO LEARN THAT BEYOND THE THREE MILE LIMIT
THERE IS
NO LAW!

The zooming phrases in newspaper headlines, superimposed over a montage of the most violent scenes, would be the opening grabber. It was the customary device and I automatically slanted it that way. When I read it, I immediately realized that this was exactly the kind of old-fashioned cliche-trailer that I wanted to avoid at all costs.

For the balance of that night, I endlessly wrote and re-wrote dozens of versions. None of them was good enough. The sun was rising when I finally hit on an approach that I liked. In documentary style, with a March-of-Time-type narrator, I wrote:

"Everybody likes to gamble, whether it's matching coins, betting a dollar on your favorite football team or going all out to try and break the casino. It's hard enough to win against an honest house but when you're gambling on the high seas the odds are stacked against you. Sometimes, to the extent of betting your life."

Bleary-eyed, I presented myself to Selzer's secretary promptly at nine. After waiting a nerve-wracking half hour, I was told to go in. He devoted about five seconds to reading the opening.

"*This* is your grabber?" he yelled. "It's crap!"

If I was going to become a professional writer, I knew I'd have to accept criticism.

"I'm sorry you think so, Mr. Seltzer," I said, "but I think it's pretty good. It gets across the story and mostly it avoids the usual cliche junk."

I'd have been just as well off if I had let my temper loose.

"I don't want any *new* cliches! You don't know the first thing about writing a trailer!"

An experienced trailer writer was hired and a week later Cerf ran his trailer in the moviola for me.

It began with a montage of violent scenes. Over them were the superimposed zooming headlines: "NOW IT CAN BE TOL D! THE EXPOSE OF THE YEAR! THRILL TO THE VIOLENCE, DANGER AND TERROR OF . . ."

20

The Gathering Storm

We were not to realize it for a long time to come, but a film that we produced in 1939 presaged the beginning of the end of our secure, innocent little world.

The project got underway in an aura of such strict secrecy that at first even we didn't know what it was all about. Over a period of a month, once or twice a week one of us would be sent to Mimeo on a rush and given eight sealed manila envelopes. Attached to each was a receipt to be signed by the recipient's secretary. It was mysterious enough to warrant trying to wheedle an explanation from the guys in Mimeo, and although they were usually willing to share confidential information, in this case we were told to mind our own business. It had the same effect as waving a red flag in front of a bull.

All we knew for certain was that the sealed envelopes contained portions of a script that Milton Krims was writing, and that upon leaving his office at night, it would be padlocked by a cop. Unlike the usual script distribution, which included every department, this was limited to J.L., H.M., Wallis, Legal, Charlie Einfeld, producer Robert Lord, Anatole Litvak and Krims.

The secret was inadvertently revealed by the latter's secretary when she opened the envelope in the presence of the delivering messenger. The script was upside down, but since many of us had developed the ability to read anything in that manner, it presented no problem. *Confessions of a Nazi Spy*. First Temporary Script.

It was one of the few revelations that at first we only talked about in awed whispers. The German-American bunds were then nearing the height of their power, and it seemed tremendously daring for us to attempt an expose. But it was also the kind of inside information that we delighted in broadcasting, and within a few days not only the studio but also the trade press were buzzing with speculation about an important anti-Nazi film that we were planning. With the cat out of the bag, Einfeld ordered the first official announcement.

Confessions of a Nazi Spy, it said, would be a carefully researched, no-holds-barred documentary. In the genre of such hard-hitting earlier exposes as *They Made Me a Fugitive From a Chain Gang*, *Emile Zola* and *They Won't Forget*, it would deal with the ideological war between fascism and democracy. But in no way would it be neutral. Rather, it would deliberately side against the Nazis regardless of any political or economic repercussions.

As hoped for, it made headlines. The American Firsters, a committee of important figures who advocated a policy of isolationism, denounced it as cheap propaganda. In Washington, though there was some pro and con, most politicians typically withheld comment until they could see which way the wind was blowing. What none of us could foresee was the approaching storm.

Production got underway with an unusual display of security. With cops stationed at the entrances of Stage 2, memos were circulated that it was off limits to all but the picture's cast and crew. Even we, usually able to ignore restrictions imposed on other employees, found it impossible to get past the guards unless we could prove we had business on the stage. No sweat. With our usual ingenuity, we merely sealed an empty envelope, typed director Litvak's name on it, added "Rush. Personal," presented it at the door, then destroyed it once we had gained admittance.

The set turned out to be a disappointment. Considering the secrecy and security, we expected to see history in the making. Instead, it seemed to be only another movie, which Litvak haranguing his cast and crew as usual, actors boredly sitting around between set-ups and the crew pulling the same dumb monkeyshines as always.

I desperately wanted to read the script, but each copy had been strictly accounted for. Ordinarily, by the time a picture started shooting, various minor departments involved in pre-production work would no longer need their copies, and they would be thrown out or returned to Mimeo. In this case, however, all departments were ordered to return their copies in sealed envelopes by special messenger so that no script could leave the lot and possibly fall into the wrong hands.

I didn't see how that could include me. It took a bit of doing, but I finally managed to obtain a copy, which was loaned to me overnight. I felt like a character in a cloak-and-dagger melodrama as I slipped it under my shirt before leaving the studio, fearful that somehow I would be apprehended.

I started reading it as soon as I got home. But like visiting the set, it proved to be a sharp disappointment. A melange of old espionage and gangster plots, it seemed a far cry from being the accusatory expose of the American Nazis that had been promised.

The picture was still in production when the first hate mail began arriving. Obviously a planned campaign, it first consisted of a trickle of letters and postal cards addressed to "The Jew Brothers Studios, Burbank, Cal." The messages were all variations on the same theme: "We are going to boycott your filthy kike movies." Those that bore names and addresses received form responses from Publicity, thanking them for their interest. It was the kind of reply that must have driven the more rabid hatemongers crazy with frustration.

At first, we laughed and joked about those poor, ignorant, prejudiced idiots. At first. Then the trickle increased to the point where each mail delivery contained dozens of similar excoriations, and there would always be one or two anonymous threats that the studio would be bombed or that some of the actors in the movie would be "taken care of." These were turned over to Blayney Matthews, and appropriate precautions were taken, but the threats remained unfulfilled.

Among our members by then were four or five German refugees, all of whom reacted with various degrees of uneasiness when they came across samples of the hate mail, pointing out how in their homeland this had culminated in the bloodbath of the Jews. The rest of us dismissed their fears as paranoid. It couldn't happen here. In our smug superiority, we dismissed the lunatic fringe as faceless misfits, all dwelling in faraway places, harmless but for the vitriol of their pens. We were wrong.

The day came when it was forcibly brought home to us that we were not inviolate within the snug walls of our little make-believe world. We had been invaded by the enemy!

Early one morning, scrawled graffiti was found on the walls of a men's room on the front lot: "LET'S TAKE CARE OF THE JEWS! BURN THE STUDIO! GET RID OF THE DIRTY KIKES!"

Months before, some employees who frequented the beer parlors and pool halls across from the Auto Gate had come across the same hate slogans and had reported it to Security. Since we had no jurisdiction over those places, all we could do was turn the information over to the Burbank police and request their cooperation. Apparently there was no law against it; at least nothing was done to stop it. But that was across the street.

This, of course, was frighteningly different. It was the work of someone—probably more than one—employed *within* the studio and thus capable of making good their anonymous threats.

The walls were immediately painted over and Security launched an intensive investigation. But within the following days similar slogans suddenly appeared elsewhere within the studio, on back lot walls and in the male extras' dressing room. Then, near the Time Office, where the crews checked in, early morning arrivals came across this chalked message on the sidewalk: "GET READY TO EXTERMINATE THE JEWS! ATTEND TONIGHT'S MEETING!"

With that, rumors started flying. For once we were rapt—and worried—*listeners*. Daily, somebody would confide:

—that over 500 employees belonged to a secret inter-studio bund and were mobilizing for a takeover . . .

—that it was the work of the night janitorial crew . . .

—that our Gun Department had been broken into and all the rifles and revolvers stolen . . .

—that Security was compiling a list of all employees with German surnames and that they would be investigated for any trace of pro-Nazi sympathies . . .

This last was deliberately mentioned in Pappmeier's presence. Being a worrier by nature, he might have believed it. It was an unkind act; we knew he was neither pro-Nazi nor anti-Semitic.

It was always one of our deepest regrets that Security was the one department whose innermost secrets remained inpenetrable. As in this case. The outbreak of graffiti was short-lived, ending as suddenly as it had started. There was talk that Matthews' investigators had uncovered the perpetrators—three or four back lot workers who belonged to a local bund, and that they had been fired and their names turned over to the FBI. We hoped it was true, but we never knew for sure.

The movie that had inspired all this completed production uneventfully, the hate mail dwindled down to its usual trickle and the furor died down. It flared up again, briefly this time, when *Confessions of a Nazi Spy* was released. Despite the timeliness of its subject matter, it was neither a critical nor box office success and I felt vindicated in my original criticism of its script.

Another happening brought the winds of change closer to home. A memo to all departments announced that, beginning the following week, members of the FBI would be at the studio for the purpose of fingerprinting and photographing each employee—eventually this operation would include every working person in the nation—and that they would be kept on file in the FBI's headquarters in Washington. For what purpose, we wondered?

There were many who claimed we could not be forced into being fingerprinted and mugged, that it would be a violation of our constitutional rights. The most vociferous of these were a number of our writers, who darkly alluded to this being the first step on our road to totalitarianism. Yet others claimed it was a good idea for all loyal Americans to be so identified and kept on file. Again, we wondered, why?

None of the reasons advanced made any sense to us, but in the continuing controversy one fact became clear: Those who were opposed were the liberals or left-wingers, while the pro forces consisted mostly of an older, more conservative group. Since the majority of us were on the side of the liberals, we were both awed and inspired to hear some of them declare that they would flatly refuse to be processed like suspected criminals being booked.

Operation Fingerprint got underway on Stage 9, and for the balance of that week there were long lines of employees, all unusually quiet and uneasy. When my turn came, I happened to be behind writer Robert Rossen. As one of the more outspoken of the liberals, I had half expected him to walk out on his contract rather than submit to what he had called ". . . an act of fascism at its worst." But there he was, along with the others who had expressed the same sentiment.

The procedure took only about a minute, and as we were leaving, Rossen turned to me. "If you ever commit a crime," he said, "be careful not to leave any fingerprints."

It was spoken in a sardonic, ruefully joking tone and I chuckled. But then, in a more reflective voice, he added, "Next thing you know, they'll be asking about our political beliefs and who our friends are."

Some years later, after finally achieving his goal of becoming an important director, Rossen was called before the House Un-American Activities Committee and questioned about his alleged communist ties. He refused to answer any of their questions.

He was subpoenaed a second time and again refused to testify. This time it resulted in his being blacklisted.

Finally, *he* sought a meeting with the committee. This time he willingly confessed to having been a member of the Communist Party. He also named a number of friends who had been party members. The blacklist was lifted and he returned to work. But his spirit had been broken. Not long afterwards, he died.

And those last words he spoke to me came back in a flood of unhappy memories.

21

Last Train From Burbank

THE HEAVIEST VOLUME of mail always arrived on Monday mornings, necessitating the eight a.m. arrival of six of us to participate in the handling and sorting. On this particular Monday, only Pappmeier, Bowers and three messengers showed up and Fred was faced with the realization that he was in trouble.

It was December 8, 1941. Singly and in pairs, most of us had patriotically rushed off to enlistment offices, all of which became so jammed with would-be recruits that everybody was told to go home and await word from our draft boards. Whereupon, some of us tardily went off to work, while others decided they might as well take the whole day off.

With less than half the normal complement finally on hand, none of the mail routes was met on schedule and Pappmeier developed an upset stomach when the rush calls backed up to an unprecedented 40-minutes delay.

There would have been harsh recriminations the following day except for the extenuating circumstances. Herding us to-

273

gether, Fred's pep talk made it clear that we were now on a paramilitary footing and that *any* goofing-off (here he glanced briefly at me) would be considered as serious as an act of sabotage and dealt with accordingly. Imbued with his fervor, we all swore to take stock of ourselves. We were now at war, and until such time as we could take up arms against the enemy, this was our only way of helping the war effort.

We actually meant it. For the next few months we buckled down to work with a singlemindedness that was beautiful to behold. Mail routes were completely covered in their alloted schedules; rush calls were expedited with swift efficiency; and "Commander" Pappmeier openly stated his satisfaction with each and every one of us. Including me.

The holidays, of course, lacked the carefree abandon of previous years. There was more loot than ever, and perhaps as a patriotic gesture to those of us who would soon be going away to war, some of the more attractive secretaries, and even a few of the minor actresses, allowed heretofore-forbidden intimacies. Withal, a pall hung over the studio. The once-distant thunder of The Gathering Storm was now overhead, and in the growing darkness we knew that, like our youth itself, an era was coming to an end.

The dawning of 1942 became the winter of our discontent. The war news was worsening. Each day saw more of us leaving for the armed forces, and for the rest, the make-believe of our business had lost its glamor. With millions of innocent people being slaughtered, it seemed almost obscene to be delivering rush memos proclaiming, "Due to the fact that our allotment of raw stock has been cut in half, no director will be allowed to order more than one printed take of each scene." Or from Story to All Writers: "Please remember that typewriter ribbons are on the priority list. You can get double the mileage from each ribbon by reversing it from top to bottom. It is absolutely essential that your old ribbon be *completely* worn out before requisitioning a new one."

One writer stopped working for three days on the patriotic grounds that, although his ribbon was completely shot from top to bottom, he didn't want to be the first to requisition a new one.

Soon everything became scarce and complaints of terrible hardships were heard from every department. Perc Westmore complained that certain makeup items were obtainable only on the blackmarket at a 500% mark-up; Orry-Kelly bitched about the scarcity of the heavy brocade material needed for *The Gay Sisters;* Set Construction was ordered to hammer out bent nails and re-use them; announcements in the commissary told us not to waste butter or sugar and then came the meatless days.

A newly signed actor named Paul von Henreid immediately had the *von* stricken from his name and German-refugee director Kurt Bernhardt emerged as *Curtis.* (Publicity considered changing his last name, too, but then somebody remembered that an actress named Bernhardt had been French, so it was allowed to remain.)

The Sales Department proclaimed that the public wanted escapism and our New York office pulled off a coup by obtaining the rights to a projected musical based on the life of George M. Cohan. The only bright spot in the deepening gloom was the fact that the movie business was approaching an unprecedented boom. In the worst of times, it was the best of times.

It was shortly after Pearl Harbor that we lost one of our best friends, a plump, middle-aged little florist named Kelly. It was he who supplied the fresh flowers for the stars' dressing rooms, the floral decorations for official functions and the bouquets or corsages that any of us needed—always on credit—for special dates. Kelly undoubtedly wasn't his real name, but it was the only one we ever knew him by. He was Japanese.

We suspected him of being a homosexual, but of the most harmless variety. Visiting our back room, and flirting with some of the guys, he would giggle madly when accused of staring at our crotches. He never denied doing so, but on the other hand, he never made a pass or offered a proposition.

One day, along with all the other Americans of Japanese ancestry, Kelly was picked up by the FBI and taken away to an internment camp. Once again the rumor-mongers went to work, the consensus being that Kelly had been a spy—no, much more than a mere spy, that he was actually the *mastermind* behind an impending invasion of the West Coast. Our informants were never able to satisfactorily explain how they knew this to be so, not that it mattered to us; it was so patently ridiculous that we never believed a word of it. Not even when our Governor Earl Warren declared there was evidence that all Japanese were Fifth Columnists. Even if that were true, we argued, what secret information could Kelly have possibly picked up at the studio?

We never saw our comedic little florist friend again. Nor—shamefully for us—did we ever try to contact him to say that, at the very least, he had our moral support.

One afternoon in 1942 one of our newcomers, Gene Stromberg, was ferrying film across the lot to Projection Room 5, where J.L. and Wallis customarily viewed the rushes. The heavy 35 mm. film cans had to be carried up a long iron stairway and all too often the round trip had to be repeated three or four times while cutters hurriedly spliced scenes together. It was one of the mindless chores that we veterans deemed necessary indoctrination for our freshmen.

Gene was handing the projectionist the last of the reels when the distant boom of anti-aircraft cannonading suddenly erupted. It was a sound that we never quite grew accustomed to, not even later with the secure knowledge that it was only practice firing with dummy shells from the artillery encampments that surrounded Lockheed. But this was the first time, and unaware that it was only practice, it was a terrifying experience.

The projectionist turned pale. "What's that?" he demanded. Gene said it sounded like an air raid. Stopping the projector, the man yelled into the inter-com, "Mr. Warner—I'm afraid there's an air raid!"

J.L. came running, followed by Max Arnow and Steve Trilling. Hearing the continuing bombardment now, they assumed the projectionist knew what he was talking about. Somehow believing that a messenger had been dispatched to lead him to safety, J.L. frantically addressed Gene.

"Tell me the truth, son! They're bombing the studio, aren't they?"

This was the first time that Gene had laid eyes on our legendary boss, understandably becoming tongue-tied under the circumstances. This only served to make J.L. fear the worst.

"Don't panic!" he cried to his underlings. "Let's get outta here!"

It was an unnecessary order. The other two were already heading pell-mell down the staircase. Sprinting for their lives like over-age athletes, they were halfway across the lot when the explosions faded away. Above, the luminous sky displayed no sign of enemy planes, the surrounding buildings remained intact and pristine. Whereupon, a bit embarrassed, they stopped running.

When Gene told us the story, groans of frustration filled the room. "You idiot!" we said. "You missed the opportunity of a lifetime. You should've said, 'Mr. Warner, sir, don't worry, I'll protect you with my own life if necessary!'"

It was a bit of joking advice that later came back to haunt us. A tall, handsome, outgoing kid, Gene had come to us through the influence of his father, who was our official studio jeweler. His ambition was to someday become a set designer. Gene was the first from our department to be killed in action. Guadacanal, August 8, 1942. He had just turned 21.

With the threat of actual air raids a growing concern, the Front Office tried to figure out some way that the studio could be spared the danger of being mistaken for Lockheed. Bert Tuttle, head of the Art Department, suggested we paint our familiar "WB" logo in huge letters atop each of the sound stages. His idea was about to be implemented when somebody else reflected, what if the Japanese pilots couldn't read English? A second dissent—perhaps the deciding one—came in the form of a handwritten note to our studio manager:

When we told our Gene Stromberg what he should have said to J. L., we didn't know our advice would soon come back to haunt us.

"I think it's a waste of time and money to try and do anything to disguise the studio. It wouldn't work. And in any case, wouldn't it seem logical for an aircraft factory to try and camouflage itself, maybe even as a harmless movie studio?"

For the record, the suggestion was made by a certain grip. Yes, the very same unknown and unsung hero who had come up with the easy way of extricating Sydney Greenstreet from the phone booth. He remained unknown and unsung; our business manager, who presented it to J.L. as his own idea, saw to that.

So the lot remained as it was, with our only planned means of protection to be a series of underground air raid shelters. One was quickly constructed for The Brothers, Wallis and a few of the other top brass. There was talk about constructing others for all 3000 employees. But except for two additional shelters for the protection of stars and the rest of the executives, the plan was never implemented.

Obviously, the rest of us were expendable.

With the outbreak of war, J.L. suddenly acquired a military rank. In keeping with his importance, it was one step above Major Albert's: Lt. Colonel in the Air Corps Reserves.

Henceforth, when we relieved in his office, we were instructed to answer the phone, "*Colonel* Warner's office." Jake of the Tailor Shop fitted him with the appropriate uniforms, which we all had to admit were a great improvement over his "second banana" civilian clothes. Striding across the lot in uniform, his braided cap jauntily cocked over one eye, he presented a dashing, heroic figure. Or, as one of us put it, "Sort of a second-rate Errol Flynn." Once, however, the uniform caused him a bit of annoyance.

It was lunchtime. Col. Warner was on his way to the Executive Dining Room (we never did get around to re-naming it "Officer's Mess") when he encountered some young Canadian Air Force officers. They promptly stiffened to attention and saluted. It really wasn't his fault that his acknowledgement was no more than a curt nod; we were shooting several war pictures, and as far as he knew, they were only a bunch of bit actors putting him on. He started to pass by when one of them spoke up.

"Excuse me, sir," he said, "but don't you Yanks return a salute?"

J.L.'s face reddened. He brought his hand up, brushing his visor, then hurried on. The Canadians looked after him and laughed.

"How in hell did he ever get to be a chicken colonel?" said another. "The dumb sonofabitch doesn't even now how to salute."

In town to pick up some training films, they left for home that day without ever learning the identity of "the dumb sonofabitch," let alone the fact that the expletive was reserved for his personal use toward others.

Still awaiting my draft call, by early Spring of 1942, I had achieved the impossible. Seniority. It was a dubious distinction. By then our department had undergone almost a complete turnover, and it remained for me and a few others, as elder statesmen, to pass the torch of learning to the new members. We spent long hours in advising them in the basic essentials:

—how to goof off while seeming to be working harder than anyone else . . .

—how to get out of taking the front lot when it was raining . . .

—or the unshaded music route when it was hot . . .

—how to charm (or coerce) visitors into good tips . . .

We lectured on 101 pleasures and pitfalls. How to take full advantage of some, and how to avoid others, all the things we had learned the hard way over a period of years. It was necessarily a crash course. There was no time for the nuances. One new member, returning after having taken his first group of visitors on The Tour, proudly announced that he had politely refused a $5 tip. Why, we demanded? He thought it was beneath his dignity to accept a gratuity.

"Next time you're offered cash," one of us advised him threateningly, "just say you're accepting it in behalf of the *poor fucking messengers!*"

Another, following delivery of fan mail to the dressing rooms, mentioned that Constance Bennett had a five-pound box of candy. When we asked for our share, he was shocked. "I didn't take a single piece. That would've been *stealing*."

My God, I thought, has our department really sunk that low? What would become of it after the last of us veterans were gone? Was it destined to become the sterile, insipid, characterless place of robot-like efficiency that Pappmeier had always hoped for? The obvious answer was too depressing to contemplate.

Among our new members—most of whom came and went before we could even remember their names—was a kid named Pierre Wilson. We had never had a "Pierre" before, and were only too happy to torment him about what we considered to be a pansy name. Especially so since Pierre, a sweet, sensitive kid of 16 was, incongruously, the offspring of tough old Whitey Wilson of the Prop Department. As noted, Wilson could get very upset about his surplus of "grand pianers." But that was something he had no control over. His mail deliveries and pickups were a different matter. With important memos from his out-of-the-way department lingering in his "Out" box sometimes for hours on end, Pappmeier would receive hair-raising phone calls, which were then visited on us.

So it really wasn't Pierre's exotic name that caused our continuing ridicule; rather, we were using him to get back at his father's bellicose attitude toward us. Within his first two weeks, Pierre apparently got the message. How he got his old man to change his attitude toward us, we never asked, but the next time one of us stopped by Prop, he was treated to an amazing reception. Whitey came out of his office to personally thank the kid for stopping by and for the first time in history phoned our office to *compliment* us on our efficiency. After which, Pierre officially became one of our group. (It was just another example of our ability to win friends and influence people. The Mafia could have taken lessons from us.)

Inevitably, the patriotic fervor of the first few war months wore off, and we gradually resumed our old, evil ways, especially Arnold Laven, Hugh Chaloupka and myself. With the recklessness and to-hell-with-it attitude of those who knew their days were numbered, we constantly sought newer and cleverer ways of putting in an eight-hour day with an absolute minimum of effort. The ultimate thrill came with our "Most Dangerous Game."

It was a running, three-handed poker party. Whenever one of us was sent on a mail route or rush, he would let the others know so that we could later rendezvous for our gambling.

Our meeting place was the Train Shed, situated behind the Music Building and reachable by fast bike within three or four minutes of wherever we were. Inside the shed, which was a small sound stage, was an actual Pullman car, complete with drawing rooms and compartments. Drawing Room "A," with a table separating the two facing seats, became our private gaming room, where we managed to meet three or four times a day.

My final day as a messenger might well be titled "Last Train From Burbank." At 10:10 a.m. I initialed the time sheet for the Music Route, informed my companions and departed. Hitting only the three stops considered essential (there were nine in all), five minutes later I was waiting in Drawing Room "A."

Within a few minutes, Arno and Hugh arrived. It was the day after payday and we all had folding money in our pockets. Loosening my tie, I glanced at my watch, noting it was 10:19. That allowed me a good ten minutes before my tardiness would be noted and require an explanation. Plenty of time to make a killing.

My pair of aces lost to two little pairs. Two pairs lost to three deuces. Three queens lost to a straight. My bankroll was down to loose change when Hugh suggested a temporary adjournment.

"We've got plenty of time yet," I said testily, looking at my watch. "It's only —" the hands had stopped at 10:19.

Four minutes later I was back in the department, with the wall clock reading 11:01. Judging from Pappmeier's expression, I knew that more than the usual explanation was necessary. Perhaps I was tired of the subterfuge . . . or maybe even of the job itself. Whatever, for the first time I had no glib, pre-prepared excuse. I merely said I had been busy on personal matters and let it go at that. (For once, it felt good to tell the truth.)

Fred had long displayed an unusual patience and tolerance regarding my non-working habits. With every right in the world to fire me, he didn't. Instead, stammering over each word, he conferred the penultimate punishment: two weeks' layoff. Except for the fact that it didn't come by way of memo from Legal, it put me in the same category as our contract people.

I went into the back room, got out of my uniform, cleaned out my locker and walked out the front door. I knew that my time as a messenger had come to an end . . . that I wouldn't be returning.

Well, I was half right. Which was still 50 percent better than most of my other predictions.

In 1949, while writing a pirate story for Errol Flynn, which he planned for independent production, he asked me to comment on the script of his next film for Warner's, a western titled *Montana*. He agreed with my diagnosis that it needed work, and when I came up with some suggestions, he liked them enough to persuade producer Bill Jacobs to hire me for a rewrite.

I had, of course, long nurtured the dream of making a triumphant return to my home studio, but when it finally came I was reminded of Thomas Wolfe's "You can't go home again." Main Reception's Grant Donley, and Al Yallen of Music Reception, were both gone, replaced by new, cold-eyed studio cops. Many of my old friends hadn't returned after the war, and those who had no longer seemed the same to me, nor did I to them.

Sadie Fryer and some of her girls, remembering my writing aspirations, made a little fuss over my return and Bill Schaefer went out of his way to welcome me back. The best compliment of all was paid me by my old friend Bert Dunne, now assistant to the head of Story. He assigned me to room 38-B in the Writers Building. During our time, it had belonged to John Huston.

Just once, I passed Fred Pappmeier on the walk outside of Mailing. We didn't exchange a single word. Obviously, he thought that I still harbored a grudge for his laying me off and I thought he might not want to shake hands out of remembrance of past aggravations. I was in the wrong. God knows, I should have apologized for all the stuttering and stomach aches I had caused him.

Withal, my return only produced a melancholy emptiness. There was no feeling of triumph. What had once been a love affair was now only a sad reminder that nothing is forever.

On the last day of my rewrite, after the obligatory act of packing all the stationery supplies I could carry, I phoned Mailing to return some material to Research. The messenger, I noted disapprovingly, was not representative of my era. Handsome, erect with a military bearing, he was coldly polite and respectful. Hoping to impress him, I casually mentioned that I had got my start in Mailing. He wasn't impressed. I inquired about some of our old legends and stories; had they survived us? He had no knowledge of any of them. I offered him a cigarette. He didn't smoke, nor could he remain to idly chat. He *wanted* to get back to work. As he left, I realized that my worst fears had come true. He was the robot who had taken over our ranks.

In utter depression, I walked over to Stage 19 to say goodbye to director Ray Enright and the *Montana* cast and crew. They were shooting a scene I had written between S.Z. "Cuddles" Sakall and Alexis Smith. Sakall, commiserating with her about something, had the line, "Don't be foolish, it'll be better." But that's not the way it came out. After four takes, his accent still turned it into "Dun't be fulla shit, it'll be better." Despite the laughter of the crew, Enright didn't find it funny.

I suggested that Sakall try, "Don't be silly, it'll be better."

It did get better, of course. My depression soon lifted and I began to see things in a different perspective. The studio had never been my *home,* nor did I *belong* there in any sense of the word. The rites of passage had been completed.

I still lovingly recalled those crazy, wonderful days of our youth; memories that would come back to me from time to time, like roaring, surging waves. Those I wanted to keep. Sometimes, too good to keep to myself, I would recount certain incidents to my family, finally prompting my son, Rick, to ask, "Truthfully, just how much fun was it?"

I thought for a long moment, trying to put it in his kind of terms.

"Well, I guess you could say it was about as much fun as you can have with your clothes on."

He was then about 16. He nodded approvingly. "Second best fun isn't bad."

One night, while my Elaine and I were watching one of our old movies on "The Late Show," I said that I had been on the set the day they had shot that particular scene and I started to launch into an anecdote.

With infinite patience, she interrupted me.

"You know how many times you've told me that story?" she said. "With all your memories, know what I would do if I were you? I'd try putting them all down in a book."

She went to bed. I sat there in the darkened room, watching the flickering shadows until The End, somehow remembering each line a beat ahead of the actors.

"There are people," wrote Saint-Beuve, "whose watches stop at a certain hour and who remain permanently at that age."

I don't think it will be permanent, but for a moment I am 17 again . . . and the best is yet to be.

THE END